God?

THOUGHTS FROM A SPIRITUAL JOURNEY

PATRICK DENNIS

Feedback is welcomed. Write: Book@DennisCreative.com. Every email will be read, and I will do my best to respond to each one.

. . .

Art at the beginning of each chapter by Megan Dennis. If you'd like to discuss commissioning Megan to do artwork for your project, please contact me.

Cover Photo by Greg Rakozy / Unsplash.

. . .

I am a principal in two different businesses. My primary work is in brand communications for a range of clients. I have also been doing some work in professional coaching. See DennisCreative.com or SurgentCoaching.com to learn more.

. . .

ISBN (Paperback): 979-8-9857396-2-6
ISBN (eBook): 979-8-9857396-3-3

To my family, my future family,
and to every young person
who has ever walked into our home
for this thing we call Group.

TABLE OF CONTENTS

God?

Years ago, I had the opportunity to get to know the gifted and award-winning cartoonist, Johnny Hart. Johnny created not one, but two nationally syndicated comic strips that ran in thousands of newspapers every day. The first was called *B.C.* The second, *The Wizard of Id,* he co-created with a cartoonist named Brant Parker.

Johnny, who died in 2007, inspired me on a number of levels. I loved our conversations.

His comic strips did not typically touch on religion; their goal was to entertain. Still, he did see Easter and Christmas as unique opportunities to use his work as a platform to encourage people to consider the claims of Christianity. He was never shy about sharing what he believed. I was amused to hear him talk about the handful of newspaper editors who often threatened not to run his "religious" strips in their papers.

Those editors typically backed down and ran the strips, but even if they had not, I don't think Johnny would have cared. I'm pretty sure he never lost sleep over these sorts of battles.

Here is an example of one such strip, a strip that is meaningful personally because Johnny hand-colored it for me as a gift.

The thing I love about this strip is that B.C., the main character, asks real questions. Throughout my adult life, I've been drawn to people with questions about God, perhaps in part because I had questions as I first considered the claims of Christianity. B.C. asks the same questions that many people would like to ask God: "Are you listening? ... How come you never show yourself? ... How do we know you even exist?"

But what if God *has* shown himself, as the later panels of the strip suggest? What if he has given us evidence but, like B.C., we have missed it, whether due to our busy lives, pre-existing beliefs, personal biases, the way we were raised, or because we've never stopped to consider that good evidence might really exist?

What if we've missed it because we've simply ignored it?

I'm convinced that God has given us more than enough reason to believe. That he has shown himself, and that there is enough evidence to lead a smart, thoughtful person to conclude that (a) God does exist and (b) Christianity is more likely to be true than not. You may disagree.

Whatever you believe, I hope you'll keep reading.

THE BIG IDEA

From the beginning, I envisioned that this would be a "what I believe and how I came to believe it" sort of book.

I have written this book to challenge curious readers to think. If you are not a Christian or aren't even sure you believe that God exists, I hope you will find this book to be both interesting and thought-provoking. If you are a Christian, I hope it will strengthen your faith.

For philosophers, theologians, and thinkers who have read books on these topics, the arguments here will be familiar. I'm not seeking to make new arguments as much as I'm hoping to pass along arguments that I have found to be compelling. In the Appendix, I will point to books that will dig into these topics in greater depth than I will do here. My goal is to scratch the surface. If you've never read a book like this, one that argues for the rationality of the Christian faith, I think you will be intrigued.

When I started this book, my goal was to write for two specific audiences. I had no plans to make it more widely available. But over the last year, it became clear that other audiences have found it to be helpful. And that is my biggest hope: that this book will be spiritually helpful.

My first intended audience is my family. My great-grandfather, whom I never knew, was a pastor in the small town of Lebanon, Connecticut. He never wrote anything like this, but I wish he had. I would have enjoyed reading it. Between the publishing of the first and second editions of this book, my first grandchild, Adelyn, was born. This is for you, Addie. And though I hope to know other possible grandchildren and great-grandchildren, if we should have any, it is obviously not a given that I will have that opportunity. So, this is for them. If even one of them reads this at some point in the future, it will have been worth my time and effort.

This book is for my incredible wife, Karey, and our amazing kids: Ryan, Megan, Ethan, and Grace, our newest daughter. It is for Luke, our soon-to-be son. It is for my dad, who loves great conversations, and for my mom, who loves the written word. It is for Bret, Kim, Caroline, Thomas, and Zachary. And for Barb, Kristen, Kim, Kevin, Elizabeth, Corinne, Amanda, Julie, Kellen, and Sarah.

I would have really enjoyed discussing this book with Bryan. It is for Ken. It is for David, Kitty, Katherine, Meredith, Aunt Ellen, and Barbara. Ellen, it might not be *Auntie Mame*, but I hope you will like it. It is for Reiko (I miss the deep-into-the-night conversations I used to have with Alan about these sorts of things). It is for the Miner clan, the Beckwith clan, Lynn, Donna, Marcy, and the rest of our family in Connecticut. And it is for the Sloans, the O'Rourkes, and the enormous Schubring side of the family (about half of Wisconsin, I'd guess).

My second audience consists of our other family: the hundreds of high school students (and now college students and college graduates) we have welcomed into our home over the last decade for this thing my kids creatively decided to call "Group." And for their families.

Group started when Ryan and Megan invited their friends and kids I had once coached in basketball to come over to discuss life, from a Christian perspective. The turnout that first week was larger than we expected.

Ryan, Gio, David, John, Mike, Jon, Nick C., Nick B., Kyle, Megan, Sara, Kelley, Elizabeth, Kathryn, Reese, Jess, and Meredith, you played a huge role in helping Group get off the ground, and it just took off from there.

During that first week, at Group, I mentioned a verse from the New Testament book of Luke in the Bible. It points to an interesting idea, whatever we believe about God or the Bible. It says that during Jesus' days as a young adult, he grew "in wisdom and stature, and in favor with God and with people."

This verse points to four dimensions of life. Each is important.

Life naturally leads us to grow in three of these four dimensions. We grow in wisdom through experience, and as we learn things and figure out how to apply that knowledge. We grow in stature, physically, without having to think much about it. And we grow in favor with people as we invest in relationships.

But that fourth dimension, the spiritual dimension, does not come as naturally to students. Nor to adults. Far too often, it is the most ignored dimension of life, even though many would argue that it is the most important of the four.

The Christian perspective on the spiritual dimension of life suggests that we were created to experience and enjoy a relationship with God. But, for reasons we'll come to later, far too many people never discover how to experience that relationship.

And before we can begin to think about a relationship with God, we need to explore more basic questions. Questions like: Does God even exist? How can we know? And many others.

As it turns out, the idea that students would enjoy having a safe place to explore these and similar questions about the spiritual dimension of life was a good one. So, that is what Karey and I have sought to provide. That and good food.

I have written this book to explore these same types of questions because so many of us—students and adults alike—wonder about them.

Group, in book form? That's the goal.

On a personal note, if you have been part of Group, you know how much Karey and I love you. No matter who you are, why you came, or what you believe, we have never ceased to be thankful for your presence in our lives. Our doors are always open, however old you are, whatever is going on in your life, and even if it has been a minute since we've heard from you.

And while I cannot possibly mention every kid who has been part of Group in this book, I will mention many of you by name in the following pages. You'll have to read on to find out where, even though I know some of you hate to read.

Beyond these audiences, I hope that students I've known or coached but who never made it to Group will read this. I can think of quite a few people who fit into this category.

And if the book finds an even wider audience, that would be great, too. I will be especially thrilled if even one person who has written off faith, is wrestling with doubt, or legitimately wonders if God even exists finds this to be helpful.

Penn Jillette Gets It

OUR FAMILY OWNS A HOME ON THE BEAUTIFUL Bohemia River on the Eastern Shore of Maryland, not far from the northern end of the Chesapeake Bay. At least a few of you who may read this book have been there with us. If so, you might remember seeing a small sign that my father-in-law, Terry, had hung on the side of the refrigerator. It said:

Some things matter very little.
Most things matter not at all.

The sign was a good reminder that much of what we tend to worry about is simply not worth our emotional energy. When I saw it, though, I often had my own variation of the thought:

Some things matter very much.
A few things matter immensely.

PENN JILLETTE GETS IT
Penn Jillette, half of the uber-talented illusionist duo Penn & Teller, has a thoughtful mind and is a gifted entertainer. He is also an atheist.

In a video posted on YouTube, Jillette talks about a fan who approached him after a show to give him a Bible.

Some might assume that this would be annoying for an atheist, but Jillette claimed not to be annoyed at all. Instead, he said he understood and respected the man. His rationale was thought-provoking:

> I've always said I don't respect people who don't [talk about their Christian faith with others.] I don't respect that at all. If you believe there is a heaven and hell, and people could be going to hell or not getting eternal life or whatever, and you think it's not really worth telling them this because it would make it socially awkward, how much do you have to hate somebody to not [do that]? How much do you have to hate someone to believe everlasting life is possible and not tell them that?
>
> If I believed, beyond a shadow of a doubt, that a truck was coming at you, and you didn't believe it, but the truck was bearing down on you, there's a certain point that I tackle you.
>
> This is more important than that.[1]

If Christianity is true—and please note that I am not assuming you believe it is—there is an eternity we will all face beyond death. That eternity is divided into two possible destinations: an eternity with God and an eternity apart from God.

Penn Jillette is right. This is more important than that.

If you have read the Preface, you already know that I am persuaded that a thoughtful and intelligent person could objectively conclude, based on evidence, that the central claims of historic, biblical Christianity are more likely to be true than not true. It is important to note here that I am not trying to make the case that these claims can be proven to be true with 100% certainty.

SKEPTICS WELCOME
Some readers will be inclined to disagree with my "more likely to be true than not" idea. I understand. These subjects are not easy. If they were, books like this would not be necessary.

If you would say, "Patrick, nothing that you or anyone else could ever write could possibly change my views," you are probably right. If your mind is that made up and closed to even the possibility that some sort of god could exist, well, I suppose the case is settled for you.

Some agnostics, who say they don't know whether some kind of god exists, have concluded they can't know and thus decide not to spend a lot of time or energy thinking about it. Some are curious and love to talk about it.

Likewise, some atheists[2] have settled the matter in their hearts and choose not to invest energy in such discussions. Other atheists remain very engaged and seem to have a passion for trying to convince theists like me—those who do believe that a god exists—that we are out to lunch. Others are curious.

If you are not convinced that a god exists but are curious, I'd suggest a simple thought exercise. If the circle below represents all knowledge, or everything that can be known, imagine drawing a smaller circle inside the larger circle to reflect how much of that knowledge you personally possess.

I'm guessing your circle will be small. My circle would be so small that it might appear to be invisible. Once you've drawn your circle, ask yourself this question: Is it possible that a god of some sort could exist somewhere in the larger circle but outside your smaller circle?

Whether you are convinced that no god exists or you simply lack the belief that one does exist, if it is even possible that a god could exist outside your smaller circle of knowledge, such thoughts are worth exploring.

Actually, could any thoughts be more important?

If you do believe in God but struggle with doubt, take courage; you are not alone. Most honest believers will admit that they wrestle with doubt sometimes. Skeptics have all sorts of doubt. I will write more on faith and doubt later in this book, but let me suggest briefly here that doubt isn't nearly as significant a problem as is *unexamined* doubt.[3]

UNEXAMINED DOUBT?

Some people don't even know why they doubt. Others have held on to their doubt for so long that it may prevent them from stopping to consider ideas that suggest good reasons to believe in God might really exist. When dealing with doubt, some people fail to carefully examine the reasons for it.

As a result, they end up uncritically trusting it. Although this is not true of all who doubt, it is certainly true of many. These people have never stopped to ask a couple of very important questions:

Could my reasons for doubt be wrong?
Should I doubt my doubt?

I'm suggesting here that, in the same way some Christians have been accused of holding onto faith blindly, some skeptics tend to do the same thing with their doubt.

But Christians are never asked to hold onto their faith blindly. Christians learn in the Bible that they should always be ready to provide reasons for the hope that is within them "with gentleness and respect."[4]

If you are a Christian, learning why you believe is important. Likewise, if you do not believe in God, you should not blindly hold onto your doubt. Knowing why one does *not* believe is also very important. If it turns out that a non-believer is wrong and Christianity is true, the result of the mistake of unbelief is incalculable.

Blaise Pascal was a brilliant French mathematician, scientist, inventor, and philosopher who lived during the 1600s. He was a renaissance man. He was also a Christian. An amazing book containing his observations on Christianity was published in 1670. The content was found after Pascal died in 1662. He had been working on a book that would defend the Christian faith.

Called *Pensées,* or, when translated from French, *Thoughts,* it is more a list of his insights than it is a typical book. But it is fantastic and still worth reading today. It has challenged thoughtful minds for more than 350 years.

In his book, you will find ideas that, together, have come to be known as Pascal's wager. I have paraphrased it here:

1. If God does not exist, but a person believes he does, that person doesn't lose much for having been wrong;[5]
2. If God does not exist, and a person correctly rejects belief, the person doesn't gain much by being correct in denying his existence;
3. If God does exist but a person does not believe, that person loses everything; and, finally,
4. If God does exist, a person who believes and discovers how to relate rightly to him gains everything.[6]

We should not make the mistake of asking Pascal's wager to do more than it should. I am not convinced that it offers a fully compelling argument that God exists. So, I don't see this as a solid enough reason to believe. Rather, I see it as a tremendous reminder that the stakes are high.

If it is even possible that Christianity is true, one should consider the evidence closely.

My hope is that these pages will provide food for thought for every reader, regardless of the person's spiritual background, because, as Penn Jillette and Blaise Pascal both recognized, this stuff really matters.

So, let's dive in.

PART ONE

Why I Believe

– SECTION ONE –

Life

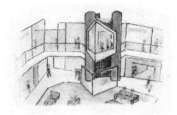

Blister Soul

On October 25, 1999, two F-16 fighter planes from the Oklahoma Air National Guard's 138th Fighter Wing scrambled to intercept a Learjet that was headed into America's heartland.

The plane they were ordered to intercept was not an enemy aircraft. It had not been hijacked. It was not carrying criminals, terrorists, drug smugglers, or anyone else who was harboring ill will toward the United States or its people.

I first read about the intercept of the jet on the internet as it happened, in real time. As the jet flew, there was speculation (later denied by the Pentagon) that our fighter pilots would be ordered to shoot it down if it approached a major city.

The Prime Minister of Canada at the time, Jean Chrétien, did authorize the Royal Canadian Air Force to shoot it down if it entered Canadian airspace without making contact. He made this decision even though he was certain that the plane's occupants had taken off with no intention of causing harm to anyone.[1]

The story was covered live, at least in part, because the jet carried a celebrity passenger, a famous professional golfer named Payne Stewart.

As someone who has played more than a little golf in my life, I have always followed professional golf with some interest. And I had recently become intrigued by Payne's story after reading about a number of powerful changes that had taken place in his life as he had begun to pursue a relationship with God.

✤ ✤ ✤

The plane had taken off from Orlando at 9:19 a.m., with Stewart, his two agents, and a golf course architect on board. It was headed for Texas, piloted by an experienced crew.

Nearly eight minutes into the flight, air traffic control received the last known radio transmission from the pilot. Approximately six and a half minutes later, an air traffic controller attempted to contact the Learjet but was unsuccessful.

The National Transportation Safety Board later determined that at some point between those two transmissions, the aircraft had suffered a loss of cabin pressurization and that the pilots had failed to receive supplemental oxygen in time. This quickly rendered everyone on the plane, including the pilots, unconscious.

The Learjet, however, continued to fly northwest, on autopilot.

At different points, the plane was intercepted by pairs of F-16s, including the two from the Oklahoma ANG. The F-16 pilots were instructed to visually inspect the Learjet and to report any signs that the pilots or passengers might be conscious.

None were observed. The cockpit windows were iced over from the inside. The Learjet pilots never responded to radio transmissions nor to the sight of the F-16s.

As the story unfolded, I refreshed my web browser repeatedly, to get updates as they were posted. I was transfixed and truly sad. I wanted to look away but could not.

I would guess I might have prayed for them. I do remember hoping that somehow, in some way, there would be a happy ending.

As the plane's flight path took them northwest, my heart went out to Payne, his companions on the flight, the pilots, and to each of their families. It felt surreal and heartbreaking to know that they were on a jet that seemed to be flying just fine, with its navigation, autopilot system, and both engines functioning properly, even as the aircraft and its passengers were in deep, deep trouble.

At approximately 12:10p.m. CDT, the plane began to run out of fuel. At 12:13, it crashed into a field near Mina, South Dakota. There were no survivors.

Even though I didn't know any of the passengers, I grieved their loss.

✛ ✛ ✛

If you could have somehow seen that Learjet 35 in flight on that fall day—sometime after the crew and passengers had passed out due to the lack of oxygen, but before you knew that fact—you might have thought how impressive the aircraft was. You might have noticed how awesome it looked, cruising at close to 500 miles per hour. You might have wondered if anyone famous was on board or where the plane was headed.

You never would have known, as you watched it fly, that as beautiful and well-built as the Learjet looked on the outside, something had gone terribly wrong on the inside.

This is not a bad description of many people today.

If we were to walk into Fair Oaks Mall, not far from my home, we'd see people who look great cruising through the mall, seemingly on autopilot, with no apparent worries. As we watched, we would have no clue that, as good as they looked on the outside, something had gone terribly wrong on the inside.

BROKENNESS SURROUNDS US

If we walked by the children's play area outside a department store, we might notice two young siblings playing. But we couldn't see that their ability to trust others had been damaged (in ways they won't come to understand for years) when their mom and dad's fighting got worse, leading to a divorce and their mom moving out.

If we grabbed a cup of coffee and sat down by the glass elevator in the atrium to watch people, we wouldn't be able to tell which ones were living under the weight of crushing stress due to the mountain of debt they had accumulated.

We wouldn't know that the gorgeous woman in line at Starbucks, whose looks turn the heads of both men and women, is dealing with debilitating depression and anxiety. Though many might notice her outer beauty, no one could see how profoundly she has struggled with an enduring sense of self-hatred.

We couldn't know that the man with the stylish haircut, expensive suit, and great shoes, who is walking by and seemingly at ease as he talks on his phone, is battling cancer and in a fight for his life.

We'd never know that the athletic 19-year-old, wearing cool jeans, a trendy shirt, and laughing with his identically dressed friends, never goes more than about 20 minutes without feeling an overwhelming and oppressive sadness caused by the impact his brother's drug addiction has had on his entire family.

We would have no clue that the quiet couple sitting near us and staring blankly into the distance, with their food untouched, had ventured out today for the first time since their toddler's funeral.

We couldn't see the fear in the life of the girl in the Apple store, buying a new phone to replace the one that was broken when she was attacked by a guy on a path near her dorm after a party.

These are just some of the people we might see at one mall, in one fairly affluent community, in one part of America. In many communities and homes, the brokenness is far more obvious.

The examples above are all related to awful realities in these people's lives. Often, however, the brokenness we experience is not related to a specific problem or difficulty.

WAYS WE SENSE BROKENNESS

Whether this brokenness is obvious and evident to everyone or more hidden inside people who look great as they cruise through a shopping mall, we tend to sense this brokenness in different ways.

Here are three:

1. A Sense that Our World is Broken

As we look at the current state of America, one of the wealthiest nations in modern history—a nation that many around the world would dream of living in—we still find crime, poverty, hunger, sickness and disease, mental health issues, addiction, broken families, broken relationships, a range of social injustices (injustices that have destroyed lives, families, and communities), and more. As I write, political and racial tensions dominate the news and are at a boiling point for many.

Despite its problems, there are still many great things about America. But one would have to be blind to miss the brokenness around us. And as challenging as things can seem in the United States today, things are worse in all sorts of places around the world. In many places, they are far worse. It doesn't take much imagination or genius to observe that the world itself seems terribly broken.

2. A Sense that Other People are Broken

If we observe that the world is broken, a logical conclusion is that it is broken, at least in part, because people are broken. Henry David Thoreau famously observed that "the mass of men lead lives of quiet desperation."[2] Albert Camus, the French philosopher who won the Nobel Prize in Literature, concluded that life is absurd. Bertrand Russell, the well-known atheist and philosopher, said, "Unless you assume a God, the question of life's meaning is meaningless."[3]

If there is no God, that means we are all flukes of nature—random accidents of chance. If there is no God, Russell was absolutely right. But even if God exists, people are not mistaken if they look at the lives around them and conclude that no matter how good people look on the outside, something has gone wrong.

My friend Derrick comments often on social media about how messed up our world is and about how messed up people are. As he looks at all that goes on in the world and the way people treat each other, he is constantly tempted to respond in anger or despair. He's not the only one.

His anger actually provides a subtle clue that God exists. If you saw the video of the death of George Floyd in 2020 and read about the details, nobody had to tell you it was wrong. You *knew* it.[4]

The fact that we would know it was wrong hints that there are absolute rights and wrongs built into our souls. The fact that we would get angry hints at our ability to judge right from wrong. But if this sense of right and wrong is somehow built into us, how did it get there? We'll come back to that later in the book.

I see brokenness in the world. I see it in other people. But if I stop there, I will likely miss the most important (but admittedly difficult) thought: that I, myself, am broken.

3. A Sense that I Personally Am Broken

We all may feel a personal sense of brokenness at times if something awful happens to us or a loved one. Still, we must not make the mistake of thinking that this sense that something has gone wrong is only the result of some terrible reality we are facing or of something bad that happens.

In our most perceptive moments, many of us recognize something that can be unsettling: that our brokenness is *within* us and not simply a result of things that have happened *to* us.

It is tempting to want to blame some person or trauma for our brokenness, sometimes for good reason. It is obviously true that many, many people have been wronged in ways that have created tremendously deep wounds. This sort of pain should not be dismissed or ignored.

But what if our brokenness runs deeper than those things that have caused us harm? What if we could remove each way we have been wronged from our past? We would still not escape this sense of brokenness.

For generations, songwriters (and poets, authors, playwrights, scriptwriters, and philosophers) have explored this theme. In the remainder of this chapter, we'll look at several songs that point, in different ways, to this personal brokenness.

SOMETHING IS MISSING

Lady Gaga and Bradley Cooper's massive hit, *Shallow*, from the 2018 film *A Star is Born*, struck a chord in the hearts of millions. The lyrics at the beginning of the song reflect what so many people feel: a sense that something is missing.

> *Tell me somethin', girl*
> *Are you happy in this modern world?*
> *Or do you need more?*
> *Is there somethin' else you're searchin' for?*
>
> *I'm falling*
> *In all the good times I find myself*
> *Longing for change*
> *And in the bad times I fear myself*
>
> *Tell me something, boy*
> *Aren't you tired trying to fill that void?*
> *Or do you need more?*
> *Ain't it hard keeping it so hardcore?* [5]

If we are honest, many of us do long for more—even in the good times—and are tired of trying to "fill that void." We too easily believe that sex, money, a career, power, success, the right house in the right neighborhood, social popularity, relationships, possessions, a great family, or some other thing will heal what ails us.

My friends Tanner and Katie recently pointed me to a Lauren Alaina song called *Getting Good*. The lyrics reflect our temptation to believe that life would be good if we could just get _____.

We may fill in our blanks differently, but deep down, we know where this road leads. We may manage to somehow get that thing we thought would fulfill us, only to discover that it doesn't work. So, we then turn to despair or change gears and begin to think we need to fill in our blanks with something new.

This is why kids beg for that must-have Christmas gift, only to turn their hearts to something new after receiving it. We did the same thing as kids. We do the same thing as adults.

The married person with a good life leaves his or her spouse. The shopaholic makes yet another unnecessary purchase. The rich person answers the question, "How much money is enough?" with, "Just a little more."[6]

I get it. I once bought a brand-new car and then—while driving it home from the dealer—caught myself admiring a different car I thought was somehow cooler than my new one.

But here's the eye-opening reality: People who have acquired or achieved the very thing we fill in our blanks with have their own blanks that they are trying to fill. This is why so many who have seemingly gained the world ask the same thing we ask: "Is this all there is?"

Or do you need more? Is there somethin' else you're searchin' for?

Actor Jim Carrey, in a college commencement speech several years ago, said, "I wish people could realize all of their dreams and wealth and fame so that they could see that it is not where they are going to find their sense of completion."[7]

Joe Gibbs has been inducted into both the NFL and NASCAR halls of fame. Joe led the Washington (then) Redskins to three Super Bowl championships. His NASCAR racing team has won five top-level, season-long championships and four Daytona 500 races. To have led teams to multiple championships at the highest level is impressive. To have done so in two different sports is legendary. But listen to Gibbs' perspective: "Every time I accomplished something like winning games, Super Bowls ... making some money, and all that, I still had an emptiness inside of me."[8]

The talented rapper NF has had two songs debut at #1 on the Billboard 200 chart, and his song *Let You Down* went triple platinum. His take on success may surprise you.

> *The most successful moment of my life was the worst—the most depressed I've ever been—literally feeling like I'd probably be happier if I was just dead. I got to number one on Billboard... My tour, every date sold out except one. So I literally had everything that I had always dreamed of happening. And I felt, well, I didn't feel happy at all... I was like, "I'm here, and if this is it, there's gotta be more for me because if this is it, it's not gonna work."[9]*

I have a friend who shared similar thoughts years ago. While in college, he had set a goal of becoming a millionaire before he turned 30. This was a goal that very few people would have even dreamed of accomplishing in his day. On his 30th birthday, he realized that he had met his goal. He called it one of the emptiest days of his life.

The experiences of these men are not uncommon, even among people who have achieved great success. Whatever we achieve, satisfaction can still seem elusive. This is a running theme in Lin-Manuel Miranda's phenomenal musical, *Hamilton*. In the show, one of the driving forces in Alexander Hamilton's life is this persistent lack of satisfaction. No matter how much he accomplished, it never seemed to be enough.

Aren't you tired trying to fill that void? Or do you need more?

SOMETHING IS WRONG

Beyond merely having a sense that something is missing, many of us wrestle with a sense that something is actually wrong, deep down inside.

My friend Ryan suggested I listen to the song *Hurt* from Nine Inch Nails' 1994 record, *The Downward Spiral*. Written by the band's frontman, Trent Reznor, the lyrics are a powerful cry of despair. Ryan also suggested I watch the music video of Johnny Cash's cover of the song. I'm glad he did. It is the single most powerful and emotionally haunting music video I've ever seen.

Recorded near the end of Cash's life, mainly inside the now-closed and run-down House of Cash (his former museum), the video has a different feel than Nine Inch Nails' version. Cash's interpretation of the song, as he looks back at life from the perspective of one nearing death, points to our brokenness, the brevity of life, and the emptiness of worldly pursuits.[10]

Here are several lines from the song:

> *What have I become, my sweetest friend?*
> *Everyone I know goes away in the end.*
> *You could have it all, my empire of dirt.*
> *I will let you down. I will make you hurt.*
> *I wear my crown of thorns, upon my liar's chair,*
> *Full of broken thoughts I cannot repair.*[11]

In just these few lines, Reznor's lyrics capture a variety of reasons people may experience feelings of personal brokenness. These feelings can come when a person: confronts the fact that he does not like who he is or who he is becoming; contemplates the pain that comes with the end of a significant relationship (whether that end comes through death or because one person has walked away); recognizes that too much of his life was invested in chasing the wrong things; recalls all of the ways he has failed or let other people down; or simply realizes his own thoughts are broken—and that he is incapable of fixing them.

Similar thoughts can be found in the Bible. The Apostle Paul, the author of a number of letters that became books in the New Testament, wrote, "I do not understand my own actions. I do not do what I want, but I do the very thing I hate." Later, he wrote, "What a wretched man I am! Who will rescue me from this body of death?" [12]

Perhaps you relate to one or several things in the previous two paragraphs. Perhaps some of the ways you experience brokenness in your own heart are very different.

Or maybe you are in a good moment in life and cannot relate to this at all because you are content with your health, family, finances, career, and relationships. If that is the case for you, enjoy this moment. But we know how tenuous such a feeling can be. We may be only one disease, death, accident, job loss, financial setback, relational breakdown, or other kind of trial away from that satisfaction disappearing.

THE ROOT OF THE PROBLEM

Even if all is well in your world at the moment, do not be surprised if, at some point, you begin to wrestle with the sense that something has gone terribly wrong on the inside.

C.S. Lewis, in *Mere Christianity*, suggested a possible reason why:

> *Creatures are not born with desires unless satisfaction for those desires exists. A baby feels hunger: well, there is such a thing as food. A duckling wants to swim: well, there is such a thing as water. Men feel sexual desire: well, there is such a thing as sex. If I find in myself a desire which no experience in this world can satisfy, the most probable explanation is that I was made for another world.*[13]

We will not find lasting satisfaction in the things of this world. The idea that we may have been made for a different world hints at a problem that some have never stopped to consider: a spiritual problem.

Bill Mallonee is an artist and musician who has recorded nearly 80 albums over the course of his career. Many people have never heard of him, even though he has written more than 2,000 songs. In one poll of the "Top 100 Living Songwriters," he was voted #65.[14]

One of Bill's songs is called *Blister Soul*. The first part of the song captures this sense that something isn't as it is supposed to be—inside us.

> *Yeah, you got this place you go*
> *It's just a trip before the fall*
> *Way past the fevered pitch*
> *Just a spit from the wrecking ball*
>
> *Said you woke up this morning*
> *Said you woke up under a curse*
> *I've heard the blues are bad*
> *but this is something worse*
> *And the ambulance driver*
> *Well he tips his hat and stares*
> *And he asks you in a grave voice*
> *'Can I take you anywhere?'*
>
> *Yeah, the thing we cannot speak of*
> *Too painful to behold*
> *Oh, this blister soul*
> *Oh, this blister soul*
> *Oh, this blister soul*
>
> *There's a smaller place you go*
> *Where there's hardly any sound*
> *Where the deals have all gone sour*
> *And the house of cards comes down*
> *And the damage is costly*
> *It's beyond all dollars and cents*
> *You can't measure it with graphs and charts*
> *or any instruments*

Yeah, the thing we cannot speak of
The secret we all know
This blister soul
Oh, this blister soul
Oh, this blister soul [15]

Mallonee suggests that our brokenness is found in our souls. He calls it "the secret we all know."

Ninety years before Mallonee wrote *Blister Soul*, G.K. Chesterton wrote a letter to the editor of a London newspaper. Chesterton was a theologian, a thinker, and one of the most prolific writers ever. He lived in Great Britain in the early 1900s and died at 62. Yet, during those 62 years, he somehow managed to write more than 100 books, 200 short stories, hundreds of poems, several plays, and more than 4,000 essays![16]

His work influenced such a broad range of writers that the list of famous authors who have praised his writing might make up a wing of a modern authors' hall of fame.

In 1905, London's *Daily News* published a piece titled, "What's Wrong with the World?" The article generated many responses, including one from Chesterton. If you had lived in London at the time, you might have expected his reply to be a long one.

You would have been wrong.

His entire response is often wrongly reported to have included four words: "Dear Sirs, I am." Actually, he wrote a short paragraph, but the core of his answer contained only three words:

> *The answer to the question, "What is Wrong?" is, or should be, "I am*
> *wrong." ... This original sin belongs to all ages, and is the business of*
> *religion.* [17]

G.K. Chesterton's answer in 1905 was, in a way, the same as Bill Mallonee's nearly a hundred years later: *I am wrong.*

This problem—the one felt or sensed by so many—is a universal one, they suggested. And a spiritual one.

Oh, this blister soul.

I should deal with a couple of possible objections some may feel at this point. First, nothing written in this chapter is meant to suggest that there aren't happy people in the world. There are. Nor does it imply that there is no good in the world. There is.

The argument here is that however much good we might see in the world, or however happy we might be in our present circumstances, there will be times when we become aware of a very real brokenness within us, and that this brokenness reflects (at least in part) a spiritual problem.[18]

Some of us sense this deeply. Others, less so. Some only become aware of it during a moment of crisis or, as Bill Mallonee wrote, "when the house of cards comes down."

Whatever you think of God, know this: if there is a God and if the central claims of Christianity are true, our broken world is behaving and functioning precisely as we should expect. We see in mankind (and in ourselves) a capacity for love, kindness, and selflessness. This is what we should expect from the human race, a people created in the image of God. Yet, we also see in mankind (and in ourselves) a capacity for selfishness, unkindness, hate, and ways we often fail to live as we ought to live. We see evil. Sometimes we see evil within ourselves. This, too, is what we should expect from the human race, a people who have fallen by turning away from God and deciding to go their own way, sometimes through active rebellion against God and sometimes through passive indifference.

If you aren't persuaded that God exists, however, it may be difficult to see the problem inside as a spiritual one, and thus one that demands a spiritual solution. This line of thinking would not have made sense to me either, at least for the first 18 years of my life.

✝ ✝ ✝

When I was a kid, I didn't think much about the brokenness in our world. I was like many teenagers—preoccupied with my own world. I might have been thinking about some girl, what I'd be doing with my friends later, or my practice schedule. Those things probably represented the depth of my thinking until one awful day during high school.

I was outside, throwing the football with some friends (if I even remember that fact correctly; memories of that day are a bit of a blur). My mom called me to come inside. Something was terribly wrong.

"Dad is very sick," she said. She had already called 911.

✛ ✛ ✛

My brother and I are blessed to have grown up with amazing parents. They were fantastic role models: fun, supportive, encouraging, and involved in our lives. I don't remember them missing a sporting event of mine. They always gave us the freedom to grow and spread our wings, as long as they trusted us. Beyond who they were as parents, they were amazing people. They were kind, generous, and loving. My ideas about how to live and parent were profoundly shaped by their example.

One of the things they often told me and my brother, however, was something I now believe I consistently misheard. They told us often that no matter what happened to us in life, they would always be there for us. In retrospect, I now know what they meant. They meant that they would always be in our corner, no matter what. That has proven to be true. They have lived it, and I have always felt it. And this has given me the courage to try all sorts of things in life.

What I heard, as a kid, was that they'd *always be here.* Of course, logically, if I had stopped to think about it, I would have seen problems with such a promise. But as I watched my dad being rolled into the ambulance that day, it rocked my world.

He might die.

For the first time, I became aware that my parents' ability to always be there for us was not really in their control. It seems ridiculous now, but I had never considered the possibility that an accident, a heart attack, or some other sickness could happen and that one or both could be gone in the blink of an eye.

I had no idea, when the ambulance took my dad away, what would happen next. At that point in my life, I'm not sure I had been to a funeral. Would my dad's be my first?

I had a great relationship with both parents. But if either of them, who I had believed would always be there for me, could be gone that quickly, it called everything into question. What else had I trusted that was false?

Clearly, this was a step toward becoming an adult. As kids, we believe all sorts of things, but then come to a point—usually in our late teens or early 20s—of deciding if we will retain those beliefs as our own and carry them forward into adulthood.

Thankfully, the EMTs, doctors, and nurses all did their thing, and my dad eventually got well. He is still beating me at golf more often than I'd like to admit. The fact that he did not die is one of the things in my life for which I am most thankful.

Obviously, though, not everyone recovers. Not all hospital trips have happy endings. Not all diseases get healed.

My wife, my mom, and all three of my sisters-in-law lost their dads far too young. My brother-in-law, Bryan, died far too early, leaving behind his wife and their four amazing kids. On Karey's side of the family, we still mourn the loss of three kids who each died in their 20s.

Perhaps losing someone unexpectedly is part of your story. If so, I am sorry. I know that such a loss is rarely far from your mind or heart. Most of us have seen significant relationships end sadly. All of us have either had or will have moments in life where the death of someone (or the very real possibility of it) shakes up everything. If you haven't—as much as I hate to write this—you will one day. And it will threaten to rock your world.

In those moments, we often wrestle with some of life's larger questions. This is what happened in my life. What would have happened in our family if Dad had died? What would have happened to him? Is there a heaven? Would he have gone there? If I died, would I go there?

Though I don't recall sitting and thinking about these types of questions, I became aware of them. Without recognizing it at the time, this began what I'd now call my spiritual journey.

It would be another year and a half until I started to discover answers that made sense.

Go Time

WHEN ONE JUMPS INTO A BODY OF WATER from the top of a tall tower, unexpected things can happen. Sadly, I know this from experience.

During the first week of my sophomore year in college, I went swimming at a quarry with friends, including my suitemates from the year before, Todd and Keith. If I had only learned one thing during my freshman year, it would have been that these guys never seemed to run out of ideas about fun things to do on a given day.

For my younger readers, hanging out with those two was like hanging out with Phineas and Ferb: *I know what we are going to do today.*

The quarry had a small beach-like area fronting a lake. Not too far out, in what turned out to be deep water, was a concrete tower that rose, I would guess, somewhere between 25 and 40 feet above the lake. My memory suggests it was closer to 40, but I don't know for sure. The height of the tower in my memory might be like the length of the fish that was caught, but somehow continues to get longer as time passes and the story of the catch is retold.

When we arrived, we watched several kids climb up a metal ladder attached to the tower as other kids jumped from the top and into the water. It didn't seem particularly tall or scary; it looked like fun.

A little more than halfway up the ladder, a rope hung down that you could grab to swing out over the water and drop in. The first time I climbed the ladder, I grabbed the rope, swung out, and let go. It felt like a trial run, of sorts. It was fun.

I swam back to the ladder and confidently began to climb.

When I got to the top and managed to get close enough to the edge to peek over, I realized that my confidence was suddenly missing in action. From the ground, I had vastly underestimated the full height of the tower.

Standing at the top, I recalibrated and saw that we were, by my new estimation, approximately 47,000 feet in the air. Somewhere in the back of my mind, I must have been aware it wasn't that tall and that my mind was playing tricks on me. Still, I couldn't shake the feeling that if an airplane flew by, we'd be looking down at it.

The top of the tower was flat and formed a decent-sized platform. A couple of kids had brought lawn chairs and beer up the ladder and were making a day of it. One guy, perhaps with alcohol-fueled courage, did a double flip on the way down. Another kid did a handstand at the edge before taking the big plunge.

I, on the other hand, was thinking about how different the view had looked from the ground. The good news was that all the kids who were jumping seemed to be surviving. The bad news showed up in a form that was actually far scarier than the drop itself.

Lightning.

One of those late-afternoon summer storms that seem to come out of nowhere was approaching. You've seen them: a bright blue sky in three directions and an ominous black sky in the fourth.

The storm was not far away and was closing fast. It occurred to me at that moment that I was the tallest guy, on top of a tall tower, above the trees, standing near a wet metal ladder, in the middle of a good-sized lake. I was soaking wet. In my mind, lightning had never seen a better target.

The fact that there were cute girls at the quarry eliminated any thought of climbing back down the ladder. A lesser man might have been paralyzed by fear at this point. I knew it was go time.

I jumped.

Half way down, everything was good. I felt stable in the air and was maintaining my balance nicely. It was a thrill, and at that point, I was blissfully unaware of what was about to happen.

Before I jumped, someone had said I should try to remain as vertically upright as possible while entering the water. That made sense. Other tips were shared. Nobody, however, had bothered to mention what perhaps was obvious to everyone but me: "No matter what happens, *keep your legs together.*"

Then I hit the water. More accurately, the water hit me. My legs were not together.

Let's just say that the water scored a direct hit. Every male who is reading this might be cringing right now. Or tempted to laugh. Laughter in the face of this sort of pain seems to be a guy thing.

In addition to the obvious reason I was experiencing pain, something else had happened that I had not expected. When I landed, water was injected into me in a way I had not previously thought possible. Water I had not swallowed seemed to now be present inside my stomach.

Somehow, I simultaneously surfaced, managed to tread water while curling up into a ball, let out a long groan, and started laughing, even in the midst of the pain. There's that guy thing again.

People say you learn valuable life lessons in college. I learned a few that day, as I often did when hanging out with Todd and Keith. In fact, it would not be an overstatement to say that a couple of the most profoundly influential things I would ever learn in life, I first learned through the two of them.

+ + +

When I arrived on campus as a freshman, I didn't know a single person apart from my orientation weekend roommate, a tennis player named Sonny. I remember thinking, as my parents were leaving after dropping me off, that I had exactly one friend at the entire school: a guy I had known for two days.

My freshman roommate, Mike, showed up in camouflage army fatigue long pants (on a very hot day) and a Sex Pistols "No Future" t-shirt. He wore earrings and a mullet before either was considered particularly cool. It turns out he was simply ahead of the curve. He was a musician and an artist, and he was into bands I'd never heard of. In one of our first conversations, he said, "I hate sports."

Uh oh.

Growing up, I played a ton of different sports. When I wasn't playing, I was watching, reading about, or talking about sports. Sports occupied a huge percentage of my mental space.

This could be a long year.

Our two suitemates, Todd and Keith, let us know pretty quickly that they were Christians and that their faith played a big role in their lives.

Yep... This is definitely going to be a long year.

I remember thinking I had heaven on one side and hell on the other, but I wasn't ready for either yet.

During the first weeks of school, I jumped into campus life with both feet. I checked out Greek Row, made friends there, and was encouraged to consider rushing.

I made other friends by getting involved with the yearbook and school newspaper. I had done some sports photography in the past and had always enjoyed it. I discovered that both publications paid their photographers. I could get sideline passes to any sporting event, use the school's expensive lenses, and get paid to do it.

On top of all of that, I got access to a great spread of free food in the press room at football and basketball games. It may have been the best college job ever; I probably would have done it for free.

The guys who lived upstairs were also incredibly fun. We played a lot of pickup basketball, and their weekly Shoot-Tennis-Balls-with-Lacrosse-Sticks-Down-the-Dorm-Hall-and-Directly-at-Each-Other-at-Midnight tournaments were epic.

It turns out, though, that the most fun guys I was able to find on campus were my suitemates. Todd and Keith really did have an endless supply of ideas for adventures. They had a fantastic group of friends, most of whom sought out the kinds of weekend fun they would not regret the next morning. That alone made them different from some of my other college friends.

But there was something else that made them different. They had a sense of purpose and direction that was different from anyone I had ever met. They drew strength and peace from their faith and really cared about people. That stood out; I did not know a ton of kids I would have described as selfless. I wouldn't have described myself as selfless.

I had never known guys who would have called themselves committed Christians until I met them. That's not to say there weren't any of those kids in my high school. If there were, I just didn't know much about their faith. A friend I really liked did invite me to his youth group—and I went once—but I had always thought, "I'm not religious."

I had always assumed that some kind of God must exist. Our family went to church occasionally on Easter or at Christmas, but I had never thought much about spiritual things.

As I got to know my suitemates, it occurred to me that somehow, and I wasn't sure why, I had formed a mental image of what a Christian who believed the Bible must be like.

It was not a flattering picture.

Looking back now, I'd say it was a caricature, based more on my imagination than on any specific people I had known. That caricature led me to assume that anyone I met who believed the Bible must not be smart, interesting, or thoughtful. They certainly wouldn't be relatable, athletic, social, or fun. And there's no way they would jump into a lake from atop a 47,000-foot-tall tower.

My caricature included the belief that Christians judge others without knowing them. Sadly, some Christians do this, but those who understand their faith with much depth generally do not. I realized that I was the one who was guilty of making unfair judgments, about Christians, without knowing them.

Todd and Keith broke just about every stereotype I held about Christians and Christianity. They were funny, social, and smart. It was more interesting to see what creative thing they'd be doing on a weekend night than to hang with other friends who had seemed to settle into a routine of seeking to find the best places to get drunk or to hook up with some random person.

THAT WAS NEW TO ME

During those first weeks of school, as I got to know Mike, it turned out that my first impressions were way off. He was laid-back, thoughtful, funny, and interesting. He introduced me to what is still some of my favorite music. And pretty quickly, we became great friends.

We also became great friends with Todd and Keith. The four of us talked about every topic possible, often late into the night. Sometimes, those conversations were about God. Todd and Keith never minded our questions. They often had better answers than I had guessed might exist. That was new to me.

I was fascinated by the way they talked about their faith. They talked about a personal relationship with God and not just a system of dos and don'ts. That was new to me.

We listened to mostly the same music, but they also listened to some "contemporary Christian" music. Some of it wasn't particularly contemporary, but some of it was. Some was very good. Sometimes, I found myself listening to it when they weren't around. One song about God kept getting stuck in my head and just seemed to speak to me. That was new to me.

They also prayed. Other than maybe my grandmother, I had not known anyone who prayed regularly. Even more interesting to me was that they kept track of their prayers and had a real expectation that God would answer. They kept a list of things they were praying for on a clipboard, and they wrote down answers as they saw them.

Did God really answer their prayers? I didn't know. But it fascinated me that they were convinced he did. That was new to me.

Very early in the year, they had explained an overview of Christianity in four points. Looking back, I guess I'd call their four points an outline that helped me learn what it means to be a Christian. I had to admit that if their outline was really what Christianity was all about, I had been clueless. I'll come back to how they explained it later, but as I heard these ideas, they resonated with something inside. That was new to me.

My suitemates also explained that Christianity rises or falls on one event in history: the resurrection of Jesus. They showed me, in the Bible, that it openly admits that if Jesus was not actually and physically raised from the dead, then all of Christianity was a fraud and a waste of time—and that Christians should be pitied most of all.[1]

That was definitely new to me.

✛ ✛ ✛

Early in that first semester, I got a call from my parents. My grandmother had suffered a stroke. Doctors said she would live, but the prognosis was not great. Todd and Keith said, "We'll pray for her."

They added her to their clipboard.

Three days later, she was released from the hospital. Her doctors couldn't explain what happened. They simply said she had taken a dramatic and inexplicable turn for the better.

I immediately thought of the clipboard and still remember thinking, "Maybe it's not so inexplicable..." I didn't fully believe yet, but at this point, the possibility that God was real (and interested in our lives) at least had my attention.

This is not surprising if God is real. There are a number of places in the Bible that reveal that God works to draw people back into a relationship with him. Still, the idea that my heart was being drawn toward belief didn't do a lot to convince my brain. I had questions.

Todd and Keith understood that I'd need to see, rationally, that this was not some kind of weird or cultish understanding of the Bible. They knew I'd need to explore whether the Bible was even trustworthy before I would seriously consider Christianity. So, they gave me books to read and pointed me to specific chapters in other books. I was surprised by my own curiosity.

I started reading.

One of the first books they gave me seemed to be intended to be more of a reference book than one to be read from cover to cover. It was called *Evidence that Demands a Verdict* by Josh McDowell. I read nearly all of it. I still had questions, but the book fascinated me. And it made sense.[2]

As I read that book, different parts of the Bible, and other books, I found myself thinking that if Christianity was really true, its answers made more sense than anything else I'd heard as to why the world seemed to be so messed up, why people seemed so messed up, and about why parts of me seemed so messed up. It explained the brokenness that surrounds us.

As I have continued to learn more about Christianity, I have come to believe, increasingly, that the Christian worldview offers the most coherent and rational answers to life's biggest questions. Some of these questions include:

- Why is there something rather than nothing?
- How do you determine right and wrong?
- How do you explain human nature?
- What is the meaning of life?
- What happens to a person at death?

Even though I wasn't consciously asking these exact questions, I did wonder about them. Most of us do, sometimes. My dad's sickness 18 months earlier had opened my eyes to questions like these. But I still had what I saw as more basic questions.

Does God exist? Was Jesus truly God? Did he actually rise from the dead? Couldn't all religions be different paths to the same God? What does "a personal relationship with God" even mean? Did God really answer Todd and Keith's prayer about my grandmother's stroke?

Perhaps you wrestle with similar questions.

Perhaps you are asking something even more basic: Could any of us truly *know* these things? Do traditional ideas about truth even apply to religion? Does belief in God demand some sort of 47,000-foot-high blind leap of faith?

We'll pause here, in the middle of my journey, and consider a couple of these questions. We'll pick up my story a bit later.

Truth

The Dress

IN MY HUMBLE OPINION, FEBRUARY 26, 2015, was one of the most entertaining days in the history of the internet. Whether you prefer the always-popular animal video or a viral social media debate, that day was a great one.

Some of you may remember that Thursday as the day that a young Scottish musician, Caitlin McNeill, nearly broke the internet. Actually, you may not remember her name or the exact date, but if you were online that day, you will almost certainly remember (unless you were buried under a rock) the now-famous photo she posted.

It was of a dress. Perhaps more helpfully, it was a photo of what both Google and Wikipedia now simply refer to as *the* dress.[1]

The photo had been taken a few weeks earlier by a woman named Cecilia Bleasdale at a mall near Chester, England. She was shopping for a dress to wear to her daughter's wedding and texted the photo to her daughter. She never could have guessed that her snapshot would become world-famous or later land her on the *Ellen DeGeneres Show*.

Her daughter showed the photo to her fiancé. The engaged couple disagreed about the color of the dress, so they posted it on Facebook. Was it white and gold, they asked their friends, or was it blue and black?

Caitlin, a musician at the wedding, was still intrigued by the photo a couple days later. She posted it to her Tumblr blog and sent a link to Buzzfeed, asking them to take a poll. Buzzfeed reposted it.

That's when basically every human being with internet access got involved in the argument. To say the photo went viral is an understatement, approximately on the same scale as saying people tend to have an opinion about Donald Trump.

Until that Thursday, Buzzfeed had never had more than 420,000 users simultaneously reading one story. A few hours after the dress went viral, more than 670,000 people were viewing the article at one time. At its peak, more than 11,000 unique users were coming to the page every second. Caitlyn's Tumblr post, at its peak, drew 140,000 views per minute.

Within 24 hours, there were 4.4 million posts about the dress on Twitter. Over time, Buzzfeed's page would draw 38+ million unique visitors. Caitlyn's Tumblr page: 73+ million. And those numbers are smaller than the millions of others who saw the dress on other social media sites, in the news, or after someone had forwarded the photo to them.

Taylor Swift wrote on Twitter, "I don't understand this odd dress debate and I feel like it's a trick somehow. I'm confused and scared. P.S. It's OBVIOUSLY BLUE AND BLACK."[2] Her post quickly received more than 265,000 likes and retweets (combined).

She wasn't the only celebrity who chimed in.

Demi Lovato: "Hold on... So people actually see white and gold...??!!"[3]

Anna Kendrick: "If that's not white and gold the universe is falling apart. Seriously, what is happening????"[4]

Justin Bieber: "And for everyone asking, I see blue and black."[5]

Kim Kardashian West: "What color is that dress? I see white & gold. Kanye sees black & blue, who is color blind?"[6]

Josh Groban took the spiritual route. He sought input from none other than the Pope: "@Pontifex, help."[7]

Ariana Grande had an entertaining take: "If one more person asks me what color I think this damn dress is..."[8]

Perhaps my favorite was from actress Rashida Jones. She wrote, "What genius pulled off this elaborate metaphor just to teach us the importance of tolerating other perspectives? #blueandblack #whiteandgold"[9]

Lost in the debate was one critically important fact: there was a correct answer to the question. This means that there was also a wrong answer. I'm guessing that most readers will recall that the dress was, in fact, blue and black.[10]

The #whiteandgold camp was wrong.

TRUTH IS EXCLUSIVE
This leads us to an important idea: truth is exclusive. The right answer excludes many possible but wrong answers.

I will admit that I thought the dress was white and gold. I've spent enough time color-correcting photos in Photoshop to be confident that I was right. According to one poll, 75% of those surveyed were with me on team white and gold.[11]

But no matter how passionately we felt, it turns out that Anna, Kim, and I—and many others—were wrong.

The right answer, that the dress was blue and black, excluded the wrong answer, that it was white and gold. It also excluded the possibility that it was brown and sky blue, or gray and teal, or any other combination of colors.

Here's a related example. If my friend Zakara asked me where I was sitting when I first saw a reference to the now-famous dress and I told her I first read about it while I was in my house, I would be making a truth claim.

She would probably believe me, but even if she didn't, a correct answer does exist.

If it is true that I read about it while inside my home in Virginia, it means I was not somewhere else. I did not read about it while I was on a beach in Cabo. I did not read about it while in a cafe, on the Metro, at my parents' house, or while I was sitting in Brooklyn's Prospect Park.

Of the many places I could theoretically have been in the universe that day, I was physically in only one. There is one right answer to the question of where I was. There are an enormous, almost incalculable, number of wrong answers.

Truth is exclusive.

CAN TRUTH BE DIFFERENT FOR DIFFERENT PEOPLE?
The answer to this question is: It depends. We first must sort out whether we are discussing an objective truth claim or a subjective truth claim. Both can be helpful.

To make an objective truth claim is to claim that the truth about a thing is rooted in the object itself and not in how someone personally perceives it. The claim that the dress was blue and black was an objective truth claim. If you were to claim that a particular bowling ball found in one specific bowling alley weighed 16 pounds, that too would be an objective truth claim. If such a claim is found to be true, it is true for everyone.

A subjective truth claim is different. A subjective truth is rooted in one's personal perceptions and therefore will not be true for everyone. A six-year-old might say that the 16-pound bowling ball I just mentioned is heavy. But my friend Andrew, a serious weightlifter, might pick up the same ball effortlessly and call it light.

Objectively, the ball might weigh 16 pounds. But these two people would have different subjective perceptions about the weight of the ball.

Imagine that my friend Mackenzie looked at a thermometer in a swimming pool and told our friend Aaron that the water temperature was 80°(F). She would be making an objective truth claim. If the water was truly 80°, it would be 80° for everybody.

But if my friends Zoe and Ioanna were swimming in that same pool, one of them might say, "The water is cold." The other might respond, "No, I think it is perfect." Neither would be wrong; each would be expressing how she subjectively experiences the objective reality that the water is 80°.

If we don't think well about the difference between objective and subjective truth, we can run into problems as we try to evaluate different sorts of truth claims.

Imagine that someone asked my friend Kayla how to spell her name, and she answered "K-a-y-l-a." In this case, Kayla would be making an objective truth claim. Her answer would be true for everyone. If that person then said, "That may be true for you, but it's not true for me. For me, your name is spelled C-a-i-l-a," it would be odd. And wrong.

This "true for you but not for me" idea does have some appeal. Everyone can go home happy. But what if this idea reflects poor thinking? Can a claim of objective truth really be true for one person but not for another in the same context?

Imagine that my friends Nick and Andrew were discussing Andrew's shoe collection, and Nick asked, "How many shoes are displayed on your wall?" If Andrew responded with a number and Nick replied, "That number may be true for you, but it is not true for me; for me, there is a different number," we'd have a disagreement to sort out. Ultimately, though, one number would be objectively true.

If my friends Gavin, Taylor, Israel, and Eugene claimed that their Westfield High School football team won three straight state championships during their high school careers, they would be making an objective truth claim. If true (and it is true), this claim would be true for everyone.

The phrase I mentioned above, "in the same context," is also important.

If my friend Emma was in the basement of her family's three-story home, she could rightly say, "The kitchen is upstairs." If Laura, Emma's mom, was on the top floor, she could rightly say, "The kitchen is downstairs." Both would be correct in their own contexts. If both were upstairs, however, on the top floor (and thus in the same context), only Laura's statement would be true.

If Emma then said, "That may be true for you, Mom, but it is not true for me," she would be wrong.

The idea that an objective truth claim can be true for one person but not for another, in the same context, simply does not work. But people can sometimes lose sight of this when they begin to think about God.

SO, HOW DO THESE IDEAS APPLY TO OUR VIEWS ABOUT GOD?

If someone claims that the central teachings of a particular religion are true, most Americans will shrug and go on with their day. They will either think, "I agree" or, perhaps, "To each his own."

When someone says, "To each his own" about religion, he may be saying, "We all have the right to believe whatever we choose." I strongly agree. This is called freedom of religion.[12] He may, however, be suggesting that whatever somebody believes can be *true for that person.* "Oh, right," he might say to someone who follows a certain religion, "that may be true for you, but it is not true for me."

There's that phrase again. It works subjectively. But claims about God are interesting because some are objective while others are subjective.

We know that religions make objective truth claims. But we also know that people from a wide range of different faith perspectives (subjectively) draw comfort, hope, meaning, and more from their faith. Their faith provides the framework through which they interpret the world.

Here is the critically important question: Is it better to evaluate a set of religious beliefs by their objective truth claims or by our own subjective perceptions or feelings about those claims?

At Group one Sunday night, we addressed this exact topic. I passed around a glass jug of spare change for the students to inspect and asked each student to write down two things on an index card. First, I asked them to write down exactly how much change they thought was in the jug. Then I asked them to write down the name of their favorite movie.

When everyone finished, they read their answers out loud, and I revealed the precise amount of change in the jug. We discovered that my friend Ana's guess was the closest to the correct answer.

I then asked something they did not expect: "Whose movie choice was the closest to correct?"

This was obviously a strange question. There was a specific amount of money in the jug—an objective standard by which people's guesses could be judged. But to say that one person's favorite movie was more correct than anyone else's was ridiculous. Movie preferences are subjective, a matter of personal opinion and taste.

I then asked this follow-up question: "In your view, is deciding what is true about God more of an objective investigation, like trying to figure out the amount of change in the jug, or a subjective preference question like the one about movies?"[13]

This should be thought-provoking for all of us because many people tend to settle on a set of beliefs about God in the same way one might decide about a purchase. A person might ask, "Which of these options do I like the most?" Or, "Which seems best?" Or perhaps even, for a few, "Which is least distasteful?"

People sometimes reject a religion because they decide, subjectively, that they don't like or even hate something it teaches. I know people who have done this. In America, our Constitution guarantees the freedom of religion, so we are free to choose what we believe about God in whatever way we'd like.

But I'd suggest that our personal (subjective) preferences, tastes, and experiences are not the best criteria to use when evaluating the claims of a religion. It is easy to imagine that a person could have a bad experience with followers of what turns out to be a true religion. Likewise, it is not hard to find stories of a person being lured into some kind of awful cult and feeling welcomed and loved while getting involved.

If my eternal destiny is on the line, wisdom suggests that a better question than what I *like*, subjectively, has to be, "Which objective truth claims about God, if any, are really true?"

All religions make objective truth claims. But can the central claims of every religion be true? If not, it would be smart to sort out which are true and which are not.

If it is possible that the central claims of some (or many, or most, or all) religions are not true, this would be important to know.

WAIT. PATRICK, YOU BELIEVE THAT SOME RELIGIONS ARE WRONG?

If I haven't been clear to this point, let me be clear now. I believe that the central teachings of some religions are false. Actually, I'll go a step further: I think you probably believe that, too. Whether people can bring themselves to admit it or not in our current cultural climate, most people do believe that the central truth claims of at least some religions are wrong.

One night during Group, we discussed whether it was okay to even ask this question. I was sitting on an ottoman in my family room and asked, "What would you think if I said, 'Starting now, you should worship, pray to, and devote your entire lives to this ottoman—it will change your eternal destiny!'?"

A senior, Colin, raised his hand. "Would we have to call it 'Goddoman?'"

Classic Colin. We all laughed, and I continued. "You'd wonder if I was serious. And if you sensed that I was serious, you would conclude that I was crazy. You would know that a man-made piece of furniture in my family room is not worth our worship or devotion."

"So, you would object at that point," I said. "You'd say, 'Wait. It would be ridiculous to worship an ottoman—you just made that up.' And, of course, you would be correct."

"So, if I then decided to create this new religion and asked you to follow it, I would expect you to (rightly) say, 'No chance.'"

"At that moment," I pointed out, "we would confirm—in theory—that you do think it is okay to believe that the central teachings of at least some religions are wrong."

To you, the reader, I'd ask: If the teachings of some religions can be wrong in theory, what about in reality? Consider three examples.

An actual religion, called Jediism, was developed from the philosophies of the Jedi Order in the *Star Wars* films. It is growing and has followers around the world. A Temple of the Jedi Order has been built in Texas.

Its tagline? "May the force be with you."

In India, there is a religion that draws people to pray to a god they believe exists in the form of a motorcycle. A British-built 300cc Royal Enfield Bullet motorcycle, to be precise. The shrine is called the Shrine of the Bullet Baba and is located just outside the city of Jodhpur.

Before anyone gets too upset with me for selecting these two religions, what about my own? What about the belief that God visited Earth in the form of a baby named Jesus, who grew up, was murdered after a sham of a trial, was buried, and then rose from the dead?

Whatever you think about these three religions, if you were to look closely at the core teachings of each and ask if all of their teachings could be true, you would certainly conclude no.

THEY CAN'T ALL BE TRUE

The world's various major religions make such different claims that the law of non-contradiction suggests it is impossible that the central teachings of *all* of them are true. A serious student of these religions will tell you that they have very different views on topics that include the nature of God, how we can know and relate to God, the afterlife, sin, forgiveness, who Jesus is, and more.

Buddhism is non-theistic, while Hinduism teaches that there are millions of gods. Islam, Judaism, and Christianity claim that there is one god (though in Christianity, God exists in three persons: the Father, Son, and Holy Spirit). So, is there a god, or isn't there? How many gods are there?

Islam, Hinduism, Buddhism, Daoism, and others do not teach that Jesus is the Messiah (fully man but also fully God), and that he came to Earth to save us. Christianity teaches that he is. This is an objective truth claim that is at the heart of Christianity. It is either true or false.

As a Christian, I have no problem with the idea that if Buddhism (or any of the world's other major religions) is true, Christianity must be false. It sometimes surprises people when they hear me say that it is possible that none of the world's religions are true.

It is not possible, however, that all of them are true.

There are a number of different reasons people feel uncomfortable pondering whether some particular religion's central claims might be false. I'll suggest five.

1. There are People of All Faiths Who are Very Sincere

If people believe something and are very sincere, we feel like it would be attacking, or at least unkind, to say we disagree with what they believe. But when done thoughtfully, we are not attacking anyone. We are comparing different systems of belief about life's most important questions.

Be careful here. The fear of offending someone who sincerely believes something can cause us to avoid considering the validity of that person's beliefs. This leads to an observation.

The sincerity of a person's belief does nothing to help us evaluate how valid or true that belief really is.

If we were to put this into a formula, it would be: Sincerity ≠ Validity. No matter how sincerely any of us may have believed that the dress was white and gold, we were sincerely wrong.

What mattered in the discussion was not the sincerity of one's belief but rather the object of one's belief. Having only a little bit of faith that the dress was blue and black turns out to be much better than having very sincere faith that the dress was white and gold.

My friend Reese recently married a great guy named Sam, who played on the University of Kansas football team's defensive line. As you might guess, Sam is not a small human being. If Sam decided to walk across a frozen pond in the winter, he would be far better off with a tiny amount of faith in ice that is five feet thick than with a very sincere, deeply held faith in ice that is 1/16th of an inch thick.

If a person sincerely believes that the ottoman in my family room will answer their prayers, the object of their faith—the ottoman—will disappoint them.

2. To Claim that One Faith Perspective is Right Seems Arrogant

It is possible to be right about something while holding that view humbly.

Of course, it is also possible to be right and arrogant. Or wrong and arrogant. Or wrong and humble. I'd suggest that a person's humility or arrogance is more a reflection of their personality and character than of whether they happen to be right or wrong about a thing.

What people are often reacting to is any claim that a particular religion is exclusively true or the *only* true religion.

But if there is a truth that may have an impact on my eternal destiny, I must get past any sort of concern about whether the central claims of that religion might seem arrogant. The critically important question, the one we can't afford to ignore, is, "Are those claims true?"

3. To Claim that Another Religion is Wrong Seems Intolerant
Consider the concept of tolerance for a moment. In today's culture, tolerance has seemingly become our highest value—in some ways, perhaps even higher than truth. We now have safe spaces on college campuses designed to protect students from a discussion of *ideas* that may hurt their feelings. In my view, this is terrible.

And the definition of "tolerant" has changed in America.

Our conversations and culture now demand not only that we tolerate ideas but that we either modify our beliefs to fit whatever is deemed to be culturally correct or remain silent with our dissent. At the risk of being a bit blunt, if you don't believe this, you haven't been paying attention to the rise of ideological censorship happening on a variety of fronts.[14]

In this new landscape, if we hold a view that is out of step with the so-called mainstream, we risk being canceled. Or being called intolerant. Or worse. But these are tricky waters. Isn't it possible that the man who would call someone intolerant might really be demonstrating his own intolerance toward the other person's view? This points us to an important concept.

Tolerance assumes disagreement.

There is a good reason I don't have to tolerate the love for Washington's NFL team that my parents, my brother Bret, my friends Tyler, Jake, Christian, Tory, Ashley, Cami, Katie, Dana, Brent, Pete, Toby, Troy, Mike, Jay, TC, and others have: I share it.

I do, however, have to find a way to tolerate the love my friends Robbie, Tom, Connor, Victoria, Katherine, Matt, and John have for the Eagles. And the love my friends Eric, Raul, Richie, Kloey, Ethan, Lilly, Tom, Kelsey, and Hope have for the Cowboys.

A football team preference, though, is subjective. As hard as this is for me to admit, there isn't a wrong answer.

Still, true tolerance is part of loving people well. During his lifetime, pastor and author Tim Keller influenced people around the world through his teaching and writing. He once posted on social media that "tolerance is not about approving an opinion you do not hold. It's about treating the person—who is saying what you can powerfully disagree with—with respect, humility, and love."[15]

This is especially important for Christians. For Christians, civility is more than a nice thought. Christians are called to love God, to love other Christians, to love their neighbors, and to love their enemies. They are even called to love Eagles and Cowboys fans. Nobody is exempt.

During a conversation with my friend Andrew over lunch, we talked about God. We listened carefully to each other's views. We did not fully agree, but we had a great conversation. It was interesting, fun, and respectful in both directions.

We have had similar conversations since then, and I feel confident we'd both say we look forward to them in the future.

Sadly, though, with so much anger and hostility in our culture, many have lost the ability to have civil conversations on topics like these—topics about which thoughtful people may disagree. This is a tremendous loss for everyone.

There are two ways that these conversations can go wrong. Too often, people can get angry at "the other side" and become mean-spirited toward those with whom they disagree. Social media has not helped. In fact, it has hurt. Immensely.[16]

People mock, attack, or even "cancel" those whose views they judgmentally decide are wrong. Karey and I have watched differing opinions cause students to walk out of friends' lives and, in two cases, out of our lives. This is awful.

On the other end of the spectrum, we can withdraw and avoid having important conversations for fear of how others might react. This, too, is awful. If my friend Valeria knew something that could change a friend's life but avoided mentioning it because she feared how her friend might respond, would that be loving?

We should be able to talk about important topics with friends, even topics on which we disagree, without having to fear damaging the relationship. Love insists that we should be kind and respectful. It does not, however, suggest we should run away from conversations where disagreement might happen. Sometimes, love demands such conversations.

Here is the really important point about tolerance: to believe that the central claims of a person's religion (or worldview) are wrong does not mean I am intolerant. It means I disagree. And it is *only* when I disagree with someone that I can demonstrate genuine tolerance.

4. What if Different Religions (or Views) Help Different People?
We know that most religions teach some things that many of us believe to be true. If a religion teaches that God exists, for example, I will agree.

Many different religions also teach things that are helpful. If a religion motivates someone to become a better spouse, parent, child, friend, neighbor, colleague, or citizen, most of us would call that good. If it were to encourage love, generosity, and kindness, most would say that those things, too, would be good.

But a question arises when we remember that different religions teach profoundly different things about the nature of God and the afterlife. Pause here for a moment and imagine—even if you don't believe this—that there is actually one true religion and that it teaches that a thing we'll call "X" must happen for a person to gain eternal life.

If one of the non-true religions taught us helpful things about how to live on Earth but failed to teach us about X, we would run into a serious problem. Imagine that a person followed an untrue religion and thus didn't learn about X, or worse, was taught that X was false.

If that person would miss out on the afterlife as a result, shouldn't we re-think our decision to call that religion good?

Following a religion that does not teach X would be somewhat like taking a self-improvement class while on the *Titanic*. The class might genuinely help and be deeply meaningful, at least in the short term. But it would not address our greatest need.

You might process this differently than I do, but I'm not sure I could say that a religion that denied X would be good—even if it truly and honestly helped someone be a better person on Earth.

5. Couldn't All Faiths Be Different Ways to God?

This is related to the question we considered earlier about whether some religions might be wrong. One reason we may feel uncomfortable seeking to evaluate the truth of a particular religion is that if it turns out not to be true, the followers of that wrong religion might face consequences for that choice.

But one of life's most consistent lessons is that our choices often have real consequences. Why would we think this might be different regarding things we choose to believe about God?

Compassion causes us to dislike the idea that the central claims of someone else's religion could be wrong. I personally know people who have drawn great comfort and strength from religious views that are very different from mine. You probably do, too. As a result, it can be tempting to comfort ourselves with seemingly modern ideas like, "No religion can claim to have the whole truth about the mystery of faith."[17] Or, "Every different religion is simply a different road to the same mountaintop."

While these ideas may help us feel better, they fail in a couple of ways.

First, most of the major world religions make exclusive truth claims. Many claim to be the only way to God. So, to suggest that there are other ways to reach God or that no one religion can have the whole truth is to disregard the very teachings of those religions.

Consider just Christianity for a moment. Jesus said, "I am the way, the truth, and the life. No man comes to the Father except through me."[18]

Here, Jesus was making a bold truth claim. It is a claim that is either true or false. You might respond, "I don't believe what Jesus taught." And that's your right, of course.

But to say that he did not really mean it when he clearly taught that he is the only way to God is to misunderstand a core teaching of Christianity.

It is clear when one studies the message of the Bible that, according to Christianity, the only hope people have of reaching heaven is to be forgiven for their sin. Further, Christianity teaches that this forgiveness is possible only through one's personal faith in Christ's sacrificial death.

If all religions lead to the same mountaintop, these core teachings of Christianity are wrong.

There is a second and similar reason why ideas like these fail.

Even if true, what human could possibly know such things? To be confident that *all* of the world's religions lead to the same mountaintop, for example, consider how much one would have to know. A person would have to know that even the most obscure (and outlandish) religions were all true.

To know that, a person would have to know more about Christianity than Jesus did, because he would be forced to correct Jesus' (presumably incorrect) teaching on a core point of Christianity. He would have to know more about Islam than Muhammad did, so he could correct Muhammad's (presumably incorrect) teaching, too. In fact, he would have to know more about nearly every religion than each of the religions' founders combined, because nearly every one of these leaders taught something very different than the idea that all roads lead to the same mountaintop.

To the person who would say that no one religion could have the whole truth about the mystery of faith, I'd ask, "Why not?"

In considering the often contradictory beliefs of various world religions, it seems far more logical to conclude that the teachings of just one religion are true—or that none of them are true—than to somehow conclude that the core teachings of all of them are true.

✝ ✝ ✝

For almost a decade, Karey and I served with a Christian ministry to college students at George Mason University. One of the things the university asked me to do was attend a monthly meeting with leaders from every religious group on campus.

One guy who showed up for these meetings did not show up for much else on campus. I'm not sure he knew any students. In these meetings, he always pushed us to offer interfaith prayer and worship services. "Interfaith" refers to people of different religions. This is different from "interdenominational," which means people from different groups within the Christian church.

This push for interfaith prayer or worship events never made sense to me. If different religions have different understandings of who God is, then to whom, exactly, would we be praying? And for what purpose? Who would we be worshipping?

Of course, interfaith discussions or service projects do make sense. Those sorts of events can be fantastic.

But during moments when we were discussing interfaith prayer or worship, I would glance at Muhammad, the leader of the Muslim Campus Ministry. We would make eye contact and smile subtly, non-verbally communicating the same thought.

How does he not understand that this makes no sense?

Muhammad and I were always friendly, and we enjoyed the fact that sometimes we became philosophical allies during these meetings. He treated me with respect. I am confident he would tell you that I treated him the same way.

But we disagreed with each other's beliefs. And both of us understood that. Never did either of us think we were simply following different roads to the same God. We taught our students different things about God.

We both knew that if his view of God was right, mine was wrong—and that if mine was right, his was wrong.

In this chapter, we have observed that truth is exclusive, and the exclusive nature of truth does apply to religion because world religions teach contradictory things. Thus, we are left to consider the probability that the central claims of at least some of the world's religions may not be true.

As we wrap up this chapter on truth, each of us must face an unsettling question: Do I—really—even care about what's true?

Most of us will react strongly: *"Of course* I do," we will say. But many of us don't.

Dr. Frank Turek, a Christian author who travels extensively to speak on the rationality of the Christian faith, made a great observation about humans. "Most people," he wrote, "are not on a truth quest. They're on a happiness quest." He went on to suggest that far too many people simply believe "whatever is going to make them happy."[19]

He is right.

If, however, you are actually on a truth quest, this brings us back to the question we'll continue to explore: How can we know which religion, if any, is true? But first, we must answer an even bigger question.

How can we know anything at all?

Llamas on the Lam

IN THE LAST CHAPTER, I WROTE THAT February 26, 2015, was a great day in internet history. That same day, before the photo of the dress appeared, two llamas captured America's attention when they attempted a daring escape in broad daylight.

During a "Meet and Greet the Llamas" event at a retirement community in a Phoenix suburb called Sun City, the two llamas saw an opening and did not throw away their shot. They took off. The llamas' owner described the scene:

> *I have two llamas running loose. We're trying to get them rounded up. Nothing is working. We have people in walkers and wheelchairs and motorized wheelchairs trying to help, but this area is so big that it can't be contained.*[1]

Apparently, you cannot stop llamas; you can only hope to contain them.

In preparing to write this chapter, I found far more great quotes about this story than I have room to share. Actually, they had me at "We have people in walkers and wheelchairs and motorized wheelchairs trying to help." If your mental image of that scene doesn't entertain you (even if you personally use a walker or wheelchair), it is safe to say that my sense of humor is very different than yours.

It got better. The llamas pulled it off. They escaped, and the chase was on. Local television stations weren't going to miss this. At least one station sent its news helicopter up to broadcast the low-speed llama chase. Llamas on the Lam—Live!

Fox News broke into its national coverage to air the chase. Anchor Shepard Smith explained why: "Because we have live pictures of llamas. What would *you* do?"[2] I don't watch much network television news, so I was not familiar with Shepard Smith, but Shepard, I was so with you on this one.

Police support was called in.

Officers would drive close to a llama, get out of the police car, and try to… Well, I'm still not entirely clear on what they hoped to do. After watching the video, I'm going to guess that police training does not include llama wrangling. The officers had no chance. The llamas would let their pursuers get close, almost as if teasing, and then bolt.

Before long, references to the chase were all over social media. I received at least one text that day from a friend who referred to it and wondered if I was watching. Seriously? How could I be expected to work at a time like this?

I tuned in immediately.

People's reactions were fantastic. A woman named Lucie Zhang posted on Twitter, "Humans sitting in offices watching llamas run around free in the sunshine. Somehow I feel like we lost."[3]

The New Republic's Rebecca Traister wrote, also on Twitter, "This is like *Thelma and Louise* if Thelma got lassoed and put inside a truck and Louise was still running free and also was a llama."[4]

When all was said and done, more than 220,000 posts about the chase had been made to Twitter in just 90 minutes.

Eventually, both llamas were lassoed and safely returned to their homes. Or to captivity, I guess, depending upon your perspective. The chase was over (No, Llama, Noooo!⁵) and a nation could get back to work. Or so it thought.

It was about to see a photo of a dress.

Stop and ponder this question: Do you believe that the llama story I just told really happened? If so, why? Could someone prove that it happened? Would you need scientific evidence?

Note that I did not ask if you would need "scientific proof." Scientists tend not to use that term. Scientists, it is said, deal in observations and theories. Mathematicians deal in proofs. It doesn't matter if you believe the llama story or not, but the question points to larger questions: How do we know that anything is true? And what level of proof do we need to believe it?

This matters because we cannot prove that the central claims of any particular religion are true with 100% certainty. If truth is exclusive, and if the claims of some religions may be false, how can we know which of those claims (if any) are true and which (if any) are false?

Let's go back to the llama story for a moment. I'm not trying to be tricky. I believe it happened. I saw part of the video as it was broadcast live. I saw news reports and references to it on social media. I have seen other evidence since then that leaves me convinced that it did really happen. I'm convinced, even though there is no scientific evidence that it happened. An event from the past can't be repeated and tested. But I do not need scientific evidence to believe all that I believe.

Some people do.

MUST A THING BE AFFIRMED THROUGH SCIENCE FOR ME TO BELIEVE?
On October 18, 2014, Karey and I attended her cousin Erin's wedding. It was held at a gorgeous home high in the hills above Santa Barbara, California. We spent much of the reception on a massive outdoor patio that overlooked the city and, beyond it, the beautiful Pacific Ocean.

During the reception, I got into a fairly deep conversation with someone about truth, religion, and the question of how we can know the things we know. He had thought quite a bit about this topic, and the discussion was very interesting.

His view (at least as I recall him explaining it[6]) was that the only way we can truly come to know anything is through science. I suggested that there are a number of ways we can come to know things, apart from science. We discussed some of them, but he disagreed. The conversation was great, but ultimately, we landed in different places.

He is not alone in his view. Nobel Prize winner Sir Harry Kroto, in a lecture at a meeting of Nobel laureates in 2011, made the same claim. Kroto said in his speech that "science is the only philosophical construct we have to determine TRUTH with any degree of reliability." The emphasized words here reflect his own emphasis in his presentation slides.[7]

The trouble with this view is that it is self-defeating. Kroto's claim—that the only things we can know with any reliability are things we come to know via science—is not a statement we can scientifically show to be true.

Do you see the problem?

According to Kroto's own statement, the only reliable way to determine if we can trust a claim would be to use science. But if we can't confirm that his own statement is true via science—and we can't—his words suggest that we can't even trust his own words! At least, not with any reliability. In fact, Kroto's statement would suggest we can't reliably know much of anything we can't use the scientific method to test.

It would have been entertaining if someone had stood up during Kroto's presentation and asked, "Can you prove that statement scientifically? No? Then why should we consider it to be reliable?"

Freeman Dyson, the theoretical physicist and mathematician who passed away in 2020, was one of the preeminent scientists of the past 70 years. The impact of his work, across a range of scientific disciplines, was astounding. Dyson believed it was "absurd" to think we could only know things through science. People who believe you can know things only through science, Dyson said in an interview, "are suffering from what

I'd call a form of scientific fundamentalism, pretending that science can explain everything or that science should explain everything. It's a sort of scientific imperialism—believing that science should be the only source of truth—which I believe is rubbish."[8]

Dr. Francis Collins, the physician-geneticist who led the Human Genome Project and is the former director of the National Institutes of Health, addressed this specific topic in an article in *The Atlantic*:

> *Scientists, by their nature, are trying to understand how nature works. And I think the message to scientists has to be [that] there are really important questions that fall outside of what science is able to address meaningfully, such as "Why is there something instead of nothing? What is the meaning of love? Is there a God? What happens after you die?" Those are not questions for which science or scientific methods can be applied.*[9]

These questions *are* important, and their answers are unknowable through science alone. Even historical events would be hard to know with any degree of reliability, according to Kroto's view.

But can we not know reliably that my friend Tally ran track at James Madison University? Can we really not know the date of D-Day or that the Washington Nationals won the 2019 World Series? Can we really not reliably know the city in which our parents were born? Can my friend Carson not reliably know that our friends Rachel, Meghan, and Gracie once served with my wife on a construction team in Kentucky together? We can't prove these things scientifically.

If you are in the "I'm not going to say I know a thing unless science affirms it" camp, you can't say you know that the llama story happened. But I am convinced that you can know.

You could have an expert review video and photographic evidence to see if either had been doctored. You could read news reports and track down eyewitnesses. You could interview the llama owners, police officers, and reporters who were there.

A thorough investigation would demand that you also consider other theories to see if a different conclusion made sense.

What other theories could explain the llama story? It could have been an elaborate hoax. The videos could have been created using CGI (this was before the days of realistic video created by AI). The news reports could have been faked. The witnesses could have been recruited and told to lie. The reporters could have been convinced to write false stories. Everyone involved could have kept this enormous hoax secret for all this time.

But is all of that likely? If this was simply a giant hoax, someone would have come forward to expose the truth, even if just for personal fame, gain, amusement, or notoriety.

Conspiracies of that size always fail because someone always talks.

Once you had finished evaluating the evidence and other possible theories, you would have to decide what standard of proof would be required to convince you.

In courts of law, there are different standards of proof required in different types of cases. In a criminal case, for example, the prosecuting attorney must convince the jury beyond a reasonable doubt that the accused actually committed the crime. In a civil case, the standard of proof is lower. There, it must be proven only that a claim is more likely to be true than not true.

What level of proof do you need to conclude that something is true?

Regarding the llama story, I'd say the evidence points to proof beyond a reasonable doubt. You may disagree.

How does all of this apply to more important discussions?

As we explore whether a god, no god, or several gods might exist, we've already noted that no religion can prove that its central claims are true with 100% certainty. But can we still say that we know things, even if we don't have 100% certainty? I'd say yes.

In the next couple of pages, we'll explore eight ways we come to know things. Then, we'll observe that beyond these types of knowledge, belief and faith play a big role in our lives every day, regardless of what we think about spiritual things.

WAYS WE COME TO KNOW THINGS

The study of knowledge is called epistemology. This is a subject that philosophers have pondered and written about for centuries.

What I offer below is not meant to be an in-depth philosophical treatment. Rather, this is a list of personal observations about ways I think a person might conclude that something is true. Of course, there may be more ways than I'll list here—and there will be overlap between these—but this list will at least get us thinking about the subject:

1. Mathematical Proof
2. Scientific Evidence
3. Direct Observation
4. The Instruction of a Teacher or Expert
5. Historical/Legal Evidence + Critical Thinking
6. Deductive Reasoning
7. Personal Experience
8. Built-in Knowledge

1. Mathematical Proof
Mathematical proofs speak for themselves.

2. Scientific Evidence
Both scientific experimentation and direct observation (which I address next) provide what we call empirical evidence. Scientific evidence is gained as scientists ask questions, do research, make observations, form hypotheses, test them, accept, reject, or refine those hypotheses, and then repeat the process as necessary.

Over the years, the problems that have been solved through the thoughtful application of science have been both amazing and incredibly wide-ranging. Though I am not a scientist, I love reading about the understanding we've gained about our world and universe through science.

3. Direct Observation
We conclude that some things are true through observation, even if we can't repeat them in the way we might repeat a scientific experiment.

Imagine that my friends Zach, Nick, Connor, Robert, Jeremiah, Lucas M., Lucas B., Charlie, T.J., Anthony, and Jack all gathered at the finish line of a marathon. Now imagine that they each counted, without comparing notes with each other, the number of runners who crossed the finish line by a certain time.

If each of these guys came up with the same number, they would all probably conclude that they knew the right number. Perhaps you'd require more than eleven observers to conclude that you knew the right answer. Whatever the number, if we were given enough trustworthy observers, most of us would conclude that we knew the truth.

4. The Instruction of a Teacher or Expert

We learn from experts in a variety of ways. The range of things we can learn to do by watching an expert demonstrate or teach on YouTube is incredible. We can read great books.

We also learn in all sorts of in-person settings, from formal classrooms to personal interactions to seminars and symposia. My friend Alyssa learned a great deal about forensic science from her professors during her time at Penn State.

I suspect that my friend Madison would say she learned about design not only from her professors but also during her summer internships.

Does this mean that we should blindly accept everything we hear from an expert or teacher? Of course not. But we will generally give them the benefit of the doubt because they have earned it. Still, we should be wise. When we hear claims of truth—even from an expert or teacher—we should evaluate those claims thoughtfully.

5. Historical/Legal Evidence and Critical Thinking

Reason and the use of logic to evaluate evidence are tools that historians, detectives, and other types of investigators use in order to draw conclusions about what happened in a given situation.

We call this critical thinking.

In his book, *An Experiment in the Development of Critical Thinking*, Edwin M. Glaser wrote that critical thinking is about examining "any belief or supposed form of knowledge in the light of the evidence that supports it and the further conclusions to which it tends."[10]

If my friend Julianna were ever to have jury duty, this is how she and her co-jurors would decide on the defendant's guilt or innocence.

Did the llama story really happen? It is a question of evidence.

6. Deductive Reasoning
Deductive reasoning is closely related to critical thinking. It allows us to know things by moving from a general principle to a specific case.

Consider these two premises: (a) all squares are rectangles, and (b) all rectangles have four sides. If both of those premises are true, we can know for sure that (c) all squares have four sides.

Here is a simple example of how one might deduce truth in real life. If my friend Kelsey knows that (a) it is dangerous to drive her car when roads are icy and (b) the roads are icy right now, she can deduce from those two premises—assuming they are both true—that (c) it is dangerous to drive right now.

We use deductive reasoning like this so often that we do it without considering the mental steps involved.

7. Personal Experience
There are things that we know based on our own life experiences. For example, I know that:

- ☐ I can ride a normal bicycle under normal circumstances.
- ☐ My friend Conor's Jeep is loud.
- ☐ Newfoundlands are absolutely enormous dogs.
- ☐ Many who have tasted Karey's chocolate chip cookies believe that they are delicious.
- ☐ My friend Carly makes people laugh.
- ☐ On a clear day, the views are spectacular from the top of Canada's Whistler Blackcomb ski resort.
- ☐ My friend Tess loves to think about and discuss ideas that really matter.
- ☐ I can (sadly) make a golf ball curve dramatically.

My own personal experiences won't necessarily convince anyone else of these truths. But I would tell you that I know each to be true.

8. Built-in Knowledge

I am convinced that there are a few things in life we just know, as if that knowledge has somehow been built into us.

One example of knowledge that I believe has been built into every one of us, whatever we think about God, is an objective system of moral values. Not everyone agrees. We will explore this idea more fully in Chapter 8.

Beyond moral values, some have argued that an innate sense that God exists has been built into each of us.

Alvin Plantinga is a widely respected philosopher who also happens to be a Christian. *Time* magazine called him "America's leading orthodox Protestant philosopher of God." In *Warranted Christian Belief,* a book that is considered to be an influential and important contribution to the field of the philosophy of religion, he explores the compatibility of faith and reason. He argues that Christian belief is not only rational but warranted, even apart from evidence or arguments. He suggests that this sense of God (he calls it *sensus divinitatis*), together with the work of the Holy Spirit, gives people a natural inclination to believe.

He makes a thought-provoking case. I will not attempt to unpack or defend his arguments here; I will simply recommend this book to philosophically minded readers to whom this might sound interesting.

✚ ✚ ✚

We've now considered eight different ways I believe people come to know things. There are almost certainly other categories one might add. For example, if my friends Laurel, Brittany, Erica, or Kaitlyn think of someone they love, how do they know that? What category does that fit into?

✚ ✚ ✚

You may reject one or more of these eight categories or believe we should categorize them differently. But even if you do, I hope you'll agree that there are at least a few different ways we come to know things.

Interestingly, however, the things we know are not always the things that cause us to take action.

WHAT IS THE ROLE OF BELIEF IN OUR LIVES?

In this chapter's exploration of how we know what we know, we haven't yet discussed the role of belief.

Belief plays an enormous role in our daily lives. I may believe something to be true, but I may be wrong. Or I may not believe something, even though it is actually true.

Either way, it is our belief that usually causes us to act.

If my friends Edson, Gustavo, Nick, and Willy all come to truly believe, during a pickup basketball game, that the gym is on fire, they are going to get out as quickly as they can. This is true whether they have 100% proof that the gym is on fire or not.

On the other hand, if the fire alarm goes off falsely at the same time every day, they might eventually begin to ignore it. In that case, if there was an actual fire and the alarm went off, they might shrug and go back to their game, believing that they were safe. If their beliefs changed and they decided the fire was real, only then would they seek to escape.

Earlier, I asked if you believed the llama story happened. I did not ask if you knew for sure. There is an actual truth; it either really did or really did not happen. Somebody knows if it really happened. The llamas' owner, the police officers, and the firsthand witnesses all might say, "I know it happened. I was there." But I was not there, so I must choose what to believe.

I have to use my reasoning skills, together with logic, as I think critically and weigh the evidence. In this case, as I've evaluated the evidence (and considered other possible explanations for the evidence), I have concluded that it is far more likely to have happened than not to have happened. If I were a gambler, I would bet that it happened.

Can I now say I *know* it happened, or is it better to say that I merely believe it happened? On a practical level, does it even matter? It does. A rational person would prefer to know something than merely believe it. But there are times when we may not be able to know with 100% certainty that something happened. In the absence of absolute knowledge, we have to make a choice about what we believe is true.

To conclude that the llama story was true demands, in a way, that we exhibit faith. Faith in the work of the reporters. Faith in the video. Faith in the eyewitnesses. Faith in our own analytical abilities.

It demands what I'd call a reasonable faith.

REASONABLE FAITH VS. BLIND FAITH

Imagine that my friends Jack, C.J., and Andrew got together at a pizza place for lunch. Just before they sat down, their minds would evaluate— incredibly quickly and without thinking about it consciously—whether the chairs looked trustworthy. Unless they noticed any reason for concern, they would start with an assumption that the chairs were fine.

They would sit down if: (1) nobody else seemed to be having a problem; (2) the chairs seemed normal; and (3) they believed that a broken chair would have been replaced by the restaurant. At this point, could they know that their chairs would not collapse when they sat down? No. But they'd still sit down because they'd believe the chairs would work as expected.

We make these sorts of decisions, by faith, every day. Reasonable faith? Yes. But by faith.

Now imagine instead that these three guys walked in and ran into our friends Kyle and Jacob, who were just leaving. If Kyle said, "Be careful with the chairs; we just saw two of them collapse when people sat down on them," and any of the three guys sat down without first testing his chair, we could reasonably call that blind faith.

We act on our faith in more serious matters, too. My friends Megan and Katrina go to different colleges. If Megan were to go on a road trip to visit Katrina, consider the amount of faith she would have to put in other drivers on the road.

At some point on her trip, she would probably have to drive on a two-lane road at, say, 45 miles per hour. If a car approaches in the opposite direction at 45mph, at least some actual danger is involved.

If both drivers stay in their lanes as they approach each other, they will avoid a head-on collision by only a couple of feet as they pass. This sort of close call will happen repeatedly, every time a car approaches.

As drivers, all of us put an enormous amount of faith, or trust, in oncoming drivers, whether we realize it or not. We can't know that a driver coming toward us isn't distracted by his or her phone. We can't know that the driver isn't drunk, high, or driving a car with faulty steering. Accidents happen every day.

But still, we get into our cars. We believe, by faith—supported by evidence and the odds—that the trip will turn out just fine. We believe that other drivers do not want to get into an accident either. We bet our lives on it. We exhibit faith, reasonably.

These examples show us how often we rely on what I'd call reasonable faith. We act on faith every day. We act on things we believe, usually for rational reasons, even if we can't prove what we believe with 100% certainty. We make the best judgment we can based on what we know, and we act accordingly.

We turn now to considering evidence for the existence of God. As the comic strip character B.C. asked in the Preface, "How do we know you even exist?"

Our job? To evaluate the evidence and make the best judgment we can based on what we know. And then act accordingly.

As I evaluated the sorts of evidence we'll consider in the next few chapters, the ideas I'll share played a big role in helping to lead me to conclude that Christianity was more likely to be true than not true and that it was more rational to believe than to not believe.

It helped move me toward what I'd call a reasonable faith... in God.

God

The Billion-Dollar Question

THE UNIVERSE IS HUGE. Almost incomprehensibly so. We can try to think about its size in at least two ways: the number of stars in the universe and the distance from one side of the universe to the other.

Let's first consider five ridiculously large numbers: 100 billion, 2 trillion, 200 sextillion, 1 nonillion, and 93 billion light-years. And also, one insanely small one: 0.0000000000000000000000000000001. We'll discuss each of these numbers in turn.

The Milky Way Galaxy, our solar system's home, contains at least 100 billion stars. Astronomers tell us that the actual number may be two to four times larger. If my friend Marianna decided to count those 100 billion stars, she'd be very tired by the end. If she could count extremely fast without taking breaks for any reason—including sleep—it would probably take her 10,000 years to count them all.[1]

Remarkably, the number of galaxies we now know to exist dwarfs the number of stars in our one galaxy. In 2016, an international team of astronomers led by Christopher Conselice of the University of Nottingham, U.K., found that there are at least *two trillion galaxies* in the known universe.[2] This is astounding.

Assuming an average of 100 billion stars per galaxy, which astronomers tell us is a safe assumption, there are at least 200 sextillion (or 200,000,000,000, 000,000,000,000) stars out there. I've seen estimates that are far higher. Put differently, imagine that we could equally divide all of the stars into groups and that every living human would somehow be given one group. Each person's group would contain more than 25 trillion stars!

If the sheer number of stars and galaxies alone doesn't amaze you, consider the universe's physical size.

The speed of light is a little more than 670 million miles per hour. That's roughly 186,000 miles per second. If my friend Pat was in a spacecraft that could travel at that speed, he could orbit Earth more than 20 times in less than the time it took you to read this sentence. He could get to the moon in 1.3 seconds, to Mercury in just under 4 minutes, and to the sun in fewer than 9 minutes. It would take him only 4.6 hours to get to Pluto.

To fully cross the universe, traveling at 670 million miles per hour, it would take Pat *93 billion years*.[3] Stop and ponder that for a moment.

If these sorts of numbers are hard for you to get your head around, don't worry. Dr. Pete Edwards is the Director of Science Outreach at Durham University, in the U.K. He said, "You'll never get your head around how big the universe is."[4]

I'm glad it's not just me.

As amazing as the size of the universe is, the current scientific view on how it got to be that size is perhaps even more amazing.

Earlier, I mentioned an absurdly small number that I'll apply here to a very short period of time: 0.0000000000000000000000000000000001 of a second. That sliver of time is shorter than one yoctosecond. A yoctosecond is one-trillionth of one-trillionth of one second.

According to the late Stephen Hawking, the famous theoretical physicist and cosmologist, this fraction of one yoctosecond is the time it took for the universe to expand (from the size of something far smaller than an atom) by 1,000,000,000,000,000,000,000,000,000,000—or 1 nonillion—times, during what he called the universe's "first phase of expansion."[5] Physicists refer to this as cosmic inflation.

Even if you struggle to grasp the size of 1 nonillion or the smallness of that fraction of a yoctosecond, this nearly instant expansion was so massive and incomprehensibly powerful that the conventional laws of modern physics fail to help us understand it. "It was," wrote Hawking, "as if a coin one centimeter in diameter suddenly blew up to ten million times the width of the Milky Way."[6]

Scientists generally believe that this inflation took place in that sliver of a yoctosecond following the Big Bang. The Big Bang, of course, is the model the scientific community holds to be the best current description of the universe's earliest moments of existence.

The phrase "best current description" is important. As new data is collected, our best estimates about the size or age of the universe may change. Scientists will almost certainly further tweak their views on cosmic inflation and the Big Bang model. New models may emerge.

I should also point out that while many Christians (including me) see the Big Bang model as a reasonable explanation of what may have happened as the result of God speaking the universe into existence, others disagree with all or parts of the model or about the universe's age.

Whatever its age—and whatever one believes about cosmic inflation or the Big Bang—over the last 100 years, there has been a seismic shift in the way scientists view our universe.

✛ ✛ ✛

One of the more memorable conversations I've ever had during a round of golf took place a few years ago at the Back Creek Golf Club in Middletown, Delaware. The club is not far from our family's river house, where we had gone to stay for a long weekend.

I decided to play golf early one morning, so I could play fast and get back to the house by the time my family was getting up and moving.

When I arrived at the club, I checked in and learned that I had been paired with another early riser. This was not a problem. Golfers who get up early to play golf usually like to play fast.

Early in the round, I learned that my playing partner had spent his career serving our nation as an astrophysicist. Once he retired, he moved from Washington, DC, to Delaware and began teaching physics and astronomy at the University of Delaware.

He was not the type of golfer who was so focused on his game that he didn't like to chat. He loved to chat. I enjoy both serious rounds of golf and social ones; this round would be social.

Because I've always been fascinated by space and the size of the universe, I started asking questions. I started with a question I knew would be easy for him: "Are there really more stars in the universe than grains of sand on Earth's beaches and deserts?" He assured me that there are.

He seemed happy to answer my questions, so I kept asking.

At some point, he said something that led me to tell him that I was a Christian. He responded, "That's fantastic! I'm an old, liberal, atheist Jew. You are younger, a Christian, and I'm guessing more conservative than me. Yet here we are, having a wonderful time playing golf together and talking about space. Isn't this great?"

It was. I was having a blast.

Several holes into the round, I asked a question I had been waiting to ask until the timing seemed right. I anticipated where the conversation might go next. "If you had to guess," I asked, "what percentage of scientists in your field believe that the universe had a beginning?"

He said (and this is a very close paraphrase, if not his exact reply): "There are other theories out there, but by now, just about all of them."

He then launched into an explanation as to why. I understood most of his explanation and did not miss his point: the universe had a beginning.

I then asked the second question I knew I had to ask.

"So, as an atheist, if the universe had a beginning, what would you say caused it?"

The tone and manner of his answer surprised me. Our golf cart was stopped when I asked, and he did not begin driving. He just sat there and looked off into the distance, nodding slowly and seemingly lost in thought. It would be his first non-animated answer of the day.

He said, as he slowly turned to face me, "Well…" followed by a long pause, "That's the billion-dollar question, isn't it?"

For the rest of our round, the conversation shifted. We talked more about space, but also quite a bit about God. The conversation was tremendous. He was honest about his struggle with my question, and his humility in the discussion impressed me.

If you are inclined to agree that the universe had a beginning, you face the same billion-dollar question: What caused it?

✛ ✛ ✛

Growing up, my understanding of God was not well-formed. I mentioned earlier that I had a vague idea that some sort of god must exist, but I had little clarity about what such a being would be like.

I remember talking with my friend Joe during high school about the idea that God created the universe. I was not religious, but I remember thinking, even then, that it would take more faith to believe the universe came from nothing than to believe some kind of creator must have created it. But I didn't have much of a reason for that belief.

So, during that first year in college, as I began reading the books that Todd and Keith gave me, I started with a basic question.

Are there good reasons to believe that God exists at all?

It turns out that there are.

In the next few chapters, we'll consider a variety of reasons. For the rest of this chapter, we'll consider just one.

THE EXISTENCE OF THE UNIVERSE SUGGESTS A CREATOR

One argument that begins to build what I believe to be a good case for God's existence is called the Kalam cosmological argument.

The argument has two premises, and if each is true, logic demands that the conclusion must also be true.

> *Premise One:* Anything that begins to exist has a cause.

> *Premise Two:* The universe began to exist.

> *Conclusion:* The universe had a cause.

Premise One: Anything that Begins to Exist has a Cause

If one could come into this discussion with no pre-existing biases, I believe that such a person would immediately agree that the first premise is true.

Peter Kreeft is a brilliant thinker, a professor of philosophy at Boston College, and a great writer. In a book he's written with Ronald K. Tacelli, they suggest that "we should grant this premise," noting that "most people— outside of asylums and graduate schools—would consider it not only true but certainly and obviously true."[7]

When have you seen a fully-grown cow spontaneously pop into existence? Or a tuba? Or a skyscraper? You haven't.

Why? Because we know that things do not pop into existence without a cause. My friends Dylan and Justin may wish, on student budgets, that Chipotle burritos would spontaneously pop into existence on their desks, but sadly for them, this just never seems to happen.

Not long ago, I was on a golf trip, headed south on an interstate in North Carolina in the midst of torrential rain. As I passed a truck, I heard something loud strike my windshield. I then noticed a series of cracks that had appeared in the glass in front of the passenger seat. These cracks had not been there when I left my home.

Let's pretend I had not heard the impact. If I had later noticed the cracks, what would I have thought? I would *not* have thought, "Wow. Those cracks just appeared, for no reason... Weird."

I would have assumed a rock or other object had struck my windshield. I might have wondered why I didn't hear it, if the glass was faulty, or how long the cracks had been there. Whatever thoughts I had, I definitely would have wondered what caused them and would never have assumed that they happened without a cause.

Of course, as we look back at the birth of the universe, there were clearly factors at play far more unusual than a rock hitting a windshield. There are some experts in quantum mechanics (the study of how tiny particles, like atoms, behave) who find that the uncertainties and unpredictability they encounter in the quantum world lead to reservations about this premise. But there are other physicists who report that their studies of quantum mechanics have pushed them toward faith in God.

I obviously have no subject-matter expertise here; quantum mechanics is an extraordinarily complex subject, even for trained scientists with very bright minds. But as I've spent time reading the perspectives of scientists with different views on this topic, I have yet to see persuasive evidence that things begin to exist without a cause.[8]

Does the idea that things begin to exist without a cause resonate with your understanding of how the world works?

Whether a cow, a tuba, a skyscraper, a burrito, cracks in a windshield, or even a universe, I believe that anything that begins to exist has a cause, even if that cause might sometimes be difficult or impossible to detect.

Premise Two: The Universe Began to Exist
Scientists have not always believed that the universe had a beginning. Early in the 20th century, scientific consensus held the opposite to be true: the universe was past-eternal. It had simply always existed.

Sir Fred Hoyle, an accomplished English astronomer, was one such scientist. Hoyle is thought to have been the first to use the term "Big Bang," during a BBC radio program that aired on March 28, 1949.

It might surprise you to learn that he actually rejected the theory, believing it to be fake science. Many reported that he used the term Big Bang in a mocking way on the radio that day. He later denied that he had used the term derisively, even though he did continue to deny that the universe had a beginning. He believed in the Steady State model, which sought to show how the universe could be eternally old even though it seemed to be expanding.

The Steady State model, though, had been in crisis since the early 1920s. Anthony Walsh, an author and professor at Boise State University, explains:

> The Steady State theory began to unravel with Einstein's famous general theory of relativity. Einstein was unsettled to find that his equations predicted the expansion of the universe, which did not fit the accepted notion in science that the universe was static and past eternal. He "corrected" his equations by adding what he termed the 'cosmological constant' representing a repulsive force to counter gravity's attraction, and thus leaving the universe static. He later called this the greatest blunder of his life, because his initial equations turned out to be right—the universe had a beginning, and was expanding.
>
> It was a Belgian Catholic priest and mathematician/physicist, Georges Lemaitre, who noted in the early 1920s that all was not right with Einstein's cosmological constant.[9]

Lemaitre, Walsh writes, "drew the opposite (and correct) conclusion," that the universe "had to be expanding, and if it was expanding, it had to do so from a finite point in time."[10]

If Lemaitre's work in the 1920s—along with that of Alexander Friedmann, Edwin Hubble, and others—started to close the casket on the Steady State model, further discoveries by Arno Penzias and Robert Wilson began to nail it shut in the 1960s.

Penzias and Wilson discovered cosmic microwave background radiation (CMBR). CMBR is the radiation in the universe that scientists believe was left over from the Big Bang. In cosmology, this was an enormously important discovery. For many scientists, it was the final piece of evidence they needed to believe that the universe had a beginning. For their work, Penzias and Wilson received the Nobel Prize in Physics in 1978.

The second law of thermodynamics is helpful, too. It leads scientists to conclude that the universe is slowly running out of usable energy. If this is true, and if the universe were infinitely old, it would have run out of usable energy by now. A loosely similar and fascinating argument from philosophy and math suggests that, due to the impossibility of crossing an actual infinite, we would not have ever arrived at today if the universe were infinitely old.[11]

Interestingly, one of the reasons some scientists initially resisted the idea that the universe had a beginning is that they believed it actually pointed to the existence of God. At the very least, it pointed to an answer that could be found only outside of science.

Fred Hoyle said bluntly that one of his problems with the idea that the universe had a beginning was that it was too tied to the account of creation found in the Bible. He said, "The reason why scientists like the 'Big Bang' is because they are overshadowed by the Book of Genesis."[12]

Don't miss the fact that, for generations, science dismissed—and some scientists even ridiculed—the biblical idea that the universe had a beginning. Eventually, science came around. The famous American astrophysicist, Robert Jastrow, put it this way:

For the scientist ... the story ends like a bad dream. He has scaled the mountains of ignorance; he is about to conquer the highest peak; as he pulls himself over the final rock, he is greeted by a band of theologians who have been sitting there for centuries.[13]

Arno Penzias said in a *New York Times* interview that "the best data we have are exactly what I would have predicted, had I nothing to go on but the first five books of Moses, the Psalms, and the Bible as a whole."[14]

In a thought-provoking 2003 paper about the Big Bang theory, Dr. Steven Ball, a physicist who is also a Christian, challenges readers who are not convinced that the universe had a beginning—and also those who might wonder if scientific inquiry is somehow at odds with the Christian faith. He wrote:

Does our worldview permit us to examine this evidence thoughtfully? One holding a solid faith in the Bible should have no fear of examining the testimony of the universe, since this too bears witness of God's handiwork. And for the one who appreciates science, but is skeptical of whether it agrees with a Christian worldview, I also urge an open mind. You will find that the evidence provided by the universe doesn't need a lot of speculative interpreting.[15]

Dr. Ball's question about whether our worldview will permit "us to examine this evidence thoughtfully" is an important one.

Fred Hoyle was so professionally respected that he was knighted by Queen Elizabeth in 1972. Still, it seems that this distinguished scientist's bias, against even the possibility that the universe had a beginning, kept him from believing the evidence that was becoming widely accepted by many of his peers.

We saw similar bias against a non-eternal universe earlier, with Einstein, in what he later called the greatest blunder of his life.

Regardless of what Hoyle or Einstein ended up believing, the prevailing view in the scientific community today is that the second premise of the Kalam argument is true. The universe had a beginning.

Alexander Vilenkin, a respected Russian theoretical physicist—and an agnostic—summed it up like this:

> *With the proof now in place, cosmologists can no longer hide behind the possibility of a past-eternal universe. There is no escape; they have to face the problem of a cosmic beginning.*[16]

If the first two premises are true, so must be the conclusion.

Conclusion: The Universe had a Cause
While discussing this topic at Group one night, my friend Cliff intuitively understood that if the universe did have a cause, the logical next question thoughtful people should ask is: "So what caused it?"

It turns out that science does not offer much help here. Scientists are quick to point out that they simply don't know much about what existed or was happening the instant before the Big Bang.

If we can't apply the scientific method to help us figure out what caused the universe—and we cannot—we find that this sort of question lives outside of the realm of what science is able to meaningfully address.

The fact that science cannot answer these questions does not harm this argument. It is important to recognize that the Kalam argument is, at its core, not a scientific argument. It is a philosophical one. And it flows from an idea: there must have been a first cause. The most basic form of this argument dates back to Plato and Aristotle.

The skeptic who hears the suggestion, at this point, that God must have been this first cause may object that this argument only shows that *something* caused the universe to exist. He might argue that it is a big leap of faith to move from believing that something caused it to believing that God did. And if this were the only argument we could make for God's existence, I might share his concern about the size of the leap. But this is not the only argument we'll consider.

I have found philosopher William Lane Craig's insight to be helpful here.

He points out that if something did cause the universe to begin to exist, that something must have been:

▫ Spaceless and timeless (because both space and time began to exist when the universe came into existence)
▫ Not material (put differently, not a physical being, because physical matter began to exist when the universe was born)
▫ Incredibly powerful (it created a still-expanding 93 billion light-year-wide universe with all of its beauty and complexities)[17]

Dr. Craig has written and spoken often about the Kalam argument. He has used it effectively in organized debates with atheists all over the world. He suggests that "spaceless, timeless, immaterial, and incredibly powerful is a good description... of God."[18] I agree.

✝ ✝ ✝

In this chapter, we have only looked at one variation of the cosmological argument. There are others. I've heard several philosophers and scientists say that they find the argument from contingency—a different form of the cosmological argument—to be compelling.

The argument from contingency, in its most simple form, makes the case that: (a) there are things around us that exist but might not have ever existed;

(b) these things are contingent upon something else for their existence; and (c) there must be some sort of thing that does not depend on anything else that explains why contingent things exist. St. Thomas Aquinas, in the 1200s, and Gottfried Wilhelm Leibniz, in the 1600s, developed slightly different forms of the argument that are worth pondering.

But neither the Kalam nor any of the other forms of the cosmological argument fully answer the question, "What is God like?" They do not specifically point to one religion. Rather, they only attempt to show that it is reasonable to believe that some kind of god exists.

I do not believe that, on its own, the Kalam cosmological argument is a "that settles it" sort of argument for the existence of a god. But I believe it is a good one. And, as I mentioned above, it is just one of several we'll consider in the following chapters.

The important question for the spiritually curious person, as Steven Ball asked, is whether your worldview will even allow you to believe that God *could* exist. And further, when a range of arguments are considered together, which conclusions make the most sense?

Let's now turn our attention to other arguments.

You Can't See a Thermal

THE SMALL PLANE TOWED OUR TWO-PERSON GLIDER high into the blue sky above Lake Tahoe, and we released the tow rope. It was time to soar.

✛ ✛ ✛

Early in our marriage, Karey and I had to attend a conference in California. We wanted to see America, so we chose to drive. We took seven weeks to do it, not counting time at the conference.

We had time but not a lot of money, so we agreed that each of us could splurge once during the trip on something we'd like to buy or experience. As we were driving our Ford Explorer out of Lake Tahoe, I saw a sign that said, "Glider Rides Over the Lake. Turn Here."

I immediately turned into the parking lot. I had found my splurge.

The glider company receptionist said they weren't busy and that I could fly—or soar, to use the term a glider pilot would use—longer than their promised minimum-length flight.

My assumption when walking into the gliderport was that our glider would be towed into the air, released, and that we would slowly descend until it was time to land. I did not know that we could repeatedly gain serious altitude during the flight.

That was before I learned about the power of thermals.

Thermals are naturally occurring columns of warm, rising air. They occur, in the most simple terms, because the sun heats the ground unevenly. When the ground is heated in a particular spot and the air above it becomes warmer than the air around it, this heated air becomes less dense and rises. The height of thermals can vary, but some have been known to rise 25,000 feet or more into the air.

Thermals and other phenomena, including ridge lifts and wave lifts, allow gliders to stay in the air far longer than I would have guessed.

In 2003, a man named Klaus Ohlmann completed a 1,869-mile glider flight in Argentina. In 1956, a pilot in the French Alps kept his glider aloft for 56 straight hours.

Birds know how to take advantage of thermals. In fact, they seem to be able to sense and find them easily. This is why you will sometimes see them soaring upward effortlessly without needing to flap their wings.

Glider pilots enter thermals and fly in tight circles to stay within the updraft and gain altitude. They then leave the thermal and soar until either finding a new thermal or landing.

I was given a safety briefing and climbed into the front seat of the two-seat aircraft. The pilot got into the seat behind me, and we were towed into the air. When we were at altitude and released the tow rope, I discovered why they call it soaring. Soaring is the perfect name for it. With no engine noise, it was eerily quiet. We were riding the wind.

After a while, we started to search the coast for a thermal. We found one and began to rise as if we were on an enormous spiral escalator. We quadrupled our altitude and left the thermal, soaring again out over the lake.

We repeated this pattern several times, and the flight was fantastic. The scenic views of Lake Tahoe and the surrounding Sierra Nevada mountains were spectacular. I did not regret my splurge.

Later, I realized I was fascinated by thermals. I did not remember ever learning about them before. As I think about thermals now, in the context of this chapter, one thing stands out:

You can't see a thermal.

You can see evidence, or clues, that a thermal exists. You can feel its power if you are in a glider that is being pushed skyward. Or if you are a bird, I suppose. But thermals are invisible.

Dr. Billy Graham, the world-renowned American minister, once made a similar observation about the wind and about God. Addressing a capacity crowd that had come to hear him speak in Cleveland's Municipal Stadium (then the home of the NFL's Browns and MLB's then-Indians), Dr. Graham asked, "Can you see God? You haven't seen him? I've never seen the wind. I see the effects of the wind, but I've never seen the wind."[1]

The fact that we cannot see God does not mean he's not there or that he does not exist. Though we can't see him, we can see the effects of his work in the world around us.

In the previous chapter, we considered how discoveries in the past century have flipped the script on the scientific community's idea about the eternality of the universe. Scientists now agree that our universe had a beginning. Some would call the miracle of the existence of the universe an effect of—or a clue that points to—the work of God. I would.

There are other clues, or effects of an invisible God's work, that point us to God. DNA, in my view, is one of many such clues.

Like a thermal, DNA is invisible to the naked eye. It plays a mission-critical role in the life of every living organism. It contains the blueprint that determines the physical traits and characteristics of all living things.

I have a friend who is a medical doctor and genetic researcher who works at perhaps the world's leading genetic research institution. She reviewed all

I've written here about DNA. As we discussed it, she said, "DNA literally provides every instruction our bodies need to live, breathe, and grow."

Even if you are not really into science, bear with me here. I think you may discover, as I have, that DNA is more remarkable and interesting than you might have guessed.

It exists in strands that are intertwined in pairs, in the famous double-helix shape that I'm sure you've seen in illustrations. Each DNA strand is ridiculously thin; one human hair is 30,000 to 40,000 times thicker.

Pause to try to imagine how thin that is.

The fact that DNA strands are so thin allows them to be packed tightly into the nucleus of nearly every one of the trillions of cells in your body. If the strands of DNA in just one microscopic human cell could be tied together and stretched out, the combined length of the strands in that cell would measure more than six feet!

There are likely at least 30 trillion cells in a typical human body. Perhaps more. If we were able to somehow take all of the strands of DNA in just one person's body and connect them end-to-end, the combined length would be at least 34 billion miles. Put differently, the length of all of the DNA strands in your body, combined, would reach Mars and back more than 120 times.[2] This is astounding.

But DNA is far more interesting than simply the length of its strands.

The DNA strands in just one tiny cell contain a staggering amount of precisely ordered information. This information can be expressed as a very long code, a sequence made up of the letters A, T, C, and G. Each letter corresponds to one of the four chemical bases that make up our DNA.

This code, contained in the DNA of just one microscopic cell, is, incredibly, three billion letters long.

The exact order of these three billion bits of information—the complex way that these four different bases are arranged—is important for DNA to create the proper RNA, which in turn creates proteins in precisely the right shape and structure to allow the cell to accomplish its function.

The order of these chemical bases is what determines whether an organism is a human, a strawberry, a penguin, or something else entirely. The DNA in each human is 99.9% identical; the remaining 0.1% is what makes each person unique.

Dr. Francis Collins, the man I quoted earlier who led the international initiative that first mapped the complete set of human DNA (the genome), obviously qualifies as a world-class expert on DNA. He wrote a book in which he called DNA an elegant language.[3]

Microsoft's founder, Bill Gates, wrote in his book, *The Road Ahead*, that "human DNA is like a computer program but far, far more advanced than any software we've ever created."[4]

This DNA code doesn't just look like a computer program of some kind—it actually works like one.

Dr. Stephen Meyer is a scientist and former professor who earned his Ph.D. from the University of Cambridge and has written three books you should read if you want to take a deeper dive into this topic.[5]

Meyer recently explained that, in 1957, Francis Crick recognized that "the chemical subunits on the inside of the [DNA] molecule were functioning just like alphabetic characters in a written language or digital characters like the 0s and 1s we use in software." Meyer called it a "stop the press moment in the history of biology."[6]

He explained:

> *Inside the DNA molecule, what we have is literally information or instructions inscribed digitally or alphabetically... in a way that provides the information necessary to build the important proteins and protein machines that keep all cells alive.*[7]

He then cited the aircraft builder Boeing's use of computer-assisted design and manufacturing as an illustration. At Boeing, he said,

> *Information in a digital form is used to direct the construction of mechanical parts or physical systems. So, if you are a Boeing engineer, you might sit at a [computer] and write code.*

That code will go down a wire, and it will be translated into another machine code that can be read at a manufacturing arm or center.

That information will be used, for example, to take rivets and put them on the aircraft wing at just the right place.

So you have digital information directing the construction of a mechanical system. Something very much like that is going on inside the cell, where the information inside the DNA is being used to direct the construction of the proteins and protein machines that are necessary for all cellular life.[8]

If this sounds complicated to you, it should. It should also sound amazing. Protein-building machines—inside each tiny cell—that are directed by a precise, three-billion-character-long code that is unique to every living organism? Incredible.

WHY SO MUCH ABOUT DNA?

When we see a series of letters that have been ordered intentionally to communicate meaning, we know that a mind of some kind must have put the letters in that particular order. The longer the phrase, the more confident we are.

Imagine that my friend Meghan walked into her kitchen and found that her husband Landon had poured the lettered tiles from a Scrabble or Bananagrams game onto the table. It is possible (though fairly unlikely) that she might find that a few tiles had randomly fallen into a line to form some short word.

If, however, she found 35 of the tiles perfectly lined up to say, "THE CAT LEAPT WILDLY WHEN IT SAW THE PICKLE," she would assume that Landon (or someone) had ordered the tiles intentionally. If she found a more personal message, like "HAVE A PHENOMENALLY GREAT TUESDAY MEGHAN," her assumption would be even stronger.

If we conclude—by looking at just 35 tiles that communicate meaning— that the tiles must have been ordered by an intelligent mind and that there is no way this could have happened randomly, what could possibly explain the origin of a highly-specific and uniquely-ordered code that is *three billion* characters long?

Dr. Meyer put it like this:

> *Whether we are looking at hieroglyphic inscriptions, or a paragraph in a book, or a section of computer code, or even information embedded in a radio signal, whenever we see information—especially when we find information in a digital or typographical form—and we trace it back to its ultimate source, we always come to a mind, and not a material process.*[9]

In his book, *Signature in the Cell,* Dr. Meyer outlines his argument for the intelligent design of the DNA information found in a cell:

> 1. *Despite a thorough search, no material causes have been discovered that demonstrate the power to produce large amounts of specified information.*
> 2. *Intelligent causes have demonstrated the power to produce large amounts of specified information. Therefore,*
> 3. *Intelligent design constitutes the best, most causally adequate, explanation for the information in the cell.*[10]

Whether the code that makes up DNA is more like written language or a computer code, the conclusion is the same. A book must have had an author. Working computer code must have had a coder.[11] The highly specific information in DNA must have had a mind behind it.

DESIGN SUGGESTS A DESIGNER

Imagine that my friends Katie, Carrie, Caroline, and Dorothy were hiking near Katie's family's house in the Blue Ridge Mountains and came upon a large, exposed rock. They might assume that the rock has been there since our planet was born.

If they stopped to think about it at all, they'd likely think the appearance of the rock was the result of millions or billions of years of just being. Perhaps it was covered by more dirt or less dirt at some point, but it was always just there.

Now imagine that they climbed to the top of the rock to enjoy a view of the valley and found a smartphone sitting there. They would not assume that the phone had always been there and that it had simply evolved into its present state over billions of years. They would assume that someone had left it behind. They would know that something so highly designed and sophisticated suggests a designer.

This has been called the argument from design. The argument was first popularized by a man named William Paley in a book he wrote way back in 1802. He used the illustration of a watch.

Paley suggested that the intricate and complex design of a watch implies a watchmaker. Because we see evidence of complexity and design in our world, he argued, we can reasonably conclude that our world must have been designed.

Peter Kreeft and Ronald K. Tacelli posed the argument like this:

1. *The universe displays a staggering amount of intelligibility, both within the things we observe and in the way these things relate to others outside themselves. That is to say, the way they exist and coexist displays an intricately beautiful order and regularity that can fill even the most casual observer with wonder. It is the norm in nature for many different beings to work together to produce the same valuable end—for example, the organs in the body work for our life and health.*
2. *Either this intelligible order is the product of chance or of intelligent design.*
3. *Not chance.*
4. *Therefore, the universe is the product of intelligent design.*
5. *Design comes only from a mind, a designer.*
6. *Therefore, the universe was the product of an intelligent designer.*[12]

When we see the complexity, order, and unity of so much in our universe—DNA and the inner workings of a cell are just two of many examples—it absolutely has the appearance of having been designed.

Many non-theists admit that things in our world appear to be designed. The difference, of course, is that they will say it has only the *appearance* of design and that it all came into being over time through an unguided process, perhaps involving natural selection and random mutation.

They would likely take issue with #3, in Kreeft and Tacelli's argument above: "Not chance."

But Kreeft and Tacelli would push back.

> *It is surely up to nonbelievers to produce a credible alternative to design. And "chance" is simply not credible. For we can understand chance only against a background of order. To say that something happened "by chance" is to say that it did not turn out as we would have expected, or that it did turn out in a way we would not have expected. But expectation is impossible without order. If you take away order and speak of chance alone as a kind of ultimate source, you have taken away the only background that allows us to speak meaningfully of chance at all.*[13]

There is a big problem with relying on chance as an answer to how life on Earth came to exist. Even if one were to grant the extremely unlikely possibility that the DNA of the first reproducing species could have come to exist in some naturalistic way, random mutation does not explain how different forms of animal life could have emerged.

While random mutation and natural selection absolutely account for changes that have occurred *within* a species, it would take a tremendous amount of faith to believe they could account for the arrival of entirely new species.

When we think of DNA as a type of information, or code, the creation of a new form of animal life would require new information in the form of new DNA, new RNA, new proteins, and new types of cells. A series of random mutations in DNA might alter future generations of an animal, but it simply would never get us to an entirely new form of animal.

Here is a different way we might think about this: Imagine what would happen if we were to take the text of a spy novel or the code from word processing software (both far less complex than DNA) and begin changing letters in the text or code randomly.

By changing letters completely at random, we *might* imagine that in at least one case, in billions or trillions of attempts, the spy novel or word processing software could be improved in some way. But we would never dream that by changing letters randomly over a long period of time, we might transform the spy novel into a dictionary or transform the word processing software into functioning missile guidance software.

In fact, the longer we randomly replaced letters, the more we would mess things up. We would eventually turn both into nonsense.

Dr. Murray Eden, a chemist and electrical engineering professor at MIT, said it this way: "No currently existing formal language can tolerate random changes in the symbol sequences which express its sentences. Meaning is almost invariably destroyed."[14]

You may believe that a cell's DNA, proteins, and protein-building machines all came to exist by chance, as a result of some unguided, naturalistic process. You may further believe that time, random mutation, and natural selection worked together to create all of the various forms of life on our beautiful planet.

But if you do, you do so by faith.

The basic version of the design argument made sense to me as I was first pondering faith in God. Since then, the more I've learned about DNA, the order and structure of our universe, and an argument called the fine-tuning argument (which we'll consider next), the more compelling I've found the design argument to be.

I believe that the designer of the universe—and the artist who created every good thing in it (all the way down to the details in DNA)—is God.

I am not alone. Thoughtful forms of this argument, for example, helped convince one of the most famous atheists of the past 100 years that there must be a God.

Antony Flew was a British philosopher who passed away in 2010. He was a professor who taught at several universities, including Oxford. For decades, he was an outspoken critic of theism. He traveled extensively to take part in debates with theists and Christians on the existence of God and wrote a number of books and articles on atheism. He was well-versed in different arguments made by theists and spent years trying to discredit those arguments.

Until he changed his mind.

The tipping point for Flew came when he concluded that there could be no satisfactory naturalistic, non-theistic explanation for the origin of the first reproducing species from DNA. Flew eventually wrote a book (with Roy Abraham Varghese) that documents why he changed his mind. The book is called *There is a God.*

In it, Flew writes:

> *Perhaps the most popular and intuitively plausible argument for God's existence is the so-called argument from design. According to this argument, the design that is apparent in nature suggests the existence of a cosmic Designer.*
>
> *I have often stressed that this is actually an argument to design from order, as such arguments proceed from the perceived order in nature to show evidence of design and, thus, a Designer. Although I was once sharply critical of the argument to design, I have since come to see that, when correctly formulated, this argument constitutes a persuasive case for the existence of God.*[15]

Flew did not convert to a particular religion. He called himself a deist, a person who believes in a supreme being who creates the universe but then stays uninvolved in it. But he had come to believe that *some* kind of God—with both immense power and intelligence—must exist.

How was he convinced? At least in part by scientific advancements in our understanding of DNA.

This is interesting because our culture seems to believe that there is some kind of enormous conflict between faith in God and science. As we prepare to wrap up this chapter and move into a chapter that will dive even more deeply into science, it is important to point out that I see no such conflict. Neither does Dr. Francis Collins.

SCIENCE... AND FAITH?

In an interview with PBS, Collins once said, "I actually do not believe that there are any collisions between what I believe as a Christian and what I know and have learned about as a scientist. I think there's a broad perception that that's the case, and that's what scares many scientists away from a serious consideration of faith."[16]

In the same interview, he suggested that people "mix up the natural and spiritual."[17] He said:

> *Science's domain is the natural. If you want to understand the natural world and be sure you're not misleading yourself, science is the way to do it. You accumulate data, you make hypotheses, you draw conclusions, you expose them to other people's critical views, and you eventually decide whether it's right.*
>
> *The spiritual world is not where science operates. The spiritual world is another part of human existence. I would argue a very critical one.*[18]

A growing number of scientists who believe in God have found that the understanding they gain through science helps them understand more about the world that God has made and thus strengthens their faith.

There are many accomplished scientists I could cite as examples, but I'll point to just one. John Polkinghorne was a British theoretical physicist who made substantial contributions in the fields of quantum mechanics and theoretical elementary particle physics. He held a prestigious professorship in mathematical physics at Cambridge University and wrote several books on quantum mechanics, including *The Quantum World*. His book, *Quantum Theory: A Very Short Introduction*, is thought to be one of the all-time best-selling books on the subject. Collectively, his books have been translated into 14 different languages.

As he progressed in his career as a scientist, Polkinghorne's faith in God grew. So much so that in his late 40s he returned to school, added a seminary degree to his list of academic accomplishments, and was ordained as a priest in the Anglican Church. By the time he died in 2021, he had written 26 books on the relationship between science and faith.

In 1997, he was knighted by Queen Elizabeth II, and in 2002, he was awarded the $1 million Templeton Prize for his work in the area of science and religion. Polkinghorne said this upon receiving the Templeton Prize:

> *I want to take science and religion with great and equal seriousness. I see them as complementary to each other and not as rivals. The most important thing that they have in common is that both believe that*

there is a truth to be sought and found, a truth whose attainment
comes through the pursuit of well-motivated belief... I believe that
I need the binocular approach of science and religion, if I am to do
any sort of justice to the deep and rich reality of the world in which
we live.[19]

Scientists observe our world and seek to learn from those observations. And the ways our lives have been improved as a result of scientific advancements are too numerous to count. Medical science alone has made a difference in the lives of billions around the world.

But, as Francis Collins, John Polkinghorne, and others have observed, there are questions that science cannot answer.

Science can tell us that we are conscious beings. But it cannot tell us about the essence or origin of consciousness. Science can tell us about the size and nature of our universe. But it can't tell us what existed before the Big Bang. Science can tell us that the universe had a beginning. But it can't tell us what caused it or why. Science can tell us that cells in every living thing contain a unique DNA code that is three billion characters long. But—apart from relying on blind chance as an explanation—it can't tell us how that code came to exist in the first reproducing species. I could go on.

As important as science is, it has limitations. And the more it teaches us about the design and order in our world—DNA is just one example—the harder it becomes to conclude that it began to exist without a designer.

✚ ✚ ✚

At this point, the skeptic may say, "Just because things appear to have been designed doesn't mean that they actually were designed by God." Or, "Just because you can't imagine how these three billion bits of information in one cell could have been precisely ordered or coded without a coder doesn't mean that God did it."

I understand these objections. So, again, I'll share this thought: the design argument doesn't conclusively prove that God exists. It simply provides another set of clues that point to the idea that belief in God is reasonable. Like an attorney's case that is built upon multiple arguments, so is the case for God.

In my journey, it was not one argument that convinced me that Christianity was true, but rather a combination of arguments.

If you have enjoyed these last two chapters, you will likely enjoy the next, as we continue to explore what we might learn about God from science, space, and the universe in which we live.

In Chapter 8, we will turn a corner and explore a wholly different sort of argument for God.

And then, in Chapter 9, we will look at perhaps the most powerful argument for the existence of God, an argument from history. We will consider the claims that this invisible God made himself visible when he chose to visit Earth.

Uncannily Perfect

IMAGINE THAT MY SON ETHAN WAS AN ASTRONAUT and that we, along with the rest of the world, were watching a live video feed of him stepping out of his lander to become the first human to set foot on Mars.

The atmosphere we would watch him step into contains less than 1% oxygen. The environment is beyond cold, with an average surface temperature of 80 degrees below zero (Fahrenheit). The conditions on Mars are completely hostile to human life.

As we watch him begin to explore the terrain, we see nothing but a barren wasteland in every direction. But later, as he passes a rock formation, we see what appears to be a structure of some kind in the distance. He moves toward it, and as he gets closer, we can see the structure more clearly. It appears to be a dome of some kind.

He finds a human-sized door—an airlock—and decides to enter. Once inside the dome, the first thing that is obvious is that there must be a power source in the building because artificial light fills the interior. The sensors in his spacesuit report that the mix of nitrogen and oxygen filling the dome is perfect for a human to breathe. The interior temperature is 70 degrees, or 150 degrees warmer than the outside of the dome. The humidity is 50%. In this environment, Ethan could actually take off his spacesuit safely if he chose (or was allowed by NASA) to do so.

He finds a spotless kitchen, complete with a refrigerator and cabinets stocked with human snacks and imperishable food. Down a hall, he discovers three bedrooms and a bathroom. Each appears to have been designed for humans. He tries the faucet in a sink, and clear water comes out. A quick test of the water proves it to be safe for a human to drink.

As we watch him explore the facility, we are in disbelief. Ethan is, too. Everyone is thinking the same thing. *How did this get here?*

✢ ✢ ✢

Credit for this illustration belongs to a philosopher and college professor named Robin Collins.[1] I've paraphrased his version, expanded it a bit, and added Ethan. After sharing the illustration in a paper, Collins asked readers what they'd be thinking if they had discovered this sort of biosphere.

I would be thinking one or more of the following thoughts:

  □ Who built this? (Note my assumption here: *It had to have been built by somebody.*)
  □ Does anyone live here now? Should I be scared?
  □ Would it be wrong to snag a couple of those snacks?
  □ This is way better than the habitat that Matt Damon's character built in the film *The Martian.*

It seems safe to assume that most people would be curious about the first question. Who built this?

You would probably conclude that it had to have been built by other humans who had completed missions to Mars without your knowledge. I have one friend who might wonder if extraterrestrials were responsible. While I'm not sure what you might think first, I can make a good guess about what you would not think. There is virtually no chance you'd think that this dome (with all of its contents) just happened to form on its own as the result of natural processes over time.

Collins makes this point in his paper. "Instead," he writes, we would all "conclude that it was designed by someone who knew exactly what would make the best possible living environment for humans."[2]

There is a larger point Collins wanted to make. Earth, and the universe as a whole, is our biosphere.

You will immediately understand this when discussing our planet: Earth provides a human-friendly habitat in a universe that is hostile to human life. Earth's unique qualities are obvious.

Our planet's atmosphere contains the perfect proportions of nitrogen and oxygen, so we can breathe. As we exhale carbon dioxide, plants absorb it and release oxygen from their leaves. Earth contains an abundance of water, and the water cycle ensures that our fresh water will stay fresh.

We are at the perfect distance from the Sun. We are close enough for it to keep us warm, but not so close that we risk being baked to death. The fact that Earth's orbit is nearly circular ensures we do not get too close or too far away from the Sun. Earth's ozone layer protects life from harmful ultraviolet radiation emitted by the Sun.

I could cite many other examples. Earth is not merely habitable for humans; it is hospitable.

But as perfect as these and other details about Earth might be for the existence of human life, there would be no Earth, no stars, and no life if the universe itself was different by even the tiniest of margins. Many scientists, whether they believe in God or not, tend to agree: the universe has either been "fine-tuned" to allow for life to exist, or at least has the appearance of having been fine-tuned.

A FINELY-TUNED UNIVERSE SUGGESTS A FINE-TUNER

The fine-tuning argument for the existence of God could be considered a grown-up sibling (or perhaps a more mature cousin) of the argument from design. Christopher Hitchens, the famous atheist, considered this to be one of the more challenging arguments for God he'd encountered in his debates with theists.

As we dive into this argument, let's first define fine-tuning.

There are dozens of values we believe to be true throughout the universe. We call them the fundamental constants. For example, the gravitational constant is a number that helps define the force of gravity. The cosmological constant is used to determine how fast the universe is expanding.

The values of at least 40 of these fundamental constants seem to have been "fine-tuned," to an almost ridiculous degree, to allow for life to exist in the universe. If the values of just one of these constants were different by even an incredibly, unfathomably tiny amount, the universe itself could not exist.

Stephen Hawking, in his famous book, *A Brief History of Time*, provided two examples. He wrote that "if the overall density of the universe were changed even by .0000000000001 percent, no stars or galaxies could be formed. If the rate of expansion one second after the Big Bang had been smaller by even one part in a hundred thousand million million, the universe would have recollapsed before it reached its present size."[3]

A science journalist at MIT, Anil Ananthaswamy, wrote that there is something "uncannily perfect about our universe."[4] This is how he explained fine-tuning in an article on the website for PBS television's science show, *NOVA*:

> *The laws of physics and the values of physical constants seem, as Goldilocks said, "just right." If even one of a host of physical properties of the universe had been different, stars, planets, and galaxies would never have formed. Life would have been all but impossible.[5]*

Here is a slightly longer explanation from the theoretical physicist, philosopher, and Arizona State University professor, Paul Davies (a man who says he is not religious in a typical sense):

> *Scientists are slowly waking up to an inconvenient truth—the universe looks suspiciously like a fix. The issue concerns the very laws of nature themselves. For 40 years, physicists and cosmologists have been quietly collecting examples of all too convenient "coincidences" and special features in the underlying laws of the universe that seem to be necessary in order for life, and hence conscious beings, to exist. Change any one of them and the consequences would be lethal. The crucial point is that some of those metaphorical knobs (of which there*

are 40) must be tuned very precisely, or the universe would be sterile. For example: neutrons are just a tad heavier than protons. If it were the other way around, atoms couldn't exist, because all the protons in the universe would have decayed into neutrons shortly after the big bang. No protons, then no atomic nucleus and no atoms. No atoms, no chemistry, no life.[6]

In Chapter 4, I quoted Freeman Dyson, a man *National Geographic* called one of the greatest figures in 20th-century physics. With regard to fine-tuning, Dyson said this: "The more I examine the universe and the details of its architecture, the more evidence I find that the universe in some sense must have known we were coming."[7]

Dyson described fine-tuning in this way:

The fact is that [there are] a number of fine-tunings that seem to be necessary to make a universe habitable the way ours is. For example, the water molecule has very special properties. The fact that ice is lighter than water—so it floats instead of sinking when it freezes— [is] absolutely essential to life in the oceans. If oceans froze from the bottom up, there would be no chance for fish to ever have been invented.[8]

"There are similar problems with nuclear physics," Dyson continued. He cited a certain energy level in carbon that was necessary in order to produce the carbon in stars.[9] Without that, Dyson said, "carbon couldn't have been produced in stars, and there couldn't be life." He went on to say that "there are a number of details of that sort that seem to have been finely tuned" to allow for life.[10]

Many widely respected scientists, including a number who do not believe in God, have observed that the universe appears to have been fine-tuned.

Sir Fred Hoyle, an atheist, admitted that a "common-sense interpretation of the facts suggests that a superintellect has monkeyed with physics."[11] Stephen Hawking, whom I quoted earlier, was an agnostic. He wrote, "The remarkable fact is that the values of these numbers seem to have been very finely adjusted to make possible the development of life."[12]

But why does the universe "seem to have been very finely adjusted?"

At first glance, there seem to be two options. Either the universe only *appears* to have been fine-tuned, even though it really has not been, or the universe truly *has* been fine-tuned to allow for life. There is a third way of looking at this that I will touch on at the end of the chapter.

Option 1: The Universe Only Appears to Have Been Fine-Tuned
If the universe has not been fine-tuned but rather only appears to have been fine-tuned, it would seem that our planet just got tremendously lucky. But just how much luck would have been necessary for chance to have resulted in these fundamental constants being so perfectly dialed in?

A 2021 article by Philip Goff in *Scientific American* magazine suggests that the odds of these constants being perfectly tuned for life—by chance— would have been "astronomically low." [13]

> As scientists have studied the fundamental principles that govern our universe, they have discovered that the odds of a universe like ours being compatible with life are astronomically low. We can model what the universe would have looked like if [just three of] its constants—the strength of gravity, the mass of an electron, the cosmological constant—had been slightly different. What has become clear is that, across a huge range of these constants, they had to have pretty much exactly the values they had in order for life to be possible. The physicist Lee Smolin has calculated that the odds of these life-compatible numbers coming up by chance is 1 in 10^{229}.

Dr. Smolin, whose work is quoted in the article, earned a Ph.D. in theoretical physics from Harvard University and has held several postdoctoral research positions. He has taught at Yale, Syracuse, and Penn State. His calculated probability (1 in 10^{229}) is almost unimaginably small.[14] Let's consider how small this probability actually is.

Estimates about the number of grains of sand on Earth tend to land somewhere between 10^{17} and 10^{19}. We'll use 10^{18}, but regardless of which is closer to correct, this illustration will still work.

Imagine that we were to choose one single grain of sand from anywhere on Earth, somehow mark it, and then replace it where we found it. Now imagine that we challenged my friend Abby to pick out that exact grain of sand, in one try, while blindfolded.

If she put on her blindfold as we transported her to the precise location on Earth where she guessed she might find it, she would then have one attempt to reach down (or dive or dig, I suppose) to try to select that one marked grain of sand. If 10^{18} is the correct number of grains of sand on Earth, her probability of success would be 1 in 1,000,000,000,000,000,000. One in one quintillion.

But let's say we wanted to make the challenge even harder on my friend Aidan, Abby's brother. Let's say we challenged Aidan to pick out one specific *atom* that we had pre-selected. But rather than limiting his choices to somewhere on Earth, Aidan had to find a specific atom from anywhere in the observable universe.

Typical estimates suggest there are somewhere between 10^{80} and 10^{85} atoms in the observable universe. Using the smaller number, the probability that Aidan would pick out the correct atom would be 1 in 10^{80}, or 1 in 100,000, 000,000,000,000,000,000,000,000,000,000,000,000,000,000,000,000, 000,000,000,000,000,000,000,000,000.

If you were Abby and faced the "easier" of the two challenges, you'd know that your probability of success, realistically, would be zero. Imagine how hard this would be at just one beach.

But Abby's probability of success would be 100 trillion trillion trillion trillion trillion times better than the probability of Aidan's success.[15] That's the difference between 10^{18} and 10^{80}.

With that in mind, consider how absurdly small Dr. Smolin's estimate of 1 in 10^{229} actually is. According to his calculation, the probability that various constants that govern our universe could have all been properly "dialed in" by chance (in such a way that the universe would be life-permitting) would be 1 in 10,000,000,000,000,000,000,000,000,000, 000,000,000,000,000,000,000,000,000,000,000,000,000,000,000,000, 000,000,000,000,000,000,000,000,000,000,000,000,000,000,000,000, 000,000,000,000,000,000,000,000,000,000,000,000,000,000,000,000, 000,000,000,000,000,000,000,000,000,000,000,000,000,000,000,000, 000,000,000.

If Dr. Smolin's math is correct, the probability of *both* Abby and Aidan succeeding on their first try (1 in 10^{98})—which, as we've seen, would seem utterly impossible—is far better than the probability of a life-permitting universe like ours being born by chance. Preposterously and unimaginably better, as it turns out.

Mathematician Amir Aczel, who wrote a book called *Why Science Does Not Disprove God*, wrote an article with the same title for *Time* magazine in 2014. He cited the work of another mathematician, suggesting the probability of the emergence of a life-permitting universe by chance was far smaller than 1 in 10^{229}:

> *The great British mathematician Roger Penrose has calculated—based on only one of the hundreds of parameters of the physical universe—that the probability of the emergence of a life-giving cosmos was 1 divided by 10, raised to the power of 10, and again raised to the power of 123. This is a number as close to zero as anyone has ever imagined.*
>
> *(This probability is much, much smaller than that of winning the Mega Millions jackpot for more days than the universe has been in existence.)* [16]

Some see these sorts of calculations and conclude that we simply got very lucky. Others know what these sorts of numbers mean. It would take an enormous amount of faith to believe that our life-permitting universe was born by chance.

Dr. Smolin's reaction to his own calculation is helpful:

> *In my opinion, a probability this tiny is not something we can let go unexplained. Luck will certainly not do here; we need some rational explanation of how something this unlikely turned out to be the case.* [17]

At this point, the skeptic finds himself facing a dilemma. He is forced to come up with an explanation as to how this sort of fine-tuning could have happened without a fine-tuner.

One theory that some have embraced as an answer is called the multiverse. This idea suggests that billions, trillions, or even far more universes exist. The greater the number, theorists argue, the more likely it is that a life-permitting universe like ours could have been born by chance.

We've all seen, in films and on television, stories involving multiple or parallel universes. In these stories, characters jump from one universe to another, all of which makes for great drama—and drama I often enjoy.

And while the idea of hopping from universe to universe is clearly something that lives only in the realm of science fiction, the concept of a multiverse should not be dismissed so quickly. Some extremely bright scientists believe that the theory has merit. But it is only a theory.

In fact, support for the existence of a multiverse is far from universal. A recent article in *Quanta Magazine* points out that many physicists hate the multiverse hypothesis and call it "a cop-out of infinite proportions."[18]

Why? Of the problems with this idea, here is one of the biggest: no empirical evidence of any kind has ever been detected to suggest the multiverse's existence. None. The idea of a multiverse is pretty much just that: a theoretical idea. It cannot be observed, tested, or measured. Freeman Dyson even went so far as to call it unscientific.

> *Unfortunately, [in the multiverse theory] all the other universes are purely hypothetical. We never shall have a chance to verify if they exist or not, so in a way, it puts the question outside of the reach of science.*[19]

Dyson said the question is outside of the reach of science because one cannot use the scientific method to test something that cannot be observed, measured, or even detected. Worse, it may never be able to be tested. Sarah Scoles, writing in *Smithsonian Magazine*, pointed this out in her article, "Can Physicists Ever Prove the Multiverse is Real?"

> *For an idea to technically move from hypothesis to theory, though, scientists have to test their predictions and then analyze the results to see whether their initial guess is supported or disproved by the data. If the idea gains enough consistent support and describes nature accurately and reliably, it gets promoted to an official theory.*
>
> *As physicists [dive] deeper into the heart of reality, their hypotheses— like the multiverse—become harder and harder, and maybe even impossible, to test. Without the ability to prove or disprove their ideas, there's no way for scientists to know how well a theory actually*

represents reality. It's like meeting a potential date on the internet: While they may look good on digital paper, you can't know if their profile represents their actual self until you meet in person. And if you never meet in person, they could be catfishing you. And so could the multiverse.[20]

In the *Scientific American* article I cited earlier, by Phillip Goff, he argues that the apparent fine-tuning in our universe does not lead to the conclusion that a multiverse exists. The article's title gives away its conclusion: "Our Improbable Existence Is No Evidence for a Multiverse."

According to experts in probability, Goff writes, multiverse theorists commit a logical fallacy known as the inverse gambler's fallacy. To understand, it is helpful to first understand the gambler's fallacy.

At a roulette table in Monte Carlo on August 18, 1913, the roulette ball, incredibly, landed on black—26 spins in a row![21] The gamblers at the table became increasingly confident after each spin that the next result would be red. So they kept betting red and lost millions of dollars.

This is an example of the gambler's fallacy. If the wheel and ball were balanced and not unfairly rigged in some way, the odds that the ball would land on red were identical to the odds of it landing on black. The results of previous spins were irrelevant when it came to what would happen on the next spin.

Imagine that, during a game night, my friends Ryan, Noah, Aron, Hannah, and Juliet were playing the board game Risk. Let's say Ryan had three armies left on Kamchatka, and he was (as we'd expect from Ryan) making a great defensive stand.

If Ryan rolled three double-sixes in a row, what would you assume would happen next? Would you guess that Ryan would be *less* likely to roll a fourth double-six because "there's just no way" he'd do it again? Or that he would be *more* likely to roll a fourth double-six because he's a battler and was "on a roll"?

Either assumption would be an example of the gambler's fallacy. In reality, Ryan would have exactly the same probability of rolling a double-six the fourth time as he did the first three: 1 in 36.

The gambler's fallacy tempts people to look at dice rolls that just happened and then make an assumption about what they think will happen next. The inverse gambler's fallacy is, obviously, inverted. It tempts people to look at the result of a current roll and then make an assumption about rolls that, in their minds, "must have" happened previously.

Let's say that my friends Claire, Savanah, Paige, Blake, Christina, and Caleb were playing Yahtzee. Imagine that Paige rolled a Yahtzee as our friend Anna walked by. If Anna assumed that they must have been playing for a while because the odds of a Yahtzee on the very first roll seemed unlikely, she would commit the inverse gambler's fallacy.

Bringing this back to the multiverse discussion, Goff suggests that some scientists see the existence of our incredibly unlikely universe and imagine that there *must have been* many universes formed before this one because we would have been far too lucky for this unlikely life-permitting one to have formed first.

This is an example of the inverse gambler's fallacy.

According to Goff, scientists who would say that the fine-tuning of our universe points to the multiverse believe that if some huge number of universes had already popped into existence, it would be more likely that a rare life-permitting universe like ours would have begun to exist, too.

But in reality, the number of universes that came into existence previously would not change the probability of any new life-permitting universe being formed by chance.

If Dr. Smolin's calculations are correct, the probability of any new life-permitting universe coming into existence by chance will be the same each time: 1 in 10^{229}. If Aczel's understanding of Penrose's calculations was correct, the probability would be even smaller. Assuming that each of these universes is independent, each universe that came into existence would face the same absurd odds against being life-permitting by chance.

Goff's conclusion is startling in its strength:

> *The reason some scientists take seriously the possibility of a multiverse in which the constants vary in different universes is that it seems to*

explain the fine-tuning. But on closer examination, the inference from fine-tuning to the multiverse proves to be an instance of flawed reasoning. So, what should we make of the fine-tuning? Perhaps there is some other way of explaining it. Or perhaps we just got lucky. [22]

Goff was not attempting to disprove the existence of a multiverse in this piece. Rather, he was seeking to show that the apparent fine-tuning of our universe is not necessarily good evidence that the multiverse exists. This is important.

If, in the future, we somehow discover evidence that makes it clear that belief in the multiverse is warranted, it would not fundamentally harm or challenge the arguments for God made in this chapter and the last. At best, it would give the atheist a slightly better explanation as to how the existence of a life-permitting universe could have begun to exist in a naturalistic way.

But, as William Lane Craig has pointed out, even in a multiverse, the probability that a life-permitting universe like ours could have come to exist by chance is still absurdly low. He points to the Borde-Guth-Vilenkin theorem, which shows that the multiverse itself cannot be extended into the infinite past. So, if there is a multiverse, it too must have begun to exist at a specific point in time. [23]

If the multiverse does exist and did have a beginning, the cosmological argument I wrote about in Chapter 5 would also apply to the multiverse.

The first option we considered, that the universe only appears to have been fine-tuned, demands that either we got impossibly lucky or that an unproven, unobserved, undetected multiverse really does exist—and that we still got impossibly lucky.

There is a second option.

Option 2: The Universe Actually *Has* Been Fine-Tuned for Life
This argument holds that the reason scientists observe the appearance of remarkable fine-tuning in so many of the fundamental constants in our universe is that it actually has been fine-tuned to be life-permitting. That a superintellect really has "monkeyed with the physics." That someone or

something designed and built this 93-billion-light-year-wide "biosphere" that was perfectly fine-tuned to allow life to exist. And that within our universe, that same someone or something also created this planet, a planet that offers an amazing habitat for human life.

If fine-tuning did happen, we have to wonder who (or what) could have possibly had the power to have done the fine-tuning. In my mind, the most reasonable answer—even if it does require faith—would be someone who exists outside of our universe and has the power to have fine-tuned his creation.

God.

✝ ✝ ✝

I mentioned earlier that there is a third way that some have suggested we view all of this. It is called the anthropic principle. In simple terms, it suggests that the reason we find ourselves in what seems to be an absurdly lucky sort of universe is that if we were *not* in this sort of universe, we never would have been alive to know it.

This argument is interesting. But it doesn't even attempt to answer the question of what could explain the fine-tuning that everyone seems to agree exists in this specific universe. For anyone interested, I will suggest a two-part video in the Endnotes in which William Lane Craig responds to this argument in greater depth.[24]

✝ ✝ ✝

You may choose to believe that this universe—the only one we can observe and that we can know exists—just appears to be fine-tuned and that we just got exceedingly, mind-bogglingly lucky. Or you may choose to believe in the multiverse and believe that we still got exceedingly, mind-bogglingly lucky.

But if you believe either, you do so, at least in part, by faith. Of course, I also believe what I believe by faith. But I'd suggest it takes more faith to believe we got preposterously lucky than it does to believe that our uncannily well-crafted universe was intentionally fine-tuned to be life-permitting by the imaginative, powerful mind who created it.

As with the prior arguments, the fine-tuning argument doesn't point to one specific God. It is simply one more argument as we continue to build the case that it is both reasonable and rational to believe in God.

In the following chapter, we will change gears completely. We'll move away from discussions of the universe, fine-tuning, science, and DNA.

It will be our final argument for the existence of God in general before we begin to consider the evidence for a very specific God.

Is that Right?

IN CHAPTER SIX, I WROTE ABOUT THE AFTERNOON I spent soaring high above Lake Tahoe in a glider. I did not, however, write about the man who piloted the glider that day.

At some point in the flight, I asked the pilot how he first learned to fly. He said he had learned just before World War II, when he was trained to fly as a fighter pilot... for Germany.

I was not expecting that, but I was very intrigued. Ever since I was a little boy, I have been fascinated by World War II, and especially by fighter planes from that era. As you probably guessed if you know me, I started asking questions.

At first, the pilot was a bit hesitant to talk about the war. I get that. The same has been true of several men I've known who experienced the horrors of combat. Perhaps it was even more true for a man who had fought against America but now lived here. So, I asked a couple of questions about the Focke-Wulf Fw 190 and different Messerschmitts flown by the Luftwaffe (the German air force) during the war. He started talking.

I asked at some point how he ended up deciding to come to America. He told me that he had become concerned about the direction of Germany under Hitler and the Nazi Party even before the war. As the war went on, his concern grew. He believed that Hitler was leading Germany down the wrong path.

Over time, he started to wrestle with a brutal decision. Should he desert and walk away from his squadron and the war without permission? Or should he keep fighting—and risking his life—for a cause in which he no longer believed?

If he had deserted and gotten caught, he would have been executed. But even worse, he said that if he had deserted, he would have put his parents' lives in danger. During the war, members of the German military understood that if they deserted or even failed to show courage, both they and their family members at home could face imprisonment or execution.

Ultimately, he said he was not willing to dishonor his parents nor to risk their safety by failing to fulfill his military commitment. His plan—if he survived the war—was to fulfill that commitment and then move to America as soon as the war ended. That's what he did.

As I think back to our conversation that day, I was interested but not surprised to hear him say he thought Hitler was wrong.[1] He knew it then, just as we know it now. But how do we know that? On what basis can we make that judgment? I'm not questioning whether Hitler was wrong—I'm sure you will agree that he was. Rather, I am asking how one would come to know such a thing.

A UNIVERSAL MORAL COMPASS?

I would suggest that this is an example of what I called built-in knowledge in Chapter 4: *we just know*. I believe that sane humans have a moral compass that points to a universal reality: some things are always and truly right, while other things are always and truly wrong.

Seeking to wipe an entire race of people off the face of the planet in order to create a so-called "master race" is wrong. We know this as surely as we know that recreational cruelty is wrong. Nobody has to tell us that torturing babies for entertainment is wrong. We know it. Rape is wrong. We know it.

We know these things in the same way that we know that courage, generosity, and self-sacrifice for the benefit of others are admirable virtues. Cultures and religions of all kinds, across the globe, affirm this.

Of course, one cannot prove that such an objective system of moral values exists universally. But even if we cannot prove it, is it reasonable to believe that such a system does exist?

I think it is.

If I had to recommend only ten books on Christianity, I'd have a hard time narrowing the list. The Bible would be a given, of course. And a book I mentioned earlier, *Mere Christianity*, by C.S. Lewis, would almost certainly be on my list.

Lewis was a writer, a professor at the famous Oxford University, and an amazing defender of the Christian faith. His books are brilliant. In *Mere Christianity*, he argues that there really is a set of universal moral values that govern our world.

> *Everyone has heard people quarrelling. Sometimes it sounds funny and sometimes it sounds merely unpleasant; but however it sounds, I believe we can learn something very important from listening to the kind of things they say.*
>
> *They say things like this: "How'd you like it if anyone did the same to you?"—"That's my seat, I was there first"—"Leave him alone, he isn't doing you any harm"—"Why should you shove in first?" "Give me a bit of your orange, I gave you a bit of mine"—"Come on, you promised." People say things like that every day, educated people as well as uneducated, and children as well as grown-ups.*
>
> *Now what interests me about all these remarks is that the man who makes them is not merely saying that the other man's behaviour does not happen to please him. He is appealing to some kind of standard of behaviour which he expects the other man to know about. And the other man very seldom replies: "To hell with your standard." Nearly always he tries to make out that what he has been doing does not really*

go against the standard, or that if it does there is some special excuse. He pretends there is some special reason in this particular case why the person who took the seat first should not keep it, or that things were quite different when he was given the bit of orange, or that something has turned up which lets him off keeping his promise.

It looks, in fact, very much as if both parties had in mind some kind of Law or Rule of fair play or decent behaviour or morality or whatever you like to call it, about which they really agreed. And they have. If they had not, they might, of course, fight like animals, but they could not quarrel in the human sense of the word. Quarrelling means trying to show that the other man is in the wrong. And there would be no sense in trying to do that unless you and he had some sort of agreement as to what Right and Wrong are; just as there would be no sense in saying that a footballer had committed a foul unless there was some agreement about the rules of football.[2]

In his typically clear style, Lewis makes a thought-provoking case for universal rights and wrongs. He argues later that these values provide the sense we all have of the way the world *ought* to be.

And he's right. We do have a shared perception about how things ought to be, and we must not ignore that. When something goes differently than we believe it ought to have gone, we say, "That was wrong." Or, "That was not fair." But this makes no sense without a standard by which to make such a judgment. If something bad were to happen to my friend Sammie, how could she have any ability to call the thing bad unless she had a clear understanding of what good and bad actually are?

This line of thinking played a role in Lewis deciding, as an adult, that his views about God had been all wrong.

My argument against God was that the universe seemed so cruel and unjust. But how had I got this idea of "just" and "unjust"? A man does not call a line crooked unless he has some idea of a straight line. What was I comparing this universe with when I called it unjust? If the whole show was bad and senseless from A to Z, so to speak, why did I, who was supposed to be part of the show, find myself in such violent reaction against it? A man feels wet when he falls into water, because man is not a water animal: a fish would not feel wet.

Of course I could have given up my idea of justice by saying it was nothing but a private idea of my own. But if I did that, then my argument against God collapsed too—for the argument depended on saying that the world was really unjust, not simply that it did not happen to please my private fancies. Thus in the very act of trying to prove that God did not exist—in other words, that the whole of reality was senseless—I found I was forced to assume that one part of reality—namely my idea of justice—was full of sense.

Consequently atheism turns out to be too simple. If the whole universe has no meaning, we should never have found out that it has no meaning: just as, if there were no light in the universe and therefore no creatures with eyes, we should never know it was dark. Dark would be a word without meaning.[3]

The Problem with Subjective Morality

An objective moral value is one that is universal and binding to every person. If objective moral values did *not* exist, all moral values would be subjective. A subjective moral value is based on one's own point of view. It is private and not binding for anyone else. But if all moral values are subjective and there is no external source of objective morality, then any argument about what is right or wrong is simply an argument between opinions.

In a world of fully subjective morality, if my friends Ben and Shea were not friends (they are, but ignore that for a moment) and Ben was able to steal a superhero-related collectible from Shea, it would not be morally wrong for Ben to steal it.

If Ben had stolen it, he would have obtained something he wanted for free. From his perspective, he'd call this good. But from Shea's perspective, this would be bad. In a world of subjective morality, whose opinion would carry more weight?

Of course, our legal system would have something to say about such a theft. Ben could be found to be legally in the wrong. But morally wrong?

In a world of fully subjective moral values, no.

One might ask at this point if a government's laws should shape one's moral values. I hope not. Consider just two examples.

First, in a vast number of nations around the world throughout history, slavery was legal. Shockingly, in many countries today, it is still not illegal.[4] If my friends Sydney and Erin moved to such a country to serve as nurses, would you suggest their new country's lack of laws prohibiting slavery should lead them to conclude that slavery is morally okay? I hope that you are shaking your head no.

The fact that my pilot believed Hitler was wrong is a second example. He was not the only German who came to that conclusion. According to historian Peter Hoffmann, more than 77,000 German citizens were executed by the Nazis for somehow playing a role in the German resistance movement.[5] Many thousands more were thrown into concentration camps, and others were never captured. These men and women's sense of right and wrong transcended their own government's definitions.

If moral values are truly subjective, however, we have no objective (true for everyone) basis upon which to conclude that Hitler was wrong. Nazi ideas about genocide and eugenics could not be judged to be more or less wrong than anyone else's ideas. Just different. And if Nazi Germany had conquered the world, we might have grown up being taught that it is acceptable to kill Jewish people, Slavic people, Black people, other non-Aryans, the sick, and the disabled, all in pursuit of the so-called master race.

But every fiber of our being screams: We *know* that Hitler was wrong. And we would still know that even if the Nazis (and the other Axis powers) had won the war.

This was illustrated in a variety of interesting ways in a streaming series from Amazon Studios called *The Man in the High Castle*. Viewers who are sensitive to mature content may want to proceed with caution, as Amazon rated the series 18+ due to its sometimes graphic violence and occasional sexual situations. The premise of the series, though, is fascinating. The drama (with a science fiction twist[6]) explores what life might have looked like in the United States if it had lost World War II.

In this alternate reality, Nazi Germany controls the eastern half of what was previously America. Japan controls the west coast. The Rocky Mountains serve as a neutral zone. One of the main characters in the series, John Smith, is a highly-ranked American Nazi military officer who is happily living with his family in what is now called the Nazi American Reich.

His family is happy—that is, until their son is found to have a disease. When the son's illness is discovered, the Nazi policy on eugenics demands that he be taken away and killed.

Smith and his wife react as you or I might in the same situation. They try to save their son. At different points, they each come to the awful realization that they had gone along with Nazi policies (or had mindlessly looked the other way) in exchange for their personal comfort, well-being, and the advancement of Smith's career. We watch their descent into crushing guilt and despair as they ponder who they have become.

Why? Because they had been ignoring what they knew to be true: Hitler was wrong. My glider pilot knew it in real life. Many other Germans knew it as well. People all over the world knew it. And we know it, too. Nobody has to tell us—we just know.

Objective moral values exist.

OBJECTIVE MORAL LAWS SUGGEST A MORAL LAW-GIVER

The existence of objective moral values is, many people believe, another thought-provoking argument for the existence of God.

Dr. Sean McDowell, an author and professor at Biola University, formulates the argument this way:

1. *If objective moral values exist, God must exist.*
2. *Objective moral values exist.*
3. *Therefore, God must exist.*[7]

We've already discussed premise two. Premise one, however, may also give a skeptic pause. Is it a leap in logic? I don't think so.

If we find that such a system of moral values is built into us, it begs two enormous and related questions: How did it get there? And how could such a universally binding system of values even begin to exist?

If these values are truly objective, they must have been defined and built into us by a third party, one that is external to the human race. And one that is very powerful. This is why the existence of objective moral values does more than suggest the existence of a moral lawgiver; it demands it.

In human terms, what law has ever been written except by the hand of one or more lawmakers? Without a universal lawmaker, how could there be universal laws?

Even the well-known atheist and philosopher J.L. Mackie recognized this. He wrote that ethics "are most unlikely to have arisen in the ordinary course of events, without an all-powerful god to create them. If then, there are such intrinsically prescriptive objective values, they make the existence of a god more probable than it would have been without them."[8]

Some skeptics may object and suggest that there are other ways a moral law could have begun to exist. Perhaps, one might argue, the moral impulses we have now evolved, as they helped previous generations of humans survive. But even if that is true (and I do not believe it is), there is no reason that such moral feelings would be binding for everyone.

You may choose to believe that there are no objective moral values or that an unguided, natural process could have instilled this value system in each of us. That is your right. But if you do, please know that you believe it, at least partially, by faith.

ADDITIONAL THOUGHTS ON OBJECTIVE VERSUS SUBJECTIVE MORALITY
There are three related ideas that seem important to mention at this point:

1. Faith in God is Not Necessary to Grasp Right vs. Wrong
Some people may assume I am arguing that a person must believe in God to know right from wrong or to make moral decisions. I am not. I'm suggesting that God has made humans in his image and has built this sense of right and wrong into each person—regardless of what that person believes or doesn't believe about God.

2. If There is No God, Oppression is Not Wrong
If there is no God, as I mentioned earlier, we are all merely flukes of nature—the result of chemistry and chance. If there is no God, there can be no binding moral values that apply to each of us. From a moral perspective, we would be no different than a rock, a tulip, or a cat. And, as William Lane Craig has pointed out, nobody judges a cat for killing a mouse; it is just being a cat.[9]

If we were the result of only chemistry and chance, we would find ourselves living in a survival-of-the-fittest sort of world. In such a world, the strong are (by definition) greater than the weak. In such a world, not even oppression could be condemned as wrong. Why? Because oppression would simply be part of the normal course of life, as the fittest rule over the less fit.

In America today, discussions about oppression are not uncommon. But to expect everyone to agree that oppression is wrong only makes sense if there is a universal system of moral values in place.

This is not to say that all atheists agree that oppression is okay. I'd guess that most thoughtful people would say that oppression is wrong, whatever their spiritual views. But if there is no God, such an opinion is subjective and is no more right or wrong than anyone else's opinion.

It should be thought-provoking for the atheist to contemplate this question: In a world of subjective moral values where there is no universal moral law, *on what basis* can an atheist say oppression is wrong?

Some might answer, "On the basis of what's good for humanity." But again, we run into the same problem. Who is to say that this answer is more valid than anyone else's? And even if you like the answer, who is to say one's view of what is "good" for humanity is better than another's? Interestingly, atheists—whether they realize it or not—actually have to borrow a concept from a theist's worldview to call *anything* objectively "wrong."

3. "Bad" Things that Happen Do Not Disprove God
Some people do not believe in God because, in their judgment, if God were real (and good), he would always prevent bad things from happening. But we've already observed that even the words "good" and "bad" don't have any objective meaning without some universal standard. So, if something a person calls "bad" results in that person doubting that God exists, things get really weird. Think about this carefully. In using "bad things" to argue that God *doesn't* exist, the atheist must use a line of reasoning that only makes sense if God *does* exist. I hope you can see the problem here.

The age-old question of why God might allow some bad thing or another to happen is a very important one. It demands more space than I can devote to it here, but I have written a very brief, three-page overview of the topic in the Endnotes.[10]

In this and the three previous chapters, we've considered arguments for the existence of some kind of god. They explain some of the reasons I believe in God. And they do demand some level of faith—a faith I'd call reasonable. I've also sought to show that a person who believes God does not exist must believe that, too, by faith.

Writers and thinkers have made other arguments for the existence of God over the years. Peter Kreeft and Ronald K. Tacelli provide overviews of twenty of them in their excellent *Handbook of Christian Apologetics*. But now it is time to turn our attention from arguments for some generic God to an argument specifically for the rationality of the Christian faith.

From the beginning of this book, I've said I believe Christianity is more likely to be true than not true and that the Christian conception of God is correct. In the chapters that follow, we'll consider why.

I believe the next two chapters offer one of the most compelling arguments we will consider for the existence of God: evidence that God Himself actually stepped into the time-space continuum and visited our planet as a person.

A person named Jesus.

Christianity

Evidence Matters

YEARS AGO, A MAN NAMED FRED KRUEGER[1] was returning to his home in Connecticut when he saw two men firing a shotgun near his property. When he pulled into his driveway, he discovered that his house was either their target or at least in their line of fire. Some of their shotgun blasts were hitting his home.

Fred was well-liked in his community and was known to be a good man. But he was also a World War II veteran who had survived combat and an intense fire as part of a tank unit. He was not going to be frightened by two fools with a shotgun.

He went inside and grabbed his .22 pistol.

When he came back out of his house, he couldn't see the two men, so he fired three warning shots: the first two into the ground and the third high into the air. He had no plans to shoot either man—he simply wanted to scare them away.

Regardless, one would soon be dead.

+++

My mom's cousin by marriage, Jim, is a man I've looked up to since I was a boy. If I were to name the men in my life who I respect the most, he would be high on the list. At the time this incident took place near Fred's home, Jim was an investigator in the Connecticut State's Attorneys' Office and was assigned to review the evidence.

On the day in question, the police arrived and discovered that the dead man was the victim of a gunshot wound. Over the next few days, detectives talked to the victim's friend, to Fred, and to others. They sought evidence and canvassed the area for witnesses. When the ballistics report came back, it revealed a key piece of evidence.

The lethal bullet had been fired from a .22 pistol.

+++

The two men with the shotgun had been in a recreation area near Fred's home, goofing off. They thought it would be fun to throw different things into the air and shoot these flying "targets" out of the sky. They had not imagined that their shotgun blasts could reach anyone's house from where they were.

So, when one of the men suddenly collapsed, it wasn't clear to his buddy what had happened. It turns out, though, that the old adage "what goes up must come down" is also true of bullets. Tragically so, in this case.

Fred's unaimed warning shot, the one he fired into the sky, had indeed come down. Astonishingly, the bullet—as it fell from high in the air—had struck and killed one of the two men who were wielding the shotgun.

As he recalled the case, Jim told me, "It was just an awful, awful situation. For everyone. A man with a young family had been killed. And Fred was a good man. But he had fired a bullet that had taken another man's life. There had to be consequences." Jim understood that his office would have to follow the evidence where it led, regardless of how he or anyone else felt about the story it told.

+++

As we continue to explore evidence for the existence of God, we too must follow it where it leads, regardless of how we may feel about God, religion, or even religious people. And much like investigators do, we should pay attention to how various lines of evidence come together to build a case.

In a court case, one single piece of evidence is often not enough to secure a conviction. But as different lines of evidence come together, the case against a defendant can become more persuasive.

In the previous chapters, we have considered just four arguments for the existence of God: the cosmological argument, the argument from design, the fine-tuning argument, and the moral argument.

You may find that none of these arguments is fully persuasive on its own. But when considered together, the case gathers strength. As we transition now from evidence for the existence of some non-specific god to evidence that Christianity is true, I believe the case will become stronger still.

A DIFFICULT ROAD
In this chapter, we will turn our attention to what I'd call one of the single most important events in world history: the resurrection of Jesus Christ.

Examining evidence for the resurrection might initially seem difficult. Not because it is hard to understand, but because we are talking about an event in the past that we didn't see. Perhaps more challenging is the fact that the story contains supernatural elements.

Christianity claims that God visited Earth as a man born to a virgin, grew up, was killed, and then rose from the dead. These are extraordinary claims.

Further, eyewitness accounts of Jesus' life include numerous other stories of miracles. So, if we are honest, we should admit from the beginning that our inclination is to not believe. Not because the evidence is bad, but because—if true—this is the most incredible story ever told.

And it is a story that has implications for each of us.

We live in a cynical, skeptical age in which people roll their eyes when any claim is made that would be out of the ordinary or (especially) supernatural. We slip into thinking, even if subconsciously, that we are too sophisticated to believe such a story. We are too easily tempted to believe that people in the past simply weren't as intelligent as we are today.

There is a name for this. It is called chronological snobbery.

Earlier in this book, I wrote that Todd and Keith had told me, early in my freshman year, that all of Christianity rises or falls on one event in history: the resurrection. It either happened or it did not.

This matters because, when considering Christianity, we are not merely considering a philosophical question. We are not considering a question of religious preference. This is not a "you should believe this because some person you love believed it and taught it to you" question. Nor is this a "you should reject this because a person you love rejected it and taught you" question. It is also not a "you should reject this because you dislike Christians or something Christianity teaches" question.

This is a historical question. *Did the resurrection happen?*

If it did not happen, the Bible admits that believers in the resurrection are to be pitied most of all.[2] But if it did happen, it changes everything. If it did happen (and if I can risk being blunt for a moment), it simply doesn't matter how much you like or dislike Christians you've met. It doesn't matter how much you like or dislike the thought of religion or whether you consider yourself to be religious. It doesn't matter how you were raised or how much you like or dislike the rest of Christianity's teachings.

Jesus had predicted that he'd die and rise again. He did not claim to merely point to God, but rather to actually *be* God. If the resurrection happened, it would give tremendous weight to all that he taught. It means that Jesus was who he claimed to be.

If it happened, it should matter immensely to every one of us.

Before I got to college, I did not understand that Christianity claimed to be a religion based on evidence and history. As I explored the evidence for the resurrection, I was fascinated.

It turns out that it is easy to find books that present this evidence. Most go into greater depth than I'll do here. Some were written by men who were skeptics when they began writing. They had set out to disprove the resurrection but found themselves compelled to follow the evidence where it led, even if they didn't initially like their own conclusions.

Albert Henry Ross was a writer from England who wrote books under the pseudonym Frank Morison. He set out to prove that the resurrection was a myth. However, his research led him to a conclusion he did not expect: that the resurrection had really happened. The first chapter of his book, *Who Moved the Stone?* is called "The Book that Refused to Be Written."

I mentioned earlier that the book *Evidence that Demands a Verdict* had been helpful in my journey. The writer, Josh McDowell, knew that if he could disprove the resurrection, he would crush Christianity. That's what he set out to accomplish. Yet McDowell eventually came to the very same conclusion as Albert Henry Ross: he became persuaded that the resurrection had truly happened.

Lee Strobel's story is nearly identical. An American journalist who earned a Master of Studies in Law degree from Yale, Strobel won awards for his work as the legal editor at the *Chicago Tribune*. He was an atheist who also set out to disprove Christianity. His research led him to faith in Christ. In 1998, he took the results of his research and wrote the best-selling book, *The Case for Christ*, a book that has since been turned into a feature film.

Simon Greenleaf played an instrumental role in the founding of Harvard Law School, the most influential law school in America. His three-volume work, *A Treatise on the Law of Evidence*, was written in 1842 and is still considered to be one of the most important legal works on evidence ever written. It helped define the rules for what is and is not considered admissible evidence in America's legal system.

While teaching at Harvard Law, as a Christian, he decided to apply the guidelines he had written on admissible evidence to the evidence for the resurrection. His analysis led him to write a book called *An Examination of the Testimony of the Four Evangelists, by the Rules of Evidence Administered in Courts of Justice.*

His conclusion? That the accounts recorded in the Gospels would stand up well in our courts of law. This is a remarkable conclusion by a brilliant legal mind.

There are other books like these that I could mention, and I have done so in the Appendix.

I understand that the skeptic may well object here: "So what? Some books have been written. That doesn't mean that these writers came to the right conclusions." This is true. The fact that I'm writing this book doesn't mean that my conclusions are fully correct.

Books like these matter, however, because they show that there is a case for Christianity that can be made on the basis of evidence, a case that many bright minds have found to be compelling. And even if I fail to make the case in this book in a way that you find to be fully persuasive, the books in the Appendix will really help if you want to take a next step by diving into these arguments more deeply.

Wisdom suggests that we should follow the evidence, whether we like where it leads or not. The question of whether Jesus Christ actually rose from the dead is that important.

FACTS ARE FACTS

Two historical facts about Jesus' resurrection have always stood out the most to me: the empty tomb and the radically changed lives of Jesus' disciples.

If you add these two facts to Jesus' own prediction that he'd die and rise again, claims that he appeared physically to many after his death, the rise of the Christian church despite opposition from the Roman Empire, and the reality that Christianity has profoundly changed the world, the evidence does indeed begin to demand a verdict.

The empty tomb and the changed lives of the disciples are particularly interesting to me because it is reasonable to believe both without having to trust only the biblical account. Simply use your mind and logic.

1. The Empty Tomb

Two important historical claims of Christianity are:

(1) Jesus of Nazareth was crucified.
(2) On the third day (counting the day he was crucified), his tomb was found to be empty.

Dr. Paul L. Maier, the Russell H. Seibert Professor of Ancient History at Western Michigan University, wrote:

> *If all the evidence is weighed carefully and fairly, it is indeed justifiable, according to the canons of historical research, to conclude that the sepulcher of Joseph of Arimathea, in which Jesus was buried, was actually empty on the morning of the first Easter. And no shred of evidence has yet been discovered in literary sources, epigraphy, or archaeology that would disprove this statement.*[3]

The claim that Jesus' tomb was empty is one that is found both inside and outside of the Bible. The fact that neither Roman nor Jewish sources ever denied the empty tomb is significant.

But even if Dr. Maier's (and others') work, from a historical perspective, doesn't persuade you, simple logic should convince you that the tomb must have been empty. If Jesus' body had been in the tomb, the earliest believers could never have convinced anyone that Jesus had risen. At least not for long.

The disciples began to preach that Jesus had risen from the dead just a short time after the crucifixion. Importantly, they began in Jerusalem, where Jesus had been crucified. Many believed in the resurrection, and the Christian church was born.

If the tomb had not been empty, the disciples' lies (or lunacy) would have quickly been revealed. Once proven wrong, when Jesus' body was shown to still be in the tomb, Christianity would have died in its infancy.

As German theologian Paul Althaus has pointed out, the claims that Jesus had risen "could not have been maintained in Jerusalem for a single day, for a single hour, if the emptiness of the tomb had not been established as a fact for all concerned."[4]

Even the Jewish leaders' response, that Jesus' followers had stolen the body, affirms the empty tomb. If they had not believed the tomb to be empty, their explanation would have made no sense.

The Jewish authorities and the Roman Empire were both motivated, for different reasons, to prove wrong the early Christians' claims that Jesus had risen. They wanted to put a stop to the spread of Christianity. All they had to do was produce Jesus' dead body.

They couldn't do it.

For me, even as an 18-year-old college student who was first pondering the resurrection, this piece of evidence seemed incredibly important. It still does.

Some might ask, "What if the disciples—or someone else—actually stole the body?" We'll explore that question in the next chapter. I'm not going to go much deeper into the evidence for the empty tomb than I've gone here because I think logic screams that it must have been empty. But other evidence does exist.

One of the world's most renowned scholars on the resurrection is Dr. Gary Habermas. He has written more than 20 books on the subject. If you want to learn more about the resurrection from a scholarly perspective, read his books. Several are listed in the Appendix.

In a statement that shows that I am only scratching the surface here, Habermas once said, "How many facts do you need to believe that America won the Revolutionary War? I can give you 21 historical evidences for why the tomb of Jesus was empty that Sunday morning."[5]

Though I believe it is safe to trust that Jesus' tomb was empty, a good investigation should also include consideration of other possible explanations. In the next chapter, we'll consider other theories that have sought to explain the empty tomb.

2. The Disciples Became Convinced That Jesus Had Risen

Consider for a moment the emotional state of Jesus' disciples after Jesus had been crucified. They were devastated.

They had encountered, in Jesus, a man who could see into their souls, who knew them the best, and yet loved them the most; a man they had seen heal sickness, give sight to the blind, and raise the dead; a man who commanded the wind and waves, all while serving others rather than demanding to be served; and a man who really seemed to be the long-awaited Messiah, yet who was humble enough to have washed their feet.

These men had left everything to follow him. For three years, they had experienced the adventure of a lifetime. They had pushed their chips to the middle and gone all in, believing that he was who he claimed to be: the long-awaited Messiah. God. But they had lost.

Whatever the dream had been, it was over. Now reeling and doubting all that they had seen with their own eyes, reality set in. Jesus was dead. It was time to slink back to their homes. Can you feel their pain? They had never quite let themselves believe that Jesus would die. Their pre-existing Jewish beliefs about resurrection would not have suggested they could expect Jesus to rise from the dead. Thus, they had not understood Jesus' prediction that he would die and rise again.

So, they did what many people might have done when Jesus was crucified: they took off.

Peter was so afraid of being found to have been with Jesus that he denied knowing him three times, twice to servant girls. These denials came less than 24 hours after Jesus had predicted Peter would deny him. Peter had responded, "Even if I have to die with you, I will never disown you." The other disciples made the same sort of promise.[6]

If you had been there after Jesus' crucifixion and had seen these men—now broken and at least some of them in hiding   you could not have imagined them one day fearlessly ignoring the threat of death in order to proclaim the Christian message. You could not have imagined it... unless something dramatically changed. And something did change, dramatically.

They all came to believe that Jesus had risen from the dead.

Whether you believe that Jesus rose from the dead or not, you can trust this: the apostles became absolutely and fully convinced, abruptly, that he did. Even non-Christian New Testament scholars generally admit this.

Think again about the disciples' fragile state immediately after Jesus had been crucified. Now consider that in the following days, this small band of brothers would gather once more. These formerly broken and fearful men would then do the astounding.

They would change the world.

Their commitment to proclaiming the news of Jesus' resurrection far and wide is what God used to transform lives, start churches, and launch a movement that continues to grow to this day. A movement that, according to a report by Pew Research a few years ago, had grown to 2.3 billion people—or more than a third of the world's population.[7]

Stop here for a moment and think about human nature. The sudden and profound change in their lives absolutely demands an explanation.

It wasn't just that these formerly frightened men had dramatically changed and were now proclaiming that Jesus had risen from the dead. That alone would be remarkable.

Rather, it was that they were doing so without concern for their own lives or personal safety. They were doing so not only despite direct resistance from the Jewish authorities but also from Rome.

In the first centuries after Christ's death, Roman persecution of Christians grew steadily. Rome may have initially thought Christianity would simply go away, but it did not. Before the Edict of Milan in 313 AD, a person in the Roman Empire who was found to be a Christian could face execution, imprisonment, or other punishments. The Roman historian Tacitus documented cruel and inhumane ways that the Roman emperor Nero had ordered Christians to be killed during his reign (54-68 AD). The persecution of Christians became even more widespread later, during the reigns of Marcus Aurelius and, later, Decius.

For his book, *The Fate of the Apostles,* Dr. Sean McDowell invested hundreds of hours over more than three years in studying the historical accounts of what happened to the apostles as a result of their proclaiming the message that Christ had risen. His conclusion? We have good historical confidence, from a range of sources (including a number of non-Christian sources), that four of Jesus' apostles were killed for proclaiming their faith. Those four were Paul, Peter, Jesus' brother James, and James, the son of Zebedee.[8]

James, the son of Zebedee, was killed by the sword. Though we do not have the same degree of confidence about how the other three were killed, many believe that Paul was beheaded, Peter was crucified (perhaps upside down), and Jesus' brother James was stoned to death.

McDowell's research led him to further conclude that it is "at least more probable than not" that Thomas and Andrew were also killed for proclaiming their faith in the resurrection.[9]

Traditions about the other apostles' deaths suggest that all but John may have also died for their faith. McDowell called accounts of these other apostles' martyrdom "as plausible as not."[10]

Because he found accounts of these other men's deaths to contain contradictions and at least some legend, he admits that we have less historical confidence than we have for the deaths of James, James, Peter, Paul, Thomas, and Andrew.

For example, he said, different ancient sources reported that Bartholomew had been: "crucified; burned to death; killed with swords; skinned alive; and put in a bag and thrown into the water." One of those accounts may be correct, but we do not have what he'd call good historical confidence in any single account.[11]

Dr. McDowell suggests that the most important thing about the persecution of the apostles is that there is no record anywhere of any of them recanting or denying their faith, despite persecution and the threat of death.[12] "The willingness of the apostles to face persecution and death," he said, "indicates their sincere belief that Jesus appeared to them after his death."[13]

Consider the example of Jesus' brother, James. During Jesus' life, James was a skeptic. Mark wrote that Jesus' siblings thought he was "out of his mind." John wrote that James had mocked Jesus and did not believe that he was God. And yet this very same man became a bold leader in the church in Jerusalem and went to his death proclaiming that the Christian message was true.

Pause for a moment here and ask yourself one really important question: What would it take to cause such a radical change in the lives of this entire group of men?

That these men would, over a short period of time, be so profoundly transformed from fearful and denying Jesus to being willing to fearlessly proclaim the resurrection despite direct opposition from the Roman

Empire is inexplicable. Inexplicable, that is, unless they had become absolutely and utterly convinced that Jesus had risen from the dead.

They had.

As I considered Christianity as a freshman in college, the facts about this radical transformation of the early followers of Christ seemed persuasive. These facts remain persuasive to me today.

There are other lines of evidence that point to the conclusion that Jesus rose from the dead, but I've only sought to focus on two so far. Whether you are convinced or not, it seems to me that a thoughtful, objective observer will at least be challenged to stop and think at this point.

There is one other line of evidence that must be considered.

At least six different historical sources reported that Jesus appeared, bodily, to a variety of people after his death. The apostle Paul, in his first letter to the church at Corinth (called First Corinthians in the Bible's New Testament), lists witnesses who had seen and interacted with the risen Christ.[14]

His list included Peter, Jesus' brother James—which would certainly explain his transformation we considered earlier—the twelve disciples together, a group of more than 500 people simultaneously, and other individuals. These people spent time with him, ate with him, and hung out with him over a period of forty days.

The skeptic may object to my citing the Bible here, but I'd ask that person to be patient; we will tackle the question of the reliability of the Bible as a historical document in Chapter 11. And this is not a "the Bible says it, so I believe it" argument. The Bible does say so, but using arguments I've already cited and will cite in the next chapter, I conclude that Jesus rose from the dead without the Bible having to be supernatural or inspired. In fact, it doesn't need to be anything other than a document of what people reported.

The different accounts of Jesus' post-crucifixion appearances should not be dismissed. John Warwick Montgomery, an attorney, professor, and theologian, addressed this in his excellent book, *History and Christianity.*

In 56 A.D., Paul wrote that over 500 people had seen the risen Jesus and that most of them were still alive (1 Corinthians 15:6 ff.). It passes the bounds of credibility that the early Christians could have manufactured such a tale and then preached it among those who might have easily refuted it simply by producing the body of Christ.[15]

The fact that we have these different eyewitness reports is at least worth pondering. I'd suggest it is compelling.

The question is, how will you process these testimonies?

As we arrive at the end of this chapter, let's remember how it started. We discussed the case of the falling warning shot and the importance of following the evidence wherever it leads, regardless of how we feel about it.

Any good investigation will not only look at the evidence for a particular theory but will also explore other possible explanations to see if they hold water. Skeptics have proposed several such explanations.

We'll explore those, and other evidence, next.

A Memorable Pregame

OF ALL THE STORIES I'LL TELL IN THIS BOOK, one of my favorites took place on December 15, 1985, in Washington, DC, at the Washington Convention Center.

It involves my favorite pro football team, someone wearing a San Diego Chicken costume while packing a loaded gun, and a pregame like no other.

✛ ✛ ✛

Seven weeks before that Sunday, a newly formed all-sports television station called Flagship International Sports TV (or FIST; remember that acronym) had invited a few thousand special guests to the Washington Convention Center for what would prove to be a memorable day.

The invitations said that the guests' names had been randomly selected from DC area residents. Recipients were informed that they would receive brunch, round-trip bus transportation from the Convention Center to RFK Stadium, and free tickets to watch Washington's NFL team take on the Cincinnati Bengals.

A *Washington Post* article on the brunch said,

> *Invitees were told to redeem their prize with fellow winners at a pregame party, where they also could enter a drawing for 1986 Redskins season tickets and a one-week, all-expenses-paid trip to Super Bowl XX in New Orleans.*[1]

Of the VIPs invited, 101 showed up. As they entered the Convention Center that morning, they noticed buses outside, warming up and running. This made sense; they had been promised a bus trip to the stadium and back. Attendees were greeted by cheerleaders, the famous San Diego Chicken mascot, an emcee in a top hat and tails, and others in typical fans' regalia. Highlights from the team's history were being shown on a giant screen.

The VIPs were then taken into a smaller room upstairs, 14-16 guests at a time. There, they were told they would be given their tickets and further details about the day. The mood was festive.

The festive mood would not last long.

As they were settling into the smaller room upstairs, the doors burst open. Heavily armed men rushed in as cheerleaders, the emcee, and even the San Diego Chicken drew weapons. Every gun was aimed at the VIPs.

There would be no football game for the special guests that day. They were taken to the buses that were warming up, but RFK Stadium was not on the itinerary. They enjoyed a one-way trip to the DC Superior Court, where they were processed as criminals.

✛ ✛ ✛

Several years prior to that Sunday, the U.S. Marshals Service had formed the Fugitive Investigative Strike Team (or FIST; see what they did there?) to address the growing number of outstanding federal fugitive warrants. Robert Leschorn, who worked for the Marshals Service, came up with a large-scale sting operation. He called it Operation Flagship.

Operation Flagship involved mailing invitations to the last known addresses of 3,000 fugitives with outstanding warrants in the Washington, DC, area.

As expected, many of those invitations were returned as undeliverable. But this took place in the era when Washington had a great football team and tickets were hard to get. Leschorn assumed, rightly, that the bait of tickets to a game would be enticing to at least some of the criminals who actually received the invitation.

On the morning of the game, law enforcement officers from a variety of agencies donned costumes and prepared for the arrival of their guests. Leschorn's assumption proved to be correct. Criminals began to show up. They had no idea that anything was wrong. Operation Flagship was a complete surprise and a fantastic success. It was one of the most successful stings of its kind in law enforcement history.[2]

A sting. Fugitives brought to justice. Subterfuge. A win for the good guys. My favorite football team. The San Diego Chicken costume as a disguise for an armed law enforcement agent. This was my kind of story. The U.S. Marshals Service had created an elaborate hoax. They created a story designed to fool people into believing that if they did X (show up at the Convention Center), the result would be that good thing Y (getting NFL tickets) would happen to them.

"It was party time, and they fell for it hook, line, and sinker," said Herbert M. Rutherford, who was the U.S. Marshal for the District of Columbia.[3]

At this point in the book, it must be asked: could the resurrection—and thus all of Christianity—be based on the same sort of hoax? Is the faith of so many around the globe a result of some giant trick or fraud? Is it a huge mistake? Simon Greenleaf pointed out that if the disciples did not tell the truth, they perpetrated one of the greatest hoaxes the world has ever seen. They started a religion that now boasts billions of followers worldwide.

"Either the men of Galilee were men of superlative wisdom and extensive knowledge and experience, and of deeper skill in the arts of deception, than any and all others, before or after them," Greenleaf wrote, "or they have truly stated the astonishing things which they saw and heard."[4]

In the previous chapter, we considered several lines of evidence for the resurrection, including arguments for the empty tomb. A skeptic, however, may say, "Even if I accept that the tomb was empty, that doesn't mean Jesus rose from the dead." This is true. An empty tomb is easier to believe than that God came to Earth as a baby, grew up, allowed himself to be killed at the hands of those he created, and then rose from the grave.

FIVE THEORIES

We will now turn our attention to five theories skeptics have proposed as alternate explanations for the facts we considered in the previous chapter.

1. The Hoax Theory: *The apostles lied.*

The hoax theory suggests that the disciples overcame their fear and sadness, most likely had to sneak past or defeat some sort of guard unit stationed at the tomb, and rolled away the massive stone. They then stole Jesus' body to help "prove" the lie they were about to foist upon the world: that Christ had risen from the dead. Finally, this theory suggests, they were willing to face persecution—and in some cases, death—to defend this lie.

This theory has always been impossible for me to believe, for several reasons. First, I have a hard time coming up with any sort of reasonable motive that might have led the disciples to want to do this.

Further, even if it had somehow seemed like a good idea to one of them, common sense screams that this sort of hoax would never have seemed like a good idea to all of them.

And even if some motive existed, I do not believe they would have had the courage or strength to pull it off. If the disciples had actually stolen the body to maintain the hoax and had been willing (for some reason) to be persecuted for it, I cannot believe that all of them would have taken this secret with them to their graves. One or more of them certainly would have admitted the hoax eventually.

And even if none of them ever admitted they had been the ones who stole the body, someone (again, knowing it to be a lie) surely would have denied believing in the resurrection, even if only to save his own skin.

I agree with an observation that has been made by many: men might die for a lie, but only if they never realize it was a lie.

In this case, do you honestly believe that *all of them* would have willingly faced persecution, torture, potential death, and, in some cases, actual death to tell the world that Jesus was alive when they knew for a fact that he was dead? I do not.

The resurrection story was not a hoax created by the apostles.

2. The Mistake Theory: *The apostles were fooled or mistaken.*
The mistake theory suggests that the apostles truly came to believe that Jesus had risen, but that all of them were wrong.

Skeptics have suggested at least three different possible ways that this could have happened:

Jesus' Body was Stolen or Moved
We have already considered the improbable idea that the disciples stole Jesus' body. But what if someone else had done it? If his body had been stolen or moved, it would be logical to ask, "Who did it?" And "Why?"

Some have suggested that his body might have been placed in Joseph of Arimathea's tomb only for a short period of time and then moved. However, Jewish laws prohibited moving a non-family member's body after it had been interred. And, again, if the body had been moved and the disciples started preaching that Jesus had risen from the dead, those who knew better would have pointed out the error.

Another possibility is that the opponents of Christianity stole or moved the body. But this seems unlikely as well. Again, the authorities were highly motivated to prove that Jesus did not rise from the dead.

If the opponents of Christianity had stolen the body, they certainly would have produced it—and possibly even paraded it around in some sort of gruesome show—to completely shut down rumors of the resurrection.

So, if neither Jesus' friends nor the authorities stole the body, could some random third party have done it?

Perhaps, but is there any possible motive for such a third party to have done this? There would have been no profit involved. Further, if there were guards at the tomb, this seems even less likely.

This possibility also fails to explain reports that many people physically encountered the risen Jesus during the 40 days that followed the discovery of the empty tomb.

Jesus' Body was Accidentally Buried in the Wrong Tomb

Although it is possible to imagine that Jesus' body could have somehow been placed in the wrong tomb, it is incredibly difficult to imagine that this mistake would not have been quickly discovered.

The disciples began preaching that Jesus had risen from the dead soon after his death. The authorities did not want to deal with this new religion, which would present a challenge to both Roman and Jewish authorities.

If Jesus' body had simply been placed in the wrong tomb, we can be sure that the authorities would have spared no expense to produce Jesus' body in order to stop the growth of this new religion.

This theory also fails to address reports of Jesus' post-death appearances.

Jesus' Post-Death Appearances were Hallucinations

Another theory about how the apostles could have been fooled has been suggested: hallucinations. This theory suggests that all of the people who reported having seen Jesus alive really only thought they had seen the risen Christ when, in fact, he was still dead. They hallucinated. But this theory, too, faces problems. I will list four.

   a. Generally, hallucinations are understood by psychologists to be unique, very personal, and subjective experiences. It would be very unusual for even two people to share the same hallucination. In the case of the reported appearances of Jesus, more than 500 people—in different places, times, and contexts—would have had to share this hallucination.

   b. Hallucinations tend to last only a short period of time that is typically measured in seconds or, rarely, minutes. After Jesus' first post-death appearance, the Bible claims that he spent time interacting with people for more than five weeks.

   c. Hallucinations, generally, tend to be related to or linked to a person's pre-existing knowledge, understanding, or dreams.

Jesus' first followers were Jewish. Their understanding of the concept of resurrection would have made it incredibly unlikely that they would have even considered the possibility that Jesus would rise from the dead.

d. Perhaps the most crushing of the problems with this theory is that if this sort of mass hallucination did happen, it would mean Jesus' body would still have been in the tomb. At that point, one of two things would have happened. Either the disciples would have gone back to somehow check the grave to see if Jesus' body was still there, or the authorities would have done it. Jesus' body would have been found, and Christianity would have been stopped before it ever had a chance to be born.

Could the disciples simply have been fooled? Again, I doubt it. What explanation best fits the facts? The disciples would have been fully confident that the Roman executioners had done their job correctly. They had been so sure that Jesus was dead that when they first heard that the tomb was empty, even they wondered if someone had taken the body. Why? The idea of a resurrection was not on their radar.

They still didn't get it.

A few days after the empty grave had been discovered—and after they had heard from Mary Magdalene that she had seen and talked to the risen Jesus—they still locked themselves into a room in fear. And even after the other disciples told Thomas that they had seen Jesus, his doubt was so great that his unfortunate nickname, "Doubting Thomas," was born. Thomas and the other disciples knew that Jesus was dead.

Until they knew that he was alive once again.

"The early Christians," Tim Keller once wrote, "did not believe because they wanted to believe. They didn't believe just because it was an inspiring story. They believed because the evidence was so overwhelming, they were forced to believe it in spite of everything they actually thought."[5]

They became so profoundly convinced that Jesus had risen that they were all willing to openly defy the Roman emperor by taking the Christian message to the world.

Consider Thomas. If he had even a hint that he might be wrong, his doubts would have paralyzed him. But he became so convinced Jesus had risen that the church in India tells us he brought the Gospel—and the reality of the resurrection—to its people.[6]

I wrote earlier that sincerity of belief does not equal validity. This is true.

But it is also possible for a truth discovery to change skepticism into sincerity. The disciples' behavior was consistent with what we might expect from people who experienced something that would change any of our lives: an encounter with a formerly dead but now-alive Savior. They knew what they had seen.

3. The Myth Theory: *The resurrection story is a myth.*
Many writers have examined the myth theory and found it to be less than compelling. Peter Kreeft and Ronald K. Tacelli, in their *Handbook of Christian Apologetics,* proposed six arguments to refute the myth theory. I will share the big idea from each of their six points, as I have no hope of making this case more clearly than they have.

  a. *The style of the Gospels is radically and clearly different from the style of all of the myths. Literary scholars can verify this.*

  b. *There was not enough time for the myth to develop... Several generations have to pass before the added mythological elements can be mistakenly believed to be facts. Eyewitnesses would be around before that to discredit the new, mythic versions.*

  c. *The myth theory has two layers. The first layer is the historical Jesus, who was not divine, did not claim divinity, performed no miracles, and did not rise from the dead. The second, [added] later, mythologized layer is the Gospels as we have them, with a Jesus who claimed to be divine, performed miracles, and rose from the dead. The problem with this theory is that there is not the slightest bit of real evidence of the existence of any such first layer...*

  d. *The first witnesses to the resurrection were women. In first-century Judaism, women had low social status and no legal right to serve as witnesses. If the empty tomb were an invented legend, its inventors would not have had it discovered by women, whose testimony was considered worthless...*

e. The New Testament could not be misinterpreted and confused with fact because it specifically distinguishes the two and [rejects] the mythic interpretation...

f. The Gospels, first, "were [actually] written by the disciples, not later myth-makers," and second, the "Gospels we have today are essentially the same as the originals." [7]

We will further explore the reliability of the Gospels (and of the Bible as a whole) in the next chapter.

4. False History Theory: *Jesus never even lived.*

Although this idea has popped up at different times, I will not spend much time on it here. Historians—including agnostics and atheists—generally agree that Jesus of Nazareth was a real, historical person. Even Bart Ehrman, an agnostic and vocal critic of Christianity, has written that Jesus "certainly existed, as virtually every competent scholar of antiquity, Christian or non-Christian, agrees." [8]

To deny that Jesus lived would demand that we reject much of what we know about ancient history and that we disagree with the weight of historical scholarship.

5. The Swoon Theory: *Jesus never truly died.*

This theory suggests that Jesus only seemed to have died—that he "swooned" or just appeared to be dead. So, after having been placed in the tomb, he got up, somehow escaped from the tomb, and was able to convince his disciples that he had risen.

But history, medicine, and logic work together to show that this hypothesis is problematic. To understand how unreasonable it is to believe that Jesus did not die on what the church now calls Good Friday, it is important to understand all that he was forced to endure that day.

I will refer to the Bible here only as a record of Jesus' sufferings. The Bible mentions the scourging (or whipping) that Jesus endured at the hands of the Romans, but without a lot of detail.

In Jesus' day, a person set to be crucified by the Romans would often have been scourged first, using a flagrum, a multi-strand whip that contained bone and/or metal balls. The flagrum was designed to literally tear into the skin and rip away chunks of flesh—a punishment intended to torture, if not kill.

The Romans believed that 40 lashes would kill a person, though they would often need to stop before 40 if they wanted to be sure that a subject did not die. We do not know exactly how many lashes Jesus received, though there is good reason to believe that his scourging was brutal. I've explained why in the Endnotes.[9]

Research by medical professionals who reviewed Jesus' physical condition throughout his ordeal suggests that his body would likely have started to fail before the cross. "Jesus' condition after scourging was serious."[10] "The torture would have left him in early traumatic or injury shock. And also, most likely, in early hypovolemic shock" (a condition that occurs as a result of blood and water loss).[11]

We tend not to think much about the crown of thorns that was pressed onto Jesus' head because it somehow seems less serious than other cruelties to which Jesus was subjected. But it likely would have "triggered a condition that causes a blinding, extraordinary amount of facial pain."[12]

In this weakened state, he was forced to carry the beam of the cross to the site outside of Jerusalem where he would be crucified. He fell several times as he struggled under its weight, until the soldiers ordered a man named Simon of Cyrene to help him.

And then came the cross. Crucifixion is one of the most horrific ways a person can die. It has been called barbaric because it is a cruel and very slow process designed to torture. The Roman troops were occupying Israel at that time, and history tells us that they crucified many in Jerusalem who dared to rise up against them. By allowing the public to witness these awful deaths, it served as a warning to anyone tempted to revolt: "You do *not* want this to be your fate."

The Roman executioners were disciplined and well-trained. They knew what they were doing and had experience understanding when a crucified person was truly dead. They were professional killers, and if they failed to execute a prisoner properly, they could potentially face execution themselves.

When they were not sure whether someone on the cross was truly dead, they broke the person's legs. This sped up the process by making it more difficult for the person on the cross to bear weight on his legs, making it harder to lift his body up into a position to breathe.

The soldiers, however, were so sure that Jesus was dead that they never broke his legs. Further, the biblical report that blood and water came from Jesus' side after they stabbed him was something that they would not have known then—but we know now—provides additional proof that Jesus had died.

Jesus' body was then taken down from the cross, wrapped in linens and spices, and taken to the tomb. A stone—which different estimates suggest may have weighed between one and two tons—was rolled into place to secure the tomb. At some point later, according to Matthew, the Jewish chief priests and Pharisees asked Pilate to have the tomb guarded to prevent the disciples from stealing Jesus' body.

Let's pause at this point and imagine that he had not really died. If, after all he had just been through, he somehow was still alive, he almost certainly would have been in what today we might call critical condition. Even escaping from the hardening linens in which his body had been wrapped would have been incredibly difficult.

At that point, while barely clinging to life and in critical condition, he would have had to: (1) remove the heavy stone, which would have been very difficult for one person to do, but especially difficult for a weakened person from the inside of the tomb; (2) find his now-scattered—and shattered—disciples; and (3) somehow convince them that he was the risen savior of the universe, who had conquered death. If guards were present outside the tomb, his escape would have been even more difficult.

The Journal of the American Medical Association chimed in on the swoon theory after reviewing the evidence. It concluded that "any swoon hypothesis is entirely irreconcilable with contemporary medical science."[13]

Though non-Christian historians tend to debate which parts of Jesus' life story they believe to be true, very few doubt that he was crucified.

Jesus died.

SO, WHERE DOES THIS LEAVE US?

If Jesus lived and died, and the disciples were not mistaken and were neither deceivers nor mythmakers, the skeptic begins to run out of good ways to explain the empty tomb. One of the strengths of the empty tomb argument is that alternate explanations are simply not compelling.

We have now considered six claims that are widely accepted to be true by a wide range of credible non-Christian and Christian historians:

1. Jesus was crucified and buried. We have first-century, non-Christian historians who affirm this, like Josephus and Tacitus. We have Christian sources from outside of the New Testament (including Ignatius, Clement of Rome, and others) who affirm this. And we have affirmations in six distinct historical books (by five authors) that were only later bound together as part of the New Testament.

2. On the third day (counting the day Jesus died), his tomb was found to be empty.

3. Neither the Roman nor the Jewish authorities ever disputed that the tomb was empty. The Jewish leaders even sought to explain the empty tomb by saying the disciples had stolen the body.

4. Jesus' formerly frightened and hiding disciples each experienced, after reporting that they had seen the risen Christ, a profoundly radical transformation. So much so that they began to courageously preach that Jesus had risen, even in the face of opposition and persecution.

5. At least four, probably more, and perhaps most of Jesus' disciples died for proclaiming the resurrection.

6. There is no record of any of them recanting their faith nor their belief that Jesus physically rose from the dead.

In addition, Jesus had predicted that he would die and rise again. And Jesus' closest followers, along with more than 500 other people in different contexts, reported that they had seen the risen Christ.

How do you process these facts?

What best explains the empty tomb, the radical change in the apostles, and the testimonies provided by Matthew, Mark, Luke, John, and Paul?

If you are not convinced but are intrigued or want to dig deeper, don't stop now. Start by reading the work of Dr. Gary Habermas. His research led him to conclude that "the most common objection to the resurrection is not that there's not enough evidence. The most common objection is, 'I don't like it.'"[14]

CHANGED LIVES... AND A CHANGED WORLD
If one concludes that Jesus rose from the dead, it is worth asking what additional evidence that person might need for the truth of Christianity. But beyond the resurrection, there is other evidence that suggests that the disciples were not guilty of creating the world's greatest hoax.

For example, Jesus fulfilled a ridiculously unlikely number of specific Old Testament prophecies that had been made about the coming Messiah— prophecies recorded long before Jesus was born. Some who have studied this deeply make a thought-provoking case that this line of evidence is a good one.[15]

There is another line of thought that is worthy of our consideration, even if a skeptic may initially want to object.

The changed lives of billions of followers of Christ through the centuries, across cultures, and around the world—and the profound changes Christianity has brought into the world—are things we should expect to see if Christianity is true. In churches in every culture where the Christian message has made inroads (and, remarkably, in many cultures where it has been banned), you will find Christians who credit Jesus for having changed their lives, often in specific and sometimes miraculous ways.

These people will tell you that they have found hope, strength, purpose, freedom, and transformation through Christ. Many will tell you that their faith has provided a peace that passes understanding and joy—even in the midst of life's various trials.

But be careful here.

I have already written that we should be wary of subjective experiences and that sincerity does not equal validity. The fact that a person believes an idea does not make that idea true. So, I am not suggesting here that stories of changed lives prove that Christianity is true.

Rather, I am arguing in the other direction. My contention is that if Christ did really rise from the dead—and Christianity *is* true—we should expect to see these kinds of changes, both in individual lives and in the world as a whole.

Everyone's story is different. But each story offers a bit of confirmation. It is, in a way, icing on the cake. If billions of lives have been changed, one would expect that the world itself would also have been changed by Christianity. And it has been, perhaps in more ways than you realize.

I don't have space here to get into this topic with the depth it deserves, but I will recommend two good books on it in the Endnotes.[16] Suffice it to say that Jesus' teachings and influence have had an extraordinary impact.

Examples are everywhere.

From human rights to the value and dignity of human life, Christ's teachings have transformed how most modern cultures view and value others. Before Christ, these ideas were simply not on anyone's radar.

Jesus' teachings made it clear that racism is a sin. Christianity's teachings on compassion and care for the less fortunate led to the founding of the first hospitals and orphanages. The Christian worldview has elevated the status of women in cultures where biblical values have been embraced. Prior to the rise of Christianity, women were viewed as second-class citizens in cultures all over the world. In some cultures, they still are.

Christianity has had an enormous impact on science and education. In America alone, our oldest and most prestigious universities—including Harvard, Yale, Princeton, and many others—were founded by Christians to glorify God and make him known in the world.

Scientific pioneers like Galileo, Boyle, Newton, Copernicus, Kepler, and many others were Christians who sought to glorify God through their discoveries and work. The famous professor emeritus of mathematics at Oxford University, John Lennox, a highly respected speaker on the interface of science, philosophy, and religion, has noted that of the Nobel Prize winners between 1901 and 2000, 65% were Christians and 20% were Jewish.[17] This suggests that the world of science has continued to be a place where theists have done truly important work.

If Christianity is true, we should expect that it would have had an impact not only in the areas listed above but also in areas including law, art, architecture, literature, music, and more. And it has. Why? Because Jesus' life and teachings were truly revolutionary.

None of this is to say that Christians (even those who have experienced genuine life change through their faith) are perfect. When Christians or a group of Christians fail to live, love, or act as they should, it damages the reputation of the church.

Let me make this more personal. If you know me, you have heard me confess openly that I fail to live out Christ's teachings perfectly. I fail at this more often than I'd care to admit. And when I fail to live, love, or act as I should, I damage the reputation of the church. Any Christian's failure to live rightly can tempt people to turn away from God. Skeptics certainly try to use this to deny the truth of the Christian message.

Further, we know that some have been deeply hurt by things that have been done by Christians—sometimes even in the name of Christianity. Even in the Bible, writers call out gross sin and sometimes sin within churches. This grieves God.

But we also know that until we die, Christians will still (sadly) battle with temptation and sin. I've never met a Christian who claims to be perfect. Therefore, it is important to recognize that the bad or even awful actions of a Christian or group of Christians do not invalidate Jesus' teachings about how we *should* live.

I once read that "an idea is not responsible for those who choose to follow it."[18] Put differently, someone once said that we don't blame Beethoven if someone plays his music poorly. Applied to Christianity, this idea suggests that if Jesus is really God, the Christian faith is still true, regardless of how wonderfully or poorly his followers obey his teachings. If anything, these failures point to our brokenness and our need for forgiveness.

If you have been wounded by the actions of a Christian or group of Christians, I am truly sorry. If you have read or heard of some wrong that was committed by a Christian or a group of Christians, I am very sorry about that as well.

But, as difficult as those things may be, I would encourage you to look beyond the failure of his imperfect followers. Look instead to the fully perfect savior, Jesus, who laid down his life for broken and sinful people like me. And you.

And regardless of how badly some of his followers may have lived or acted, Jesus' impact on the world has been unrivaled in all of history.

Consider the words of James Allan Francis' famous four paragraphs called *One Solitary Life*:

> *He was born in an obscure village, the child of a peasant. He grew up in another village, where he worked in a carpenter shop until he was thirty. Then, for three years, he was an itinerant preacher.*
>
> *He never wrote a book. He never held an office. He never had a family or owned a home. He didn't go to college. He never lived in a big city. He never traveled 200 miles from the place where he was born. He did none of the things that usually accompany greatness. He had no credentials but himself.*
>
> *He was only 33 when the tide of public opinion turned against him. His friends ran away. One of them denied him. He was turned over to his enemies and went through the mockery of a trial. He was nailed to a cross between two thieves. While he was dying, his executioners gambled for his garments, the only property he had on Earth. When he was dead, he was laid in a borrowed grave, through the pity of a friend.*
>
> *Twenty centuries have come and gone, and today he is the central figure of the human race. I am well within the mark when I say that all the armies that ever marched, all the navies that ever sailed, all the parliaments that ever sat, all the kings that ever reigned—put together—have not affected the life of man on this Earth as much as that one, solitary life.* [19]

As powerful as Francis' words are, Jesus' impact—if he truly did rise from the dead—reaches far beyond just the difference he made while on Earth. If Jesus is God, the impact of all he did and taught reaches into eternity.

The best records of his life and teachings are found in the Bible. This is one reason the Bible matters. But many people ask if the Bible can be trusted. It is an important question.

We will tackle that next.

The Collection

IMAGINE THAT MY FRIEND BECKY DECIDED to pursue a law degree. Let's say that she worked hard in law school, graduated, put in the 400+ hours of study it takes to prepare for the bar exam, passed it, and went on to land a job with a criminal defense firm. She looked forward to becoming a trial lawyer, defending the innocent, and ensuring that the guilty would receive fair trials.

Fast forward several years, and imagine that my friends Tori, Riley, Anne, and Kate were at dinner with Becky when Riley asked for Becky's help. She said that her boyfriend, Chad, had been arrested and wrongly accused of a crime. She was sure he was innocent. And she was scared.

Becky agreed to take his case.

At the heart of Chad's defense would be five eyewitnesses. Becky thought each would be credible and convincing. The witnesses did not know each other, came from different walks of life, and had no motive to help Chad. His case looked solid to Becky. As required, Becky gave the witnesses' names to the prosecutor before the trial.

Each witness had a slightly different take on some of the details, as eyewitnesses do, but their stories lined up in all the ways that mattered. They knew what they had seen; Chad had been an innocent bystander.

Just before the trial, Becky learned that the prosecutor had made a motion to suppress, or disallow, the testimony of all five of her key witnesses. She was not happy.

When she arrived for the hearing, she saw that the prosecutor had printed her witnesses' statements and that he had bundled them together into one document. His document, oddly, had a title page. He had titled it *The Collection.* When he stood to explain his motion, he made a show of waving the document in the air as he argued that:

1. Each of the five testimonies was included in *The Collection;*
2. *The Collection,* as a whole, seemed biased—the whole thing pointed toward Chad's innocence, and therefore
3. All of the testimonies in *The Collection* should be suppressed.

If you are even half awake as you read this, you will recognize how absurd such an argument would be. The prosecutor—the one who had bound *The Collection* together in the first place—was desperate. He was grasping at straws. No prosecutor would dare make such a motion; the judge would be angry that the prosecutor had wasted the court's time.

Becky shook her head in disbelief. Her *goal* was to call witnesses whose testimonies would prove Chad's innocence. The fact that the prosecutor had bundled the testimonies together did nothing to weaken any of their stories. The idea that a testimony should be thrown out simply because it has been bundled together with other testimonies is ridiculous.

However realistic or unrealistic this scenario is from a legal perspective, the prosecutor's rationale in this imagined case is not terribly different from the rationale some people use when thinking about testimonies found in the Bible. If it's in the Bible, some people assume it can't be trusted.

But this line of thinking needs to be challenged. A historical document (like any single book in the Bible) should not be rejected simply because it has been bound together with other documents. Instead, the content of an author's writing should be viewed and evaluated on its own merit.

Consider just one claim: that Jesus appeared alive to many after his death. It is not wrong to say, "The Bible makes this claim." But it is more helpful to recognize that there are six separate and stand-alone historical documents that each make this claim. These documents were written by five different authors, each writing in a different context. It was only later that these six historical documents were bound together as part of the Bible.

The fact that these six separate documents exist, historically speaking, carries more weight with historians than if just one source document existed. The fact that they were eventually pulled together into a larger collection is not a good reason to reject any of them.

I know that any mention of the Bible in a discussion with a skeptic will often raise red flags for that person. I get it: the Bible contains some wild stories and radical ideas.

But shouldn't we expect that a collection of books that claim to be the word of God would contain stories and ideas that are quite different from what we might call a more "normal" book? If God does exist and did inspire the biblical writers to write what they wrote, should we be surprised that the Bible is different from all other books? We should not.

Still, it is reasonable to ask: Are there reasons to trust that it is historically reliable? There are.

QUESTIONS TO ASK WHEN EXAMINING AN ANCIENT BOOK

To help determine whether any ancient book should be considered historically reliable, we can start by asking three questions: Does the book's own content disqualify it? Do external sources prove the content of the book to be false? And finally, do we have reason to believe that the book has been accurately passed down to us? Let's apply these three questions to the Bible.

1. Does the Bible's Content Disqualify It?

This question is one of internal consistency. It looks at whether errors or real contradictions that would disqualify the Bible are contained *within* it. Historical documents that fail in this way disqualify themselves and are deemed not to be reliable.

The Bible is both an extraordinary and an extraordinarily unique book. In fact, it is a bit misleading to think of it as one book at all. Rather, it is an anthology of sorts—a collection, you might say—of 66 different books written by more than 30 different authors.

The biblical authors included kings, scholars, shepherds, fishermen, a military general, a physician, a priest, and others. They wrote on three different continents, in three different languages, over a period of nearly 2,000 years. But despite this wide range of contexts, their writings reflect profoundly consistent themes and a consistent overarching story. This sort of consistency supports the Bible's credibility.

Skeptics, however, sometimes argue that there are places where the Bible contradicts itself. I've talked to people over the years who have said the Bible is full of contradictions. A few times, when it seemed appropriate, I've asked them if they would show me a contradiction that bothered them. They typically couldn't name one; they had simply repeated this claim that they had heard about the Bible from someone else.

That's not to say that apparent contradictions do not exist; they do. But they can be explained. Often, they are not contradictions at all. They are simply differences. This distinction is important.

The fact that a story might be told in two different ways does not mean that either version is false.

For example, some have observed that the Gospels—the four biblical accounts of Jesus' life—seem to disagree on the number of angels present at Jesus' tomb when it was found to be empty. Matthew and Mark mention one angel's presence. Luke and John mention the presence of two angels.

But neither Matthew nor Mark reported that there was *only* one angel at the tomb. Further, Matthew and Mark seemed to focus on how the stone got rolled away. Luke and John, on the other hand, seemed to focus more on the discussion with the women who had shown up and on how many angels helped Jesus get out of the tomb.[1]

Let's consider for a moment that the Gospels were written by four different men in different places. They wrote with different purposes and different audiences in mind.

The fact that these four authors recorded different perspectives on the same events should not surprise a thoughtful reader. This happens all the time.

Imagine that my sister-in-law, Kim, her friend Susan, and Kim's daughter, Sarah, stopped by our house to drop off a box for Karey. Let's further imagine that two of our friends—neighbors both named Beth—were talking in front of our house when Kim pulled up, and that Kim and Susan got out of the car to say hello. And imagine that neither of the two Beths noticed Sarah, who had stayed in the back seat of the car, texting a friend.

Now, imagine that I was leaving my house later that day to run errands as Karey pulled into our driveway. I would tell her where I was headed. I might also mention, "Kim stopped by to drop off a box for you. It's in the garage." I might not feel the need, as we crossed paths briefly, to share every detail of Kim's visit. Still, my statement would be true.

If either Beth happened to run into Karey later that day, she might mention that she enjoyed talking with Kim and Susan when they stopped by. This would provide new (and also true) information for Karey.

Karey would receive even more information if she later got this text from Kim: "Hey. I stopped by this morning with Sarah and Susan and left a box in the garage for you." Kim's text would be true.

Finally, imagine that three different reporters each wrote a story that included details about Kim's visit. If one writer quoted only what I said to Karey, a second mentioned only what Beth said to Karey, and a third cited only Kim's text to Karey, a person reading these accounts might find them to be contradictory. But would any of them be wrong?

This is obviously an imagined scenario. So, let's now turn our attention to a slightly different but real-life example.

On February 23, 2021, the famous professional golfer, Tiger Woods, was in a horrible car crash just south of Los Angeles. When I heard about it, I visited the websites of different news outlets that were providing live coverage from the scene of the accident. I was immediately struck by what seemed to be contradictory reports. First, I heard a reporter in a helicopter say that it had been a single-car accident. Then, I switched websites and heard a different newsperson claim that three cars were involved.

As it turned out, this apparent contradiction was easily explained. We see here, again, how two people might describe the same scene using language that—at first glance—can seem to be contradictory.

The first reporter was correct when he said that it had been a single-car accident. No other vehicle had struck or been struck by Woods' SUV.

The second reporter, who said that three cars were involved, was also telling the truth. When Woods' SUV veered across the median, a car in the oncoming lane stopped short to avoid it. That person's car had then been rear-ended by a third car.

Woods was technically in a single-vehicle accident. But three cars were involved. Did the reporters seem to report different things? Yes. Were their accounts truly contradictory? Here, the reporters were telling the same (true) story in different ways.

Of course, there are other types of apparent contradictions to which skeptics will point. Mark Strauss, a seminary professor, has written a great article on apparent contradictions in the Gospels and the types of situations that might cause something in the Bible to appear to be a contradiction when it is not.[2] But it should not surprise us when different people (with different perspectives, different information, and different communication goals) tell the same story in different ways. In fact, we should actually expect them to do so.

We see this in the Gospels. Interestingly, the variations between the four gospel accounts were what really got the attention of one of America's best-known cold-case detectives when he first read the Bible.

Before he retired, J. Warner Wallace invested his life in solving homicides in Southern California. His work, and commentary on other cases, have been broadcast on CourtTV and national television shows, including *NBC News*, *Dateline*, and *Fox News*.

Wallace grew up as an atheist. He shared his father's view that Christianity was a delusion. But when his wife suggested that they try going to church, he agreed. He was confident he would never embrace the Christian message but thought the church might have something helpful to offer him and his wife as parents.

During their first visit, the pastor claimed that Jesus was the smartest man who had ever lived. Wallace wasn't so sure. Then, the pastor claimed that all of western civilization had been founded upon the teachings of Jesus. Wallace thought, "That's not true."[3]

But he did want to learn more about the wisdom of Jesus, so he bought a Bible. As he began to read through the eyewitness accounts of Jesus' life, Wallace noticed that they had what he called "a compelling texture." So, he decided to apply the same template he used in his criminal cold cases to examine these documents.[4]

He recognized that the way the reports from the eyewitnesses were written in the Bible reminded him very much of the eyewitness accounts he was used to seeing in criminal cold cases.[5] Wallace said:

> I don't have access to the original eyewitnesses—sometimes it is 35 years later, and they are dead. I don't even have access to the people who wrote the reports about the original eyewitnesses, because those guys are dead. So, I'm looking at reports of eyewitness accounts where I have no access to either the eyewitnesses or the report writer. What does that sound like to you? Those are the Gospels.[6]

As he read, he was neither surprised nor bothered by the places in the Gospels where there seemed to be variations in the accounts. As we have already observed, differing reports are typical when more than one person describes the same event. In fact, police detectives say that if witnesses' stories match too perfectly at a crime scene, they get suspicious. Wallace has spoken about this often.

During his career as a detective, he said, he realized "that no two eyewitnesses ever agree."[7]

> When I get called out to a murder scene, the first thing I ask the dispatcher is, "Is there an officer on the scene? Yes? Separate the eyewitnesses." Why do I ask them to separate the eyewitnesses? Because I don't want to get there and get four exact, repeated stories because they have been sitting around talking to each other for an hour before I got there and they got their stories together. I expect them to come at it with some things that will even seem self-contradictory at first. Things that will look different from the [other] accounts. Questions

raised by one witness that will be answered by the other. That's the nature of true, reliable eyewitness accounts. And once you know that, you are able to puzzle the accounts back together.[8]

I do not share Wallace's story in an attempt to suggest the New Testament is true because he came to believe it to be true. Rather, I share his story because it affirms what common sense should tell us: that witnesses often have different perspectives on things they saw.

To Wallace, these variations made the Gospels more credible—not less. Wallace has written quite a bit about apparent contradictions in the Bible. His article, *Ten Principles When Considering Alleged Bible Contradictions,* is one helpful example.[9]

Beyond the question of contradictions, some people may be tempted to say that the Bible's content disqualifies it because it contains records of supernatural events and therefore must be false. But such an objection is simply evidence of the objector's bias against the supernatural. I'll further address this objection later in this chapter.

In Frank Turek and Norman Geisler's book, *I Don't Have Enough Faith to Be an Atheist,* they point to yet another sort of internal evidence for the Bible's credibility. They offer a list of things that would have been unlikely to have made it into the Bible if it had been an invented work of fiction.[10]

They observe that the New Testament writers:

- □ Included embarrassing details about themselves
- □ Included embarrassing details and difficult sayings of Jesus
- □ Included demanding sayings of Jesus
- □ Carefully distinguished Jesus' words from their own
- □ Included events related to the resurrection that they would not have invented
- □ Included more than 30 historically confirmed people in their writings
- □ Included divergent details
- □ Described miracles like other historical events: with simple, unembellished accounts
- □ Challenged their readers to check out verifiable facts, even facts about miracles [11]

If the New Testament writers had set out to create a false religion and had made up these stories to support their big lie, Turek and Geisler are right; they never would have included these sorts of details. They would have cleaned up each apparent contradiction.

Further, we find that stories throughout the Bible are unvarnished. The Bible never shies away from pointing out the (often serious) flaws in the lives of even some of its greatest characters. This kind of authenticity is internal evidence that—at least in my view—strengthens the Bible's credibility.

When we examine the Bible's content, we find that it does not disqualify itself. At this point, one might ask, "But is there reason to believe that the Bible's record of history is truly trustworthy?" Here, we'll apply a second question that should be asked of any ancient book to the Bible.

2. Do External Sources Prove the Content of the Bible to be False?

This question considers evidence from outside the document being examined. It compares external evidence about events, people, locations, and historical references with the content of the document in question. Archaeology, books, letters, and maps from the same era are some of the sources that can help confirm a document's historical reliability.

The study of archaeology has been a tremendous ally in confirming historical facts found in the Bible. Over the centuries, there have been many biblical stories and facts that have been called into question or called false, only to have later been proven correct—often by archaeology.

Here is one example. It is widely believed by New Testament scholars (even many non-Christian scholars) that both the Gospel of Luke and the Book of Acts were written by the same person, a physician named Luke. Some have called the book of Acts "part two" of the Gospel of Luke. Together, these books make up more than one-fourth of the entire New Testament.

Luke's influence was enormous. But in the late 1800s, some began to challenge the historical reliability of his work. Critics felt that archaeology had not provided enough support for much of what Luke wrote.

This led an archaeologist, William Ramsay, to investigate. As an atheist, he rejected Acts as an accurate record of history. He reportedly thought it to be a book of fables. So, he moved from Scotland to Asia Minor and invested years of his life trying to show that Luke had gotten it wrong.

But he couldn't do it.

The more time he invested, the more he was forced to admit that Luke's work was excellent. From the smallest details to descriptions of geography, terminology, people, titles, and events, Ramsay concluded that Luke was "a historian of the first rank,"[12] and that he "should be placed along with the greatest of historians."[13]

Ramsay's conclusions matter: he was later knighted in England as the result of his distinguished scholarship. He went on to receive three honorary fellowships from Oxford colleges and nine honorary doctorates from universities in Europe and North America. By the time he died, he had written more than 20 books and was considered to be one of the world's leading authorities on the history and geography of Asia Minor. Ramsay's first-hand research led him to become a Christian—a conversion that surprised many when they learned of it.

His conclusions, however, should not be surprising.

Colin Hemer, in an important book called *The Book of Acts in the Setting of Hellenistic History*, listed 84 facts from the latter part of the Book of Acts alone that have all been confirmed by historical and archaeological research.[14] The more we've discovered, the more confidence we have in Luke's work as a historian.

But it isn't just Luke's writings that pass what some have called this external evidence test. If Luke and Acts are found to be trustworthy historical documents, this would suggest that the other Gospels—which tell essentially the same story as Luke did—should also be carefully considered.

And archaeology confirms far more than just the historical accounts found in the four Gospels.

Nelson Glueck, an American rabbi, academic, and archaeologist, played an enormous role in the discovery of many archaeological sites of biblical importance. Glueck said, "It may be stated categorically that no archaeological discovery has ever controverted a Biblical reference. Scores of archaeological findings have been made which confirm in clear outline or exact detail historical statements in the Bible."[15]

Even today, digs in many areas of biblical significance are yielding fascinating discoveries. For example, in 2021, a group of 21 scientists reported, in a highly technical, peer-reviewed journal, astonishing findings from the Tall el-Hammam archaeological site in modern-day Jordan.

Evidence from the now-15-year-long dig north of the Dead Sea revealed a city that was incinerated by a firestorm that was, incredibly, 1,000 times more powerful than the atomic bomb dropped at Hiroshima! It generated temperatures exceeding 3,500°(F). Those working on the site believe they've found the Old Testament city of Sodom.[16]

Other archaeologists, however, who are working in an area south of the Dead Sea, believe *they* have found the city of Sodom. Who is correct? As I write, it is unclear. But, given time, it seems likely that continued archaeological work will eventually shed light on the question.

And while this specific question is unsettled at the moment, that is exactly my point: questions like this are still being actively investigated by people with very bright minds. Every year, *Christianity Today* magazine runs a tremendous article on the year's top 10 discoveries in biblical archaeology.

This sort of archaeological research and writings from ancient extra-biblical authors have provided a compelling and growing body of evidence that affirms the historical reliability of the Bible.[17]

But this leads to a third question we should ask.

3. Has the Bible Been Accurately Passed Down to Us?
This question examines whether we can have confidence that the content in today's version of the Bible is essentially the same as the content in the original versions. Here, historians consider the number of copies of a document that have been discovered and the elapsed time between the original writing of a document and the earliest copies we have found.

The more copies or fragments of an ancient document that are found, the more able we are to ensure consistency between older copies and newer ones. The smaller the time span between a copy we have and the date the original was likely to have been written, the less likely it is that an error could have crept into the document.

So, when compared to other ancient documents that are considered historically reliable, how does the Bible hold up? Incredibly well, actually.

New Testament scholars Stanley Porter and Andrew Pitts wrote, "When compared with other works of antiquity, the New Testament has far greater (numerical) and earlier documentation than any other book. Most of the available works of antiquity have only a few manuscripts that attest to their existence."[18]

I won't dig into all of the numbers, but they are eye-opening. There are far, far more full and partial manuscripts of the Bible than there are for any other famous book of antiquity. As of 2017, more than 66,000 full and partial copies of the Bible had been discovered, more than 41,000 of which are ancient. By contrast, we have only 238 ancient copies or fragments of Plato's most famous writings. We have even fewer copies of many other important works of antiquity.[19]

The Histories, by Herodotus, is one of the most significant historical works ever written. We have 106 ancient copies or fragments of it, but few would suggest that we should doubt its historical reliability. Similarly, nobody seems to doubt that the works of Homer, Tacitus, Sophocles, and others have been accurately transmitted to us, even though we have comparatively tiny numbers of copies and fragments of their works.[20]

When compared to the more than 41,000 full and partial ancient copies of the Bible that we have, the difference is astounding.[21]

Further, the gap in time between when the New Testament was likely to have been written and the date of the earliest copies and fragments of the New Testament we have found is much smaller than the time gap for other ancient books.

Together, these numbers show that the Bible has stronger bibliographical support than any other ancient book. Far stronger, in fact.

Still, some people wonder if the Bible has changed over time, whether due to copying errors, translation problems, or cultural considerations. This question is understandable. Until the 1450s, the only way to create a new Bible was to copy it by hand, a process that could take a scribe 15 months or more to complete.

Because of the manual nature of the work, errors did happen at times. Scribes were human. But some people make a bad assumption at this point, believing that these errors would multiply, like that old telephone game you may have played as a kid.

The telephone game started with a person whispering an initial message to someone else, who would whisper it to a third person, and so on. This would continue until the person at the end would repeat, out loud, a message that was usually wildly different from the original.

Applying this assumption to the way the Bible was copied would make sense if each scribe had only the previous scribe's version of the Bible and if all previous versions were destroyed every time a new copy was made. But this is not the case.

The scribes who copied the Bible cared deeply about their work. Were mistakes made? Of course. Sometimes words were duplicated or left out. Occasionally, an entire line might be left out or repeated. Some copies are better than others. But if a scribe noticed an oddity in a copy made by a previous scribe, he could review earlier versions to get it right.

If we were to correct the telephone game analogy, the actual process might look more like this: My friend Erin would write a message and give it to several friends, including Nina. Nina and Erin's other friends would copy it. If our friend Olivia received a copy from a mutual friend, she could check it against Nina's—or Erin's, or other copies—to be sure that the message was still accurate. If my friends Natalie and Danielle later received a version to pass along, they too could check the message they received against any earlier copies to ensure that the message was still accurate.

Today, biblical scholars have access to thousands of ancient manuscripts and fragments that they can compare to ensure accuracy. Computers are improving this process further.

Dr. Peter Gurry is an expert in textual criticism, the process of examining an ancient text in an attempt to discover what it originally said. In a 2021 interview, Dr. Gurry made a remarkable claim. He said that the best versions of the New Testament we have today are likely *closer* to the original than the versions people had access to 500 years ago.[22]

SO WHAT?

None of the three tests we've considered prove that the Bible is God's word. Rather, they help show that the Bible doesn't disqualify itself, that outside facts do not disqualify it, and that the Bible we have today has been reliably passed down to us.

Historically speaking, the Bible is a trustworthy collection of 66 books. If you want to claim that the Bible is historically unreliable, you certainly have that right. But to be consistent with yourself, you should probably also deem the works of Homer, Sophocles, Plato, and every other ancient writer to be unreliable as well.

WHY SOME PEOPLE DOUBT THE BIBLE'S RELIABILITY

Because the Bible makes a variety of remarkable claims, it is not surprising that some doubt its reliability. Here are three possible reasons a person might wrestle with this sort of doubt.

1. A Belief that Every Supernatural Claim Must Be False

When people say, "The Bible can't be trusted," what are they really saying? Obviously, *some* things in the Bible can be trusted. Historians and archaeologists have confirmed a tremendous number of historical facts, places, and references in the Bible.

Many who claim that the Bible can't be trusted have a pre-existing belief (or presupposition) that any record or story of a supernatural event or miracle must be wrong. These sorts of presuppositions can be problematic. When such a person confronts a supernatural claim (like the claim that God exists, that he came to Earth as a baby, or of miracles reported in the Bible), it can be difficult for that person to examine this sort of claim fairly. Such a person's rejection of the Bible's historical reliability will likely have more to do with his or her own biases than with the Bible itself.

I've met more than one person who has said: (1) he doubts that the Bible is reliable, but also admits (2) that he has not read much of it, and yet (3) he trusts that other works of antiquity (say, Aristotle's works) are reliable. Often, stories of miracles are what give these people pause.

This sort of thinking reveals an important bias. If a person rejects the Bible as historically reliable based on the assumption that it could not possibly be trustworthy if it reports miracles, this is simply flawed thinking.

With that sort of presupposition in place, why bother to examine the Bible at all? Such a person's conclusion will be decided before the examination.

For the materialist, who believes that matter is all that exists and that everything can be explained by physical processes, the bias against the supernatural is overt. It is not hidden at all.

But here is a thought that should give the materialist pause: Unless you can prove that God does *not* exist—and you cannot—you cannot prove that miracles do not exist. If God does exist, however, the possibility of miracles is unavoidable.

So, if a book—in this case, the Bible—makes a claim that some supernatural event happened, the skeptic needs more reason than just personal bias or a pre-existing belief to reject that claim. As Simon Greenleaf wrote, "In examining the evidence of the Christian religion, it is essential to the discovery of truth that we bring to the investigation a mind freed, as far as possible, from existing prejudice."[23]

2. A Belief that New Ideas are Always Better than Old Ones

Owen Barfield was a British philosopher and a member of a literary group that called themselves the Inklings in the 1930s and 1940s. J.R.R. Tolkien, who wrote *The Lord of the Rings* trilogy, and C.S. Lewis were the most famous of the Inklings. Barfield is credited with coming up with a term I mentioned earlier, "chronological snobbery." Lewis also wrote about it. Barfield defined it as a belief, "fueled by the modern [idea] of progress, that all thinking, all art, and all science of an earlier time are inherently inferior, indeed childlike or even imbecilic, compared to that of the present."[24]

Put more plainly, chronological snobbery assumes that modern ideas are better than older ideas because we've come so far. Barfield and Lewis pointed out that, rather than rejecting ideas simply because they are old, we should instead consider whether those ideas still have merit.

They recognized that even if an idea was old or became culturally unpopular, it might still be true.

The results of this logical fallacy are obvious when considering the Bible: *all* of its ideas are old. Chronological snobbery could tempt a person to assume that we've simply advanced or moved beyond the "outdated" teachings in the Bible and that we now "know better."

When confronted with controversial teachings or miraculous stories from the Bible, the modern person is tempted to believe things like: "The writers and eyewitnesses lived and wrote in more primitive times. They aren't as sophisticated as we are today. We never would have fallen for that."

Barfield and Lewis called this chronological snobbery. I call it modern arrogance. What really matters is not how old an idea is, but whether the idea is true.

3. A Dislike for Some Particular Teaching in the Bible

I mentioned earlier that some people reject the Bible not on the basis of whether it's true but because they don't like something it teaches. Some people hate some of its teachings. I get it. There are difficult passages in the Bible. A thoughtful reader will almost certainly wrestle with the sense that some ideas and stories—perhaps especially in the Old Testament— can be hard to comprehend or accept.

But if God is God, it would be surprising for him to always think, act, or lead in ways that make sense to finite humans like us.

My interest has always been in trying to figure out if there are good reasons to believe that the Bible's central claims are true. And, if there are, in then seeking to discover how to reconcile some of its difficult teachings with what it teaches about God's character.

The bottom line is that if Christianity is true, its teachings really matter, regardless of how I or anyone else may personally feel about them.

It is worth noting that even parts of the Bible we clearly understand can still be difficult. I've not been able to verify the original source, but it has been reported often that Mark Twain once said, "Some people are troubled by the things in the Bible they can't understand. The things that trouble me are the things I can understand." Regardless of who first said it, I suspect this is true for many of us. It gets to the heart of what really bothers some people about the Bible.

As my friend Sean said recently, "People want to discredit the Bible not because it contradicts itself, but because it contradicts *them*."[25]

If we were to read just the Sermon on the Mount (found in the book of Matthew in the New Testament) and note the way Jesus calls us to live, we'd see that it is radically different from how the world tells us to live. And radically different from how our own hearts often tell us to live.

We are called to deny ourselves and to put God first. To love our enemies. To pray for those who persecute us. To self-sacrificially put others' needs above our own. To forgive those who have hurt us. Anyone who has tried to live out just these few ideals knows how hard it is to do. And there are certainly ideas in the Bible that are polarizing in different ways. But again, the question that is far more important than, "Do I like these teachings?" must be, "Is there reason to believe that they are really inspired by God?"

If you have doubts about the Bible but have never explored those doubts, consider the following thought experiment:

Imagine that my friend Allan discovered a deed and ownership documents in his name for a beautiful beach house in Corolla, North Carolina.[26] But let's say he ignored them, thinking, "They are probably fake." If his doubt kept him from looking more carefully into the authenticity of the documents, we would call him foolish. But in this scenario, I believe Allan would do whatever it took to learn if the papers were genuine.

To not apply this same care to our views about the Bible would also be foolish. It is the most remarkable book ever written. It is the most widely printed, translated, and sold book in history. By far. I feel safe asserting that it is the most widely read book in history. More importantly, it claims to be "the power of God for salvation to everyone who believes."[27]

None of these things prove that the Bible is true. They prove that it is unique. But if it is even possible that the Bible really is God's word and is the power of God for salvation, its claims are worth our time and consideration.

I believe in the reliability of the Bible for reasons I've already shared. But if you are looking for 100% proof that the Bible is true, you may not find it on this side of heaven. As we'll see in Chapter 16, this may be in part because God values faith.

✝ ✝ ✝

We've now considered arguments that God exists without really needing to use the Bible. We've considered the idea that God performed the greatest miracle ever when he created our massive universe—also without our having to cite the Bible. And we've considered evidence for Jesus' resurrection without having to rely solely on the Bible's supernatural claims. When you add the testimonies in the New Testament to the evidence above, the case for Christianity grows stronger still.

From early in this book, my contention has been that Christianity is more likely to be true than not true. I began to believe that as a college freshman. Today, I am more convinced than ever. I'm convinced by the evidence I've shared. I'm convinced by logic. I'm convinced by the impact Jesus' teachings have made in the world and in people's lives. And I'm convinced by the ways I've seen God work that defy other explanations.

Does my belief require faith? Of course. But it requires what I'd call reasonable faith. You may not be so convinced. And that is fine. Each of us is on our own journey. I've never assumed that this book would fully convince every reader.

Rather, I hoped to show at least two things.

First, I hoped to show that there are rational reasons for a thinking person to believe that God exists and that Jesus is who he claimed to be.

Second, I hoped this book might spark a curiosity or desire that would motivate readers to explore these arguments in greater depth. If this is the first book you've read that presents a rational defense of the Christian faith and you have enjoyed it, please continue the journey by reading some of the books I've listed in the Appendix.

But now, we will pivot from why I believe to what I believe and explore the Bible's answer to the most important question we could possibly ask.

How can a person experience a right relationship with God?

- PART TWO -

What I Believe

Redemption

She's My Friend

"WHATEVER THEIR PLANNED TARGET, the mortar rounds landed in an orphanage run by a missionary group in the small Vietnamese village."

I had flipped open an old issue of *Reader's Digest* magazine that was sitting on a table in the barber shop's waiting area. In just 21 words, the writer grabbed my attention as I waited to get a haircut. The title of the article was "No Greater Love."

I kept reading:

> *The missionaries and one or two children were killed outright, and several more children were wounded, including one young girl, about eight years old.*

> *People from the village requested medical help from a neighboring town that had radio contact with the American forces. Finally, an American Navy doctor and nurse arrived in a jeep with only their medical kits. They established that the girl was the most critically injured.*

Without quick action, she would die of shock and loss of blood.

A transfusion was imperative, and a donor with a matching blood type was required. A quick test showed that neither American had the correct type, but several of the uninjured orphans did.

The doctor spoke some pidgin Vietnamese, and the nurse a smattering of high-school French. Using that combination, together with much impromptu sign language, they tried to explain to their young, frightened audience that unless they could replace some of the girl's lost blood, she would certainly die. They then asked if anyone would be willing to give blood to help.

Their request was met with wide-eyed silence.

After several long moments, a small hand waveringly went up, dropped back down, and then went up again.

"Oh, thank you," the nurse said in French. "What is your name?"

"Heng," came the reply.

Heng was quickly laid on a pallet, his arm swabbed with alcohol, and a needle inserted in his vein.

Through this ordeal, Heng lay stiff and silent.

After a moment, he let out a shuddering sob, quickly covering his face with his free hand.

"Is it hurting, Heng?" the doctor asked. Heng shook his head, but after a few moments another sob escaped, and once more he tried to cover up his crying. Again the doctor asked him if the needle hurt, and again Heng shook his head.

But now his occasional sobs gave way to a steady, silent crying, his eyes screwed tightly shut, his fist in his mouth to stifle his sobs.

The medical team was concerned. Something was obviously very wrong. At this point, a Vietnamese nurse arrived to help. Seeing the little boy's distress, she spoke to him rapidly in Vietnamese, listened to his reply, and answered him in a soothing voice.

After a moment, the patient stopped crying and looked questioningly at the Vietnamese nurse. When she nodded, a look of great relief spread over his face.

Glancing up, the nurse said quietly to the Americans, "He thought he was dying. He misunderstood you. He thought you had asked him to give all his blood so the little girl could live."

"Why would he be willing to do that?" asked the Navy nurse.

The Vietnamese nurse repeated the question to the little boy, who answered simply, "She's my friend."

The author, Colonel John Mansur[1], USAF, Ret., concluded the article perfectly, with Jesus' words:

Greater love has no man than this, that he lay down his life for his friends.[2]

Most of us have heard stories of people who made instinctive decisions to risk or lay down their lives to save others. Stories like this often happen in times of war. And stories of this kind of selflessness and self-sacrifice move us profoundly.

They should.

But in this story, we learn of a little boy who did not simply react instinctively. Rather, he paused and thought about it before making an intentional decision. He *decided* that he was willing to die so his friend could live. Of course, the doctor and nurse had not asked him to die, but he thought that's what they were asking of him.

A small hand waveringly went up.

Amazing. The story of Heng's courage and love for his friend is beautiful. And it is an excellent reminder that, in a similar way, God has demonstrated his love for us.

When Jesus first said, "Greater love has no man than this, that he lay down his life for his friends," he had to be looking ahead to the day that he would intentionally decide to lay down his life for us. After all, he called himself the good shepherd and said that "the good shepherd lays down his life for his sheep."[3]

Even if you've heard this many times, it is still hard to fathom. That the God of the universe, who had come to Earth as a man, would allow himself to be killed at the very hands of the people he created seems crazy. Why would Jesus have done that?

My son, Ryan, asked that exact question when he was young. He was five years old, if I remember correctly, when he asked if the two of us could have a business meeting. I said, "Absolutely, Ry. Let's have one tomorrow. We'll have a business lunch."

He agreed, and we formally shook hands to seal the deal. He smiled as I made a point of showing him that I had added our lunch meeting to my work calendar.

The next day, we headed out to Spartans, a restaurant our family enjoys in Burke, Virginia. I still remember where we sat, and I will never forget one part of our conversation.

> *Ryan: Dad, do you know about the soldiers in Star Wars?*
>
> *Me [confident that Ryan had never seen Star Wars]: Yep.*
>
> *Ryan: Could they kill God?*
>
> *Me: Interesting question. What do you think?*
>
> *Ryan: I don't think so.*
>
> *Me: Why—wait, have you even seen Star Wars?*
>
> *Ryan: No. But I know about it.*
>
> *Me [not sure how, but nodding]: I think you are right. They couldn't kill God. But you know that those soldiers aren't real, right?*

Me: You know that Star Wars is a made-up movie?

Ryan: Yeah.

Me: Even if they were real, they couldn't kill God.

Ryan: But soldiers killed Jesus, right?

Me: Yes... Yes, they did.

Ryan: And Jesus was God?

At this point, I thought, it's one thing to be engaged in a deep theological conversation with a five-year-old. It is quite another thing to realize he has you on the ropes.

Me: Yes. And that's a great point, Ryan. But Jesus allowed them to kill him.

Ryan: Why did he do that?

Me: Because of his love for people.

Now, Ryan seemed to be deep in thought, his eyes fixed on the ceiling above me. I was also deep in thought. My mind was spinning as I tried to wrestle with how to explain to a five-year-old that Christ was our substitute when he died (and what that had to do with love). But I knew I should let him speak next.

Ryan: Hey Dad, look at that awesome fan!

That was it. The ceiling fan had captured his attention, and our conversation shifted gears. That's how conversations with five-year-olds go. I knew we would have opportunities to continue this discussion later.

But his question is one many have asked: Why did he do that?

When people ask this question, there are two very closely related but slightly different questions they might be asking: one of effectiveness and one of motive.

First, a person could be asking, "What difference would Jesus' death make?" Or, put differently, "What good could possibly be accomplished by his death?" As my friend Charlotte asked me once, "If Jesus was doing this great stuff on Earth, why did he have to die? Wouldn't it have been better if he had stayed alive?"

Those are questions we'll consider in the next two chapters.

But the person could also be asking, "What would motivate him to be willing to lay down his life?" Part of his motive was certainly related to the question of what his death would accomplish. But part of his motivation was love.

Years ago, I was given a recording of a remarkable modern parable called *The Parable of the Strings*.[4] Set to music, it artistically re-told the biblical story as if God had created man to play music in tune with him. In the parable, God put Adam and Eve in the garden and gave them perfect sets of strings so that they could play music together. The music was a metaphor for the relationship that God created us to enjoy with him.

When God put them in the garden, he warned them that their strings would corrode if they ate fruit from one forbidden tree. That they'd have to leave the garden, and they wouldn't be able to play music together any longer. Here's how God reacts in the parable when they eventually do eat from the tree:

> God: Don't you see? We can't make music together anymore. We are no longer in tune.

Then, as he sent them out of the garden, God said quietly:

> I can fix this, but you have no idea how much it is going to cost.

That last line is phenomenal. A theologian somewhere might quibble with the phrase "*can* fix this," as if God would somehow have been surprised by this turn of events. But even if we have to grant a bit of creative license to the writer, I love the way it reflects God the Father's love for Jesus and for the world.

God must have known, before he even created mankind, that when he gave humans the freedom to live how they wanted, they would turn away from him. He must have known that the relationship he designed us to have with him would be broken. And therefore, he surely understood how costly the "fix" would be.

To fix it, God the Father knew he would have to watch Jesus, his only son, die a terrible death on a cross.

To fix it, Jesus knew he would have to willingly choose to go to the cross. The night before his death, he understood how agonizing the next day was going to be physically, spiritually, and emotionally.

Emotionally, he knew that he would be mocked by the very people he was choosing to die for, and that he'd be ridiculed by crowds seeking to humiliate him. He knew that his closest friends would betray him and that all who loved him would be crushed by this turn of events.

Physically, he knew that he was facing all that we discussed in Chapter 10. Luke—a doctor—records that Jesus was so deeply aware of how brutal the next day would be that, as he prayed that night, "his sweat became like drops of blood."[5]

But beyond the physical and emotional toll it would take, he knew how difficult it was going to be on a spiritual level. His dread was so real that he asked God the Father if there was another way. As we will see in the following pages, there was not.

So, Jesus, God in the form of a man, who had only come to serve, allowed the soldiers to brutally whip him. He allowed the soldiers to (mockingly and painfully) press the crown of thorns onto his head. And he allowed the soldiers to crucify him.

Like Heng, Jesus made an intentional decision to willingly lay down his life. Unlike Heng, who volunteered to die for a friend but ultimately did not have to die, Jesus did die a very real death—for a race of people who had turned their backs on God.

The Bible tells us that "God demonstrates his love for us in this: while we were still sinners, Christ died for us." That one verse, Romans 5:8, captures what we are talking about here. (I should pause and note, for readers who are new to the Bible, that when I cite a Bible verse, like Romans 5:8, it is simply an easy way to refer to the fifth chapter and eighth verse in the book of Romans.)

In Hebrews 12:2, the writer of Hebrews uses a powerful phrase to describe Jesus' decision to lay down his life, writing that, *"for the joy set before him,"* Jesus "endured the cross, despising the shame, and sat down at the right hand of the throne of God" (emphasis mine).

Scholars have suggested a couple of different possible explanations for what "the joy set before him" means. Some suggest it means the joy of accomplishing the mission God the Father had given him. Others have written that it refers to the joy of knowing his death would make forgiveness possible and that it would enable many to eventually be with him forever, in heaven. Because those two ideas are so completely linked, I believe that both are true.

John 15:13, as I mentioned earlier, says, "Greater love has no man than this, that he lay down his life for his friends."

Don't miss the profoundly amazing truth here. The idea of God's love is not some abstract, hard-to-understand theoretical or philosophical concept. He proved it.

And he proved it despite the unfathomably high cost.

The first part of the famous verse, John 3:16, reminds us that "God so loved the world that he gave his only Son."

We are talking here about the same God who spoke our incomprehensibly huge universe into existence; who knows the exact number of stars the universe contains and calls them each by name (Psalm 147:4); who wrote the DNA code—and knit you together in your mother's womb (Psalm 139:13); and who knows the number of hairs on your head (Luke 12:7).

This is the same God who created us in his image, making humankind unique among all of the creatures. And this is the same God who created us to enjoy a relationship with him, both now and for all eternity. When we read in the Bible that "God is love," don't take that thought lightly.

God so loved the world that he gave his only Son.

But none of this answers the question of what his death accomplished. Before we can answer that, we must understand that even though God is love and that he created us to enjoy a relationship with him, there's a problem. And the problem is an enormous one.

The relationship we were created to have with God has been broken... By us.

Hero or Criminal?

On May 12, 2017, a 22-year-old named Marcus Hutchins, working from his parents' home on a cattle farm near the west coast of England, saved the internet.

If this claim—made in the cover story of *Wired* magazine's June 2020 issue—sounds remarkable to you, it should.[1]

On that Friday, one of the worst ransomware cyberattacks in internet history was unleashed. The attack came in the form of a bit of computer malware called WannaCry—no relation to my friend Wanna—and it spread with ferocious speed.[2]

Within just a few hours of its release, the virus had infected more than 230,000 computers worldwide. When all was said and done, it had crippled computers in more than 150 countries.

The attack was not aimed at any one company or entity but rather spread wherever possible—to businesses, non-profits, educational institutions, the healthcare industry, governments, and personal computers around the world. From global companies including FedEx, Hitachi, Boeing, Nissan, and many others, to the UK's National Health Service, to a large Russian bank, to Germany's rail network, to Chinese universities, to law enforcement agencies in India, and far beyond, the reach of WannaCry was extraordinary.

Data security firms around the world went into full crisis mode, allocating massive resources to try to stop the spread of the virus. Hutchins, working from his bedroom, succeeded.

He was able to reverse engineer the virus and discover what is known as a "kill switch" that had been carefully hidden in the code of WannaCry. The kill switch would allow the original programmer to stop the virus, if desired.

Here's how the kill switch worked: Whenever WannaCry infected a new computer, this kill switch code caused WannaCry to try to contact a specific website with a very weird domain name that did not actually exist. If no website was found at this strange URL, the malware would continue its destructive work and render the computer unusable. Hutchins discovered this, quickly registered the odd domain name, and put up a simple website there. WannaCry was neutralized.

In its very short lifespan, the virus was estimated to have caused between $4 billion and $8 billion worth of damage globally.

In the computer hacking community, Hutchins was hailed as a hero and eventually found himself in the spotlight.

It was not a spotlight he wanted.

A few months later, while in Las Vegas, Hutchins was arrested by the FBI.

He was not arrested for anything related to his great work to end the WannaCry cyberattack. Rather, he was arrested for software he had created several years prior, while he was still in his late teens. It was called Kronos, and it was not a good thing. Hackers around the world used Kronos to help them steal money from unsuspecting internet users.

During the time between his work on Kronos and his cracking of the WannaCry malware, Hutchins had begun using his hacking skills for good, rather than destructive, purposes. But it was too late. His work on Kronos came back to haunt him.

The title of the cover story of *Wired* magazine was:

> *The ~~Hero Criminal~~ Hacker who Saved the Internet.*

Stop for a moment and consider this question: In your opinion, was Marcus Hutchins a hero or a criminal? You could argue either side. I believe that he was both. To me, this was the most interesting part of the story. Most of us understand that every human—including you and me—has the capacity to act and think in ways that are both great and terrible. I touched on this in Chapter 1. Personal self-analysis, psychology, sociology, history, the Bible, and common sense all point to this reality.

Marcus Hutchins initially used his hacking skills in ways that others exploited to hurt people financially. Then he did a 180.

In court, he was found guilty of the charges that had been brought against him. When he had to stand before Judge Joseph Stadtmueller for sentencing, the judge's ruling was fascinating.

Although Judge Stadtmueller did not downplay Hutchins' crimes, he clearly weighed the turn Hutchins had made toward using his hacking skills for good.

Here is *Wired's* recap of the final ruling:

> *Stadtmueller delivered his conclusion: "There are just too many positives on the other side of the ledger," he said. "The final call in the case of Marcus Hutchins today is a sentence of time served, with a one-year period of supervised release."*
>
> *Hutchins could hardly believe what he'd just heard: The judge had weighed his good deeds against his bad ones and decided that his moral debt was canceled. After a few more formalities, the gavel dropped.*[3]

This is exactly how many people assume that God will judge us when deciding whether to allow us into heaven. He will, people are tempted to believe, weigh our good deeds in life against our bad deeds and make a decision.

If Christianity is true, however, there are two serious problems with this idea. First, it completely misunderstands how important God's holiness—and our lack of holiness—really are. We'll come back to this.

There is a second and related problem with this idea that God will weigh the scales between our good and bad. It suggests that if we *are* somehow good enough, we can earn our way into heaven. But that raises a question. If we could earn our way into heaven by being good, how good would we have to be?

HOW GOOD DO YOU HAVE TO BE?

For nearly a decade, Karey and I were part of a Christian ministry called Cru. We served students who wanted to explore issues of faith at George Mason University.

A number of students who were involved were athletes, and I led a Bible study that included several GMU wrestlers. The wrestlers were crazy in all sorts of great ways. They were also amazing young men. I enjoyed every minute I spent with them.

Several of them were not shy about talking about their faith with other students. One year, a couple of the wrestlers and I decided to invite their teammates and other athletes who lived in their dorm to take part in what we called a focus group. It wasn't a focus group in the strictest technical sense of the word, but I promised that I would bring plenty of pizza, ask interesting questions, and listen to their opinions without ever injecting my views.

On the night of the event, we had a great turnout. We gathered in a study lounge of Dominion Hall, the dorm where many of the athletes lived. Some wrestlers showed up, as did several basketball players I knew, track athletes, and other students.

One of the guys who came was the point guard on the GMU basketball team. He was perhaps the most highly visible athlete (if not student) on the Mason campus, and he thought it sounded interesting. Either that, or he just wanted free pizza.

A couple of Christians showed up as well. I asked them not to talk but rather to simply be great listeners.

At the start of the evening, most of the students shared that they believed that some kind of god probably does exist. Here's how the next part of the conversation went:

> *Me: Do you believe there is such a thing as heaven?*

> *Virtually everyone: Yes.*

> *Me: Does everyone get into heaven?*

> *Nearly all: No.*

> *One student: Yes.*

> *Me, to that student: So, does that mean you believe Hitler is in heaven?*

> *That same student: Actually... [long pause] I doubt it. Maybe everyone doesn't get into heaven.*

> *Me, to everyone: How would someone get into heaven?*

> *Nearly everyone: By being a good person.*

> *Me: How good do you have to be?*

> *Everyone: Um... What?*

> *Me: If everyone doesn't get in, how good is good enough?*

> *Me: Let me put it differently. Where is the dividing line?*

> *Me: Can someone who has committed three murders get into heaven? Or is the limit two? Or seven? Can a serial rapist get in?*

Me: What about someone who has never murdered, raped, stolen, or been unfaithful to his spouse—but who has spent his life as a lying, nasty, unforgiving, hateful, racist?

When you ask these questions in a group, one of two things happens. Either everyone looks at you blankly or everyone talks at once. This night, it was the latter. I just sat back and listened, as promised. Everyone had ideas, but any time someone suggested a possible answer, four others immediately shot it down, sometimes in colorful language.

The conversation was fantastic. And it went absolutely nowhere. This did not surprise me.

As they began to realize that there were no answers that seemed fair, they asked me for my opinion. I refused to chime in. Eventually, the point guard got exasperated. He said to me, "Come on, Patrick. Seriously. You would not have asked us that if you didn't have an opinion. Tell us what you think."

I did have an opinion. A strong one. But I had made a promise I knew I had to keep. I shook my head and shrugged my shoulders. "I'm here to listen tonight. Not talk. Sorry."

Over time, they landed in an interesting and, I think, insightful place. They concluded that, with any sort of dividing line, the gap between the two people (on one side, the person going to heaven who is the closest to not getting in; on the other, the person not going to heaven who is the closest to getting in) would be too small to draw the line anywhere. They argued a bit longer before they eventually settled on the idea of a balance, as mentioned above. That God would weigh each person's good against the bad and make a decision.

They asked me again what I believed. I said, "I promised not to talk about what I believe and that we'd stop the focus group after 59 minutes. Once we finish, if anyone wants to hang around, I'll stay too, and we can discuss it more. I could share some of my thoughts at that point."

At the 59-minute mark, I ended the event and thanked them for coming. Only a couple of students left; everyone else stayed. I think it was about 10 p.m. at that point. From there, we had one of the best group discussions about faith and Christianity that I've ever experienced with a group of non-Christians. By the time we finally wrapped it up, it was closing in on midnight. The pizza was long gone.

Over the course of the evening, other students stopped in to see what was going on. They sat down to listen and jumped into the fray eventually. Some left to go get their roommates. We finally wrapped up the evening with just about as many students in the room as had been there in the beginning.

The things the students agreed on that night were revealing. Not all groups would agree on these five points, but this group seemed to generally agree that:

1. Some kind of god probably exists.
2. Assuming that there is a god, there is probably a heaven.
3. A person gets to heaven by being good.
4. They, their friends, and their families were all definitely good enough to get into heaven.
5. Hitler most definitely will not be there.

I share this story because I've talked to a lot of people who believe all five of these points. Perhaps you are one of them.

For these students, there was definitely a line that could be crossed beyond which someone would *not* go to heaven. They just had no idea where the line was. Yet they somehow had complete confidence that neither they nor their loved ones had crossed that line. When the meeting had officially ended, they asked me again to share my views. Here is something pretty close to what I remember saying that night:

> *First, we have to admit that what we think is fair—or good—in our limited understanding is probably not the exact same way God would define it. He has far greater wisdom, understanding, insight, and visibility into our hearts than we do. Second, when we talk about good versus bad, we are usually comparing ourselves to other people. We are not comparing ourselves to God.*
>
> *This is a huge problem. He is holy, and we are not. But bottom line, if there is no fair dividing line, it seems to me that there are really only*

two reasonable answers about how this might work. Either everyone deserves to get into heaven, or nobody deserves it.

None of you believe that everyone is getting into heaven. We've already talked about that. Neither do I. The Bible definitely does not teach that everyone will go to heaven.

That leaves the second option: that nobody is good enough to deserve to go to heaven. That's where the Bible lands.

They weren't expecting that.

Several of them started talking at once, with the objections you would expect. Or maybe, with objections similar to your own:

Wait, what?

Nobody's perfect!

That can't be right.

You don't really believe that nobody gets in... do you?

God is love. He is forgiving!

Then we got into the heart of true Christianity—a discussion of our biggest problem and the lengths to which God went to solve it. I told them that Christianity offered the best news possible, but before people can truly understand how good the good news is, they have to fully understand how bad the bad news is.

The same thing is true for anyone reading this book.

The bad news, put simply, is that none of us—not even the best people we know or have read about—deserve to go to heaven as a result of our own goodness. Not one of us.

This is problematic for many of us because, however we've lived, we want to be able to view ourselves as good people. We have helped the old lady cross the street. We have returned the wallet we found and the cash, even if we peeked to see how much money was there. We have thrown some change into the Salvation Army kettle in December and have brought food to the homeless guy on the corner.

So, like the George Mason students I mentioned earlier, even though we know we aren't perfect, we see ourselves as generally good people who are deserving of heaven.

This is not the message of the Bible.

WE WANT JUSTICE... SOMETIMES
When it comes to wrongs committed, you can be encouraged. There is a lot of talk in our culture today about injustice. And there is good news.

All who have done something that is hateful, mean, dishonest, racist, or in some other way wrong in God's eyes, or who have committed some sort of injustice against you (or others), will have to answer to God one day for their sin. This is good; we want God to punish those who have hurt us and those we judge to have done wrong.

Those people, we are quite sure, deserve it.

Unfortunately, though, this cuts both ways. If the Bible is true, our own wrongs also deserve to be punished. This is where things get difficult.

We do want wrongs to be punished. Just not our wrongs. So, we say "nobody's perfect" when pondering our own failures and how we fall short of the ways God would want us to live. But while the idea that nobody's perfect is true, it is also a cop-out. In a sense, it is us hoping that God will grade on a curve: *I'm not as bad as the next guy.*

So, if we can find some way—often by comparing ourselves to others—to view ourselves as good, we can take comfort in thinking that we deserve heaven. But, again, this is not what Christianity teaches. God does not grade on a curve.

According to the Bible, the biggest problem we'll ever face is what it calls sin, because our sin is what separates us from God.

Professor and theologian Dr. Wayne Grudem has written that a good definition of sin is "any failure to conform to the moral law of God in act, attitude, or nature."[4]

Because God is holy, he cannot merely dismiss or ignore our sin. So, to return to the "God will weigh our good against our bad" idea, here is the problem. We assume that if our good were to outweigh our bad, we'd get a green light into heaven. If our good and bad were to somehow balance out perfectly, God would have to sort it out. And if our bad were to outweigh our good, we'd get a red light.

But Christianity teaches that our sin has caused a red light. It has created a divide between us and God that no number of good works could ever overcome.

My friends Harrison, Micah, Trey, and Josh are brothers. Each is physically fit. But if they went to Virginia Beach and jumped into the Atlantic Ocean to see who could come the closest to swimming to Spain, their fitness would only take them so far. Regardless of who won, the winner would likely only make it a fraction of one percent of the way to Europe before needing to be rescued.

I do not share this illustration to claim that some people get closer to heaven than others by being better people. I share it to reflect the fact that attempting to cross the divide between us and God by being good has no hope of success, no matter how good a person may be. None of us would ever get close.

I AM SINFUL

When we think of sinful people, we have no problem calling a tyrant or murderous dictator who starves or kills his own people sinful. We have no problem calling a murderer, rapist, or child molester sinful.

But it is jarring to think of the late Mother Teresa of Calcutta as someone who was deeply troubled by the depth of her own sin. It is jarring to read that the Apostle Paul, who wrote much of the New Testament of the Bible, called himself the worst of all sinners. And it is jarring to think of the best, most moral people we've ever met as sinful. Because if those people— people who seem, at least compared to others, to be amazingly good—are sinful, we face an uncomfortable truth: we too are sinful.

I know that I am sinful. That is the one part of the biblical message that I've never struggled to believe.

My guess is that if you are willing to be honest, you will admit that this is true of you, too. Most of us understand that if there is a perfect God, we fall far short of his perfect standard. Many of us have seen ways that our own sin can be destructive.

Of course, we understand that. We're not perfect. But still, we want to think of ourselves as good.

But this doesn't square with the biblical ideas that our very nature is sinful, that our hearts are desperately sinful[5], and that we are rebels who have turned our backs on God.

This sinful nature—which drives our inclination to rebel against *any* authority—shows up early in life.

I've heard people say that children are born good. I usually wonder if those people have raised children. I don't remember ever having to teach my kids to lie. Or having to teach them to push each other down to get their way. Or having to teach them to do an end run around a rule they didn't like. No, they pretty much came out of the womb with those instincts. We all did.

One day, when my daughter Megan was about three years old, she was jumping off of her bed in a way we thought was dangerous. She was fearless, and we didn't want her to get hurt, so we made it clear that she had to stop.

When I walked into her room, she was standing on her bed and about to do it again. Karey walked in behind me. "Megan," I said as I kneeled to talk to her, "if you do that again, you are going to be in trouble, and I'm going to have to punish you. I don't want to have to do that. Do you understand?"

She looked up at me sweetly, with her angelic little face, and said, "You gotta do what you gotta do, Daddy."

Then she jumped.

It was hard to even get angry. Her response was hilarious. "You gotta do what you gotta do!?" *From a three-year-old?*

I had to turn away so Megan wouldn't see that I was about to burst into laughter. When I did turn away, I noticed that Karey was long gone. She had bailed. I was 100% sure she was in the other room, laughing. I needed to pull it together. Megan had to face the music.

But her bold, brazen rebellion is a great picture of our human nature. And that very same nature leads us to rebel against God himself.

In a book by my friend Randy Newman, he shares a great story about a young woman in Ireland who had to think outside the box to teach the rowdy boys in her religion class about our rebellion against God:

> She dressed in less than fine clothes and said they were going to have a play day with modeling clay and paper-mâché. "Today we are going to create a world," she told them. "We're going to use these things to make our own little planet, and tomorrow we'll make creatures to put on our planet." The boys responded with much joy!

> As you might guess, [the boys] chose to inhabit their newly created planet with creatures that all looked like Godzilla, fire-breathing dragons, and sharp-toothed goblins.

> For several days, they 'played' with their creatures on their planet and had a grand old time. Then one day the teacher announced: "We need some rules for your creatures. They're biting each others' heads off, falling into the water and melting (remember that they were made of clay and paper-mâché), and ruining the planet."

> So the boys put together a list of rules, one of the first being, "You must obey us, your creators!"

> After a day or two of playing by the rules (or else experiencing the dragon equivalent of a timeout), the young teacher began a class with another announcement: "The creatures have decided not to obey your rules."

> [Boys] are not known for their subtlety. "What!?" they cried.

"They are not going to obey your rules. They told me. They've got free will. They don't like your restrictive rules. Now, go play with them. But remember that they are not going to do what you say."

One by one, the boys expressed outrage. "But we made them!" they insisted.

"So what?" she replied.

Finally, one boy from the back of the room stood up, hands on hips, and yelled at the top of his lungs, "I'll break their #^$@% legs!" [6]

This story, Randy points out, helps "drive home the audacity of our sin, the sheer gall of creatures telling their creator to buzz off (or worse!)."[7]

As a race, we have gone our own way. We've told God with our lives, "Buzz off." Or, "You gotta do what you gotta do." We have brazenly rebelled. And our sin has caused the brokenness—both personal and societal—that we talked about in Chapter 1.

THE CONSEQUENCES OF MY SIN

If the Bible is true, man's sin—our sin—has broken everything.

Again, Dr. Grudem's perspective is helpful.

It is not just that some parts of us are sinful and others are pure. Rather, every part of our being is affected by sin—our intellects, our emotions and desires, our hearts (the center of our desires and decision-making processes), our goals and motives, and even our physical bodies.[8]

Our rebellion against God is why the world is so broken. God loved us enough to give us the freedom to choose whether we'd follow him or not. As a race, we turned away, and away from the life he invited us to enjoy.

Our decision had consequences.

It is important to note here that the Bible does not teach that any of us are as bad as we can possibly be. Rather, the Bible teaches that because of our sin, our *situation before God* is as bad as it can possibly be.

The Bible uses strong language to describe the spiritual condition in which our sin has left us. It describes each of us as being "dead" in our sins.[9]

In Romans 3:23, we learn that *"all* have sinned and fall short of the glory of God" (emphasis mine). Three chapters later, we learn in Romans 6:23 that "the wages of sin is death."[10] What each of us deserves is a spiritual death. A spiritual separation from God.

I haven't even used the Bible's strongest language here. The Bible calls sinful people "objects of God's wrath."[11] But how are we to make sense of this? God created us in his image. He is love. But we are objects of his wrath because of our sin?

Actually, yes. One explanation I've found to be helpful is from A.W. Tozer's classic book, *The Knowledge of the Holy* (emphasis mine in the third paragraph below):

> *Because God's first concern for his universe is its moral health, that is, its holiness, whatever is contrary to this is necessarily under his eternal displeasure. To preserve his creation God must destroy whatever would destroy it.*
>
> *When he arises to put down [sin] and save the world from irreparable moral collapse, he is said to be angry. Every wrathful judgment in the history of the world has been a holy act of preservation. The holiness of God, the wrath of God, and the health of the creation are inseparably united.*
>
> *God's wrath is his utter intolerance of whatever degrades and destroys.* **He hates [sin] as a mother hates the polio that would take the life of her child.**[12]

We understand a mother's hatred for a disease that would kill her child. If sin is killing us and is the root cause of the world's brokenness (whether we sense it or not), we can understand why God would hate it.

So, if our sin has left us in a state of spiritual death and we can't earn our way to heaven by being good, we find ourselves in a terrible place. No matter how good we think we are and no matter how well we compare to others, we find ourselves headed for an eternity apart from God.

We find ourselves headed for hell.

Even as I type the word hell, I am aware that most readers will recoil as they read it. It is no fun for me to write. It is no fun for any of us to ponder. But Jesus had a lot to say about hell.

And if hell is real, as Penn Jillette once observed, it would be unloving of me to ignore it.

One Christian writer addressed people's reactions to mentions of hell:

> What's the general response of most sensitive people to the idea of hell? Here's the primary and most popular response: "How can a loving, just God create and fill a place like hell? That's not fair. It's not right. The punishment does not fit the crime. If I tell one lie or steal a pack of gum or say a curse word when I stub my toe, I get eternal torment?"
>
> Am I close? Isn't this where most people's logic lands? "It's not fair."
>
> But to discount the enormity of God's severity, as if we aren't that bad and deserve mostly kindness, is to discount the enormity of God's holiness. It is very easy, in this trajectory of logic, to switch things up, completely disregard the Scriptures and teachings of Jesus, and move into the idea that it's we who are good and God who is fallen.[13]

That last sentence is worth reading again. When we learn something about God that we don't like or find to be unpleasant, we declare that God must be wrong. Not us.

We don't like the idea of hell, so we pass judgment on God. We define sin in our own terms and not his, so we can assure ourselves that we really aren't *that* bad.

Hell is not fair, we judge.

But if God is real, this is an arrogant assumption for us to make. We underestimate the significance of God's holiness. This makes it easier to compare ourselves to others and conclude that we are deserving of heaven.

But we are not.

This is the problem G.K. Chesterton, Bill Mallonee, A.W. Tozer, Wayne Grudem, and so many others have observed. Our sin, and not anything else we can imagine, is the biggest problem any of us will ever face because its consequences last beyond the grave.

It is a bigger problem than depression, anxiety, or an emotional breakdown. It is a bigger problem than a relational breakdown, an awful medical diagnosis, a crippling injury, the loss of a loved one, or financial ruin. It is, in fact, a bigger problem than anything we can imagine in this world.

When it comes to heaven, our sin has caused a red light.

Like the Learjet from the first chapter, we are in a desperate situation. We are cruising through life, and our outer shell might even look great while we are doing it. But spiritually speaking, we are dead on the inside. And we are facing the wrath of a holy God because of our sin.

Fortunately for us, the story does not end there.

But Still, He Wept

WHEN I STARTED THIS BOOK, I WAS A PRISONER in my own home. My family didn't want me to leave. My friends didn't want me to leave. My enemies didn't want me to leave. The United States government asked me not to leave, though they never threatened criminal prosecution if I did leave.

One visitor did stop by to see me every few days. His name was Jack. He and my daughter were dating at the time, so it is possible that he was here to see her, but I am pretty sure he was actually here to visit me during my confinement.

I began writing in 2020, and I was imprisoned, willingly, by a strange, invisible captor: the coronavirus. Known more formally as COVID-19, the virus seemed to hit the world hard and spread with remarkable speed. In some areas, the number of patients needing help initially overwhelmed some hospitals.

I am thankful for the doctors, nurses, and first responders who served others with courage and selflessness during those uncertain days.

Beyond the physical toll of the coronavirus, there has also been an economic toll that has had an enormous impact on a wide range of industries and on an enormous number of lives. It left many families reeling, both physically and financially.

Yet for all of the fear, upheaval, closures of businesses and schools, loss of financial well-being, sickness, and loss of life, it has accomplished at least one thing that might be called good.

In my lifetime, it is difficult to remember anything that has done as good a job as this pandemic of shining a spotlight on the foolishness of trusting in our own self-sufficiency.

As Americans, the fact that we are not as self-sufficient as we'd like to believe can be a bitter pill to swallow. Humans (perhaps especially Americans) do not like being faced with the reality that so much of the control we believe we have in life is an illusion. The notion that I am not the master of my own destiny feels somehow almost un-American to write.

During the pandemic, a U.S. Army colonel commented on the impact it was having on his unit: "Usually when we encounter a problem, we figure out a solution—and go solve it. But in this case, we just have to sit here."[1]

As my friend Karlie would say, the pandemic has hit different.

It has shown that the things in which people often place their trust—their money, career, relationships, and health come to mind—can disappear in the blink of an eye. This thought can be deeply troubling and may contribute to the stunning rise in reports of anxiety among Americans in the months following COVID-19's arrival.

Imagine being in the shoes, for just a moment, of someone who got COVID-19 and was hit hard by it. (I hope this is a theoretical exercise and you weren't personally hit hard by the virus.) You would have had a significant problem. You would have had a problem that you would have been incapable of fixing on your own.

You would have needed help from someone outside yourself—help from someone with the intelligence, knowledge, and resources to solve the problem.

This imagined COVID situation is not a terrible picture of our spiritual condition, apart from a right relationship with God. Our sin is a problem. An enormous problem, actually. It is a far bigger problem than COVID-19. And our sin, too, is a problem we are incapable of fixing on our own.

Though I don't think Eminem was writing about sin as the monster in his life in his song, *The Monster*, these lines are gripping:

> *I need an interventionist*
> *To intervene between me and this monster*
> *And save me from myself and all this conflict*
> *'Cause the very thing that I love's killing me*
> *And I can't conquer it.*[2]

I've always appreciated the honesty and vulnerability in some of Eminem's songs. Here, even if he did not intend to do so, he paints a great picture of our inability to conquer the sin problem that faces every one of us. We need an interventionist. Actually, we need more than an interventionist.

We need help from someone outside ourselves—help from someone with the intelligence, knowledge, and resources to solve the problem. We are guilty. We need forgiveness.

We need a savior.

This idea, however, flies in the face of all things American. Our nation has always been characterized by a 'can-do' spirit. Got a problem? Get to work. Roll up your sleeves and, as the Army colonel said, go solve it. We are a nation of people who, in our pride, hate the thought that we would ever need help from the outside.

We don't like the idea that we might need a savior because we want to earn whatever we get. We believe we can solve our own problems. But if we can't solve this one, what then?

Thankfully, God has provided a savior. His name is Jesus Christ.

On what I'll call my friend Katie's unusual "goodness scale" of one to ten, where ten is the upper limit of good, Katie would rate this news as about a 47 billion. Out of ten. I warned you that her scale was unusual.

When I told her I was going to write this, she replied, "47 billion isn't high enough."

It's not just that Jesus came to Earth; it's that he did so knowing he would one day have to die to knock down the dividing wall between us and God. And that he would thus make it possible for all who would turn to him to find forgiveness for their sin.

When we hear "God is love," it can sometimes feel like a nice greeting card sentiment—until we remember how much his love cost. Until we remember that because of his love, God the Father had to watch his only son go through a sham of a trial at the hands of his own creations, be tortured, and ultimately be killed.

When one considers what Jesus went through for a people in outright rebellion against him, it seems reasonable to say that his death was the most stunning display of love in all of history.

JESUS CHRIST
There are at least four important things about Jesus that anyone who wants to understand Christianity should know.

1. He is Fully God. And Fully Human.
When we say that God sent a savior to Earth, this was not a case of God sending a savior in the same way as he would send an angel or a messenger. In this case, it was God himself who showed up, in the person of Jesus. Theologians call this (God coming to Earth as a man) the incarnation.

The belief that Jesus is both fully God and fully man has been a central teaching in every major branch of the Christian church since the first century.

In the early church, if Christians got this wrong, they typically erred by believing that Jesus was fully God but not fully man. This fascinates me. Jesus' miracles and his resurrection were so broadly and deeply believed that early Christians found it easier to believe that he was God than that he was a man.

Today, it is just the opposite. People are happy to call Jesus a great moral teacher or a great man, but not God.

At the risk of offending someone who has said this, the idea that he was only a great man but not God makes no sense. If Jesus was not God, he was absolutely not a great man. He was either a great teacher and also God, or he was dishonest and thus an awful teacher.

A great teacher, but *not* God? No chance.

My favorite rock band—and in my mind, there is no close second—is U2. The band's lead singer, Bono, has been open about his Christian faith. He is also open about the fact that he's made some missteps along the way. (Haven't we all?)

In a biography that was the result of a series of interviews Bono did with French writer Michka Assayas, Bono challenged the idea that Jesus could have been a great teacher but not God.

> *Look, the secular response to the Christ story always goes like this: he was a great prophet, obviously a very interesting guy, had a lot to say along the lines of other great prophets, be they Elijah, Muhammad, Buddha, or Confucius. But actually, Christ doesn't allow you that. He doesn't let you off that hook.*
>
> *Christ says: "No. I'm not saying I'm a teacher, don't call me teacher. I'm not saying I'm a prophet. I'm saying: I'm the Messiah. I'm saying: I'm God incarnate."*
>
> *And people say: "No, no, please just be a prophet. A prophet we can take... But don't mention the M word! Because, you know, we are going to have to crucify you." And he goes: "No, no, I know you're expecting me to come back with an army and set you free from these creeps, but actually I am the Messiah." At this point, everyone starts looking at their shoes and says: "Oh my God, he's going to keep saying this."*
>
> *What you are left with is either Christ was who he said he was—the Messiah—or a complete nutcase. I mean we're talking a nutcase on the level of Charles Manson.*[3]

"I'm not joking here," Bono continued. "The idea that the entire course of civilization for over half of the globe could have its fate changed and turned upside down by a nutcase, for me, *that* is farfetched."[4]

C.S. Lewis shared similar thoughts 53 years earlier (thoughts that may well have influenced Bono) in *Mere Christianity*:

> *A man who said the sort of things Jesus said would not be a great moral teacher. He would either be a lunatic—on the level with a man who says he is a poached egg—or else he would be the Devil of Hell. You must make your choice. Either this man was, and is, the Son of God, or else a madman or something worse. You can shut him up for a fool, you can spit at him and kill him as a demon or you can fall at his feet and call him Lord and God, but let us not come with any patronising nonsense about him becoming a great human teacher.*[5]

To ponder the idea that Jesus is both fully God and also fully man is to wrestle with a mystery. How could this be possible? A man who is also God? God, who is also a man? The idea that Jesus has two natures is both a mystery and a miracle.

Both of Jesus' natures are important. The fact that he is fully human matters to theologians for a few reasons, but I'll focus on one reason it should matter to all of us: he can relate to everything we will ever go through.

The shortest verse in the Bible is found in John 11:35. It says, "Jesus wept." If you ever felt motivated to memorize a verse of the Bible, this would be a good place to start.

This verse is tucked into the story of the death of a man named Lazarus. Lazarus and his two sisters, Mary and Martha, were very close to Jesus.

When Lazarus got sick, Mary and Martha sent someone to deliver a message to Jesus, asking him to come quickly. Jesus did not come quickly, however. By the time he arrived, Lazarus had died. The sisters were distraught and upset with Jesus for not having returned sooner.

When he saw the two of them crying, John tells us, Jesus was "deeply moved in his spirit and troubled." (John 11:33)

Two verses later, we learn that Jesus wept. This is interesting because Jesus had already made it clear that he knew that Lazarus would die. And he knew he would raise Lazarus from the dead. Put differently, he knew exactly what was about to happen and knew that he would ultimately make it turn out well.

But still, he wept.

His heart broke when he saw his friends heartbroken. He never minimized their pain. He did not say, "Mary, Martha, chill. I got this." He did not discourage or ignore their crying. Instead, he wept with them.

This was the king of the universe, through whom everything that exists was created, weeping—despite knowing that he had the situation totally under control.

We learn a lot about Jesus here. Among other things, we learn of his compassion for our pain. Jesus is not a distant and untouchable king in a castle on some hill, removed from—and unmoved by—the problems of his people.

Have you ever been tempted to sin? Jesus has. Ever dealt with anxiety or stress? Jesus has experienced both, intensely. Have you ever been abandoned by someone you loved in a time of need? Jesus has. Have you been betrayed by a friend? Jesus has. Have you ever felt unfairly accused or attacked? Jesus has. Have you felt hungry or tired? Or angry at things you've witnessed? Jesus has felt each of those things. Like we have.

Perhaps you are going through something right now that feels brutally difficult or, in some way, wrong. If Christianity is true, this story should give you great comfort. You can know that Jesus cares.

The writer of Hebrews reminds us that we should "approach the throne of grace with boldness, so that we may receive mercy and find grace to help us in time of need." (Hebrews 4:16)

The fact that Jesus is fully human was evident in his compassionate response to Mary and Martha's grief. That he was also fully God meant he had the power to do something about that grief. The same is true today.

We are invited to boldly approach this compassionate and powerful king's throne so that we may find grace to help.

The fact that Jesus is fully God makes him different from every other religious leader in history. Other religious leaders were advisors, or spiritual guides of sorts, who pointed the way to their respective gods. Those leaders' bodies are all in their tombs.

Only Jesus actually claimed to be God. His life, miracles, and resurrection supported his claim. Jesus was fully God. And fully man. He did not come to merely advise or point the way.

He came to die.

2. He Died in Our Place

Jesus said in Luke 19:10 that he came into this world to "seek and save the lost." But for him to save the lost—to be the savior—he had to die.

But why?

That was part of the question Ryan asked during our lunch that day at Spartans. It is the question my friend Charlotte asked me: "If Jesus was doing this great stuff on Earth, why did he have to die?" Put differently, what difference could Jesus' death make? These are great questions.

Not long ago, I was on the verge of falling asleep when I got a text from a high school student who was wrestling with this exact question. I will share part of our text exchange with the student's permission. I have edited it lightly for clarity and spelled out any abbreviations.

> Student: *Why did Jesus have to die? I know it seems basic.*
>
> Me: *That is a really important question. Jesus had to die because God's justice and holiness require him to punish sin.*
>
> Student: *OK, but what does Jesus have to do with our sin?*
>
> Me: *In order for God to be a just (or right) judge, he has to punish sin. When Jesus died, the worst part was not his physical death on the cross, but rather that, while he was on the cross, God poured out his anger at our sin onto Jesus. Jesus literally took the punishment we deserved for our sin upon himself. This is amazing. Everything I've ever done wrong in life, or thought wrong—every lie I've told, every*

bad motive, every selfish, hateful, lustful, or otherwise wrong act or thought—has been an offense against God. God punished Jesus for it, instead of me. Jesus took my place, so I would not have to face that punishment.

Student: But doesn't God forgive our sins?

Me: Yes, but there was a cost involved. He doesn't forgive simply by ignoring sin or by just being a nice God. It's like this. Imagine a judge in a courtroom whose daughter came before him, and he found her guilty of breaking some law and had to sentence her to pay a big fine. [A girl wouldn't be allowed to stand trial before her dad in a courtroom, of course, but stay with me here.] Imagine that she cried out to her father, "Dad! It's me. You know I can't pay that!"

As an honest judge with integrity, he must uphold the law. The sentence must be handed down, and the fine must be paid. He cannot (because of love or kindness or fatherly concern) simply ignore his responsibility to find her guilty. Imagine the dad then pausing the trial, taking off his robe, and walking around to the front of the bench, as a dad, and paying the fine his daughter was supposed to pay.

The judge has now done the right thing. He handed down the sentence and ensured that the fine would be paid. But he literally took her punishment upon himself.

You asked if God forgives our sins. Yes, but Jesus had to choose to die and take our punishment so that we could be forgiven—even though we didn't deserve it.

The conversation went on, and the student began to understand. Jesus was our substitute. This is what the Bible is talking about in First Corinthians 15:3 when it says, "Christ died for our sins." There are a variety of passages in the Bible that talk about this idea. Let's explore a few of them.

In the Old Testament, a prophecy about the coming savior, written long before Jesus was born, predicted that he would be "pierced for our transgressions, and crushed for our iniquities." It continues: "The punishment that brought us peace was on him, and by his wounds we are healed." (Isaiah 53:5 NIV)

In the New Testament, there are several passages that remind us that Jesus died in our place. In Romans 3:25, Paul used a word that, when translated into English, is unfamiliar to many. He wrote that God sent Jesus as a "propitiation" for our sin. The book of First John uses the same word: "In this is love, not that we loved God, but that he loved us and sent his Son to be the propitiation for our sins." (1 John 4:10)

Propitiation can be loosely translated as "the sacrifice" or "the satisfaction" for our sins. Jesus' death satisfied God's anger toward our sin.

Peter wrote that Jesus "bore our sins in his body on the tree, so that, having died to sins, we might live for righteousness; by his wounds you have been healed." (1 Peter 2:24) Later, he wrote that Christ "suffered for sins once for all, the righteous for the unrighteous, that he might bring you to God." (1 Peter 3:18)

Wayne Grudem explains what it means that Jesus "bore our sins in his body on the tree":

> *God the Father, the mighty Creator, the Lord of the universe, poured out on Jesus the fury of his wrath: Jesus became the object of the intense hatred of sin and vengeance against sin which God had patiently stored up since the beginning of the world.*[6]

Grudem's observation that Jesus "became the object of [God's] intense hatred of sin" reminds us, yet again, that as much as we like thinking of God as love—which he is—we must not lose sight that the biblical God is also holy and righteous. Jesus' death means that all who trust in his sacrifice on the cross will never have to be the object of God's fury.

The last line of Grudem's quote refers in part to the end of Romans 3:25, which paints a picture of a righteous God who was patient even as his anger was building as he watched sin destroy generation after generation. But he always had a plan. God's plan was Jesus.

I can fix this, but you have no idea how much it is going to cost.

Jesus died in our place, for the joy set before him. He became our substitute when he willingly laid down his life so we could escape God's fury at our sin. *At my sin.* Amazing.

And then he didn't stay dead.

3. He Rose from the Dead.
We explored evidence for Jesus' resurrection in Chapters 9 and 10. If Jesus did rise from the dead, as he had predicted, it proves that he is who he claimed to be. God.

4. He is the Only Way to God.
I mentioned in Chapter 3 that Jesus claimed to be "the way, the truth, and the life" and that "no one comes to the Father except through me" (John 14:6). When he said that, he meant exactly what it sounds like he meant. He was claiming to be the *only way* to God.

This is a bold statement, and not one that is particularly politically correct these days. But, as we discussed earlier, Jesus' claim was either true or false.

You can disagree, but please know that this is at the very heart of Christianity. *Jesus is God's only solution for man's sin.* We, as the human race, utterly rebelled against the God of the universe. And in the most extraordinary display of love ever, he took upon himself the punishment we deserved for our rebellion.

Without Jesus' death on our behalf, we would have no hope of forgiveness. Without forgiveness, we would have no hope of spending eternity with God in heaven.

Peter said it like this when he was called before the Jewish high priests, rulers, scribes, and elders in Jerusalem (in Acts 4:12): "There is salvation in no one else, for there is no other name under heaven given to people by which we must be saved."

Thank God that he sent a savior.

But merely having a mental understanding of these four facts about Jesus Christ will not save us. That's why the following chapter is the most important chapter in this entire book.

Now Pitching for the Red Sox

FOR TEN YEARS, I OWNED A COMPANY I LAUNCHED in 1999 with a friend and business partner named Kevin. Working with Kevin was fantastic. He is one of the best (and funniest) human beings I have ever known.

I've known Kevin to get up early on snowy mornings and go out in his truck when the roads were dangerous. His goal? To drive around our area looking to see if anyone needed help or needed to have a car pulled out of a ditch. Maybe other people do that, too. I've just never met anyone else who does.

He is also the kind of person who often finds himself walking into seemingly normal situations and then walking out later, having had experiences that defy explanation. I could tell you a number of these stories, including the time Kevin and I flew to Chicago to see a Cubs game at Wrigley Field to celebrate our company's fifth anniversary.

We walked into the stadium with tickets for seats in the upper deck. We ended up being able to choose between using Dusty Baker's personal tickets, just a few rows from the field near home plate (Dusty was the Cubs' manager at the time), and sitting equally close using a Cubs player's unused personal tickets.

This story might surprise you if you don't know Kevin, but it isn't even his best story about visiting an iconic baseball stadium.

While he was still dating his now-wife, Chrissy, they went to visit her family in Massachusetts. Like everyone in New England, Chrissy's family loves the Boston Red Sox, so they decided to go to a game at Boston's historic Fenway Park.

Fairly early in the game, Kevin was surprised to hear this, from the public address announcer:

Now pitching for the Red Sox, number 41, Bill Pulsipher.

Kevin wasn't even aware, as he walked into Fenway that day, that Bill had recently signed with Boston. Bill had bounced around the majors after having dealt with some injuries, and as Kevin watched Bill warm up, he thought back to their days as teammates in high school. He wondered if he could catch up with his old friend after the game.

When Bill was taken out of the game, Kevin left his seat and wandered down into the bowels of Fenway Park.

He eventually found a security guard and explained that he was an old friend and ex-teammate of Bill's and would really like to say hello after the game. He was hoping to find out where the players would leave the stadium once the game had ended. The guard, however, directed Kevin to a hallway with an unmarked door and no external doorknob—a door that led into the Red Sox clubhouse.

The guard told Kevin to knock on the door and said another guard or a clubhouse attendant would likely answer, someone who might be able to deliver a message to Bill.

Kevin found the door, knocked, and it opened. The person inside agreed, with no promises, to try to deliver Kevin's message and asked Kevin to wait. A few minutes later, the door opened again, but this time it was not the clubhouse attendant who opened the door. It was Bill himself.

He had been icing his arm after coming out of the game and caught Kevin by surprise when he opened the door. The two got some good time together and caught up on each other's lives, with Bill still in his uniform. Eventually, Kevin returned to his seat with Chrissy and her family.

I still shake my head at the thought of Chrissy's family in the stands, watching the game, wondering why Kevin had been gone so long. They could not have guessed that he was actually hanging out with a Boston player—during the game.

Here's why I share that story: It was not Kevin's charm that allowed him to get time with Bill that day. It was not that (at least when compared to other people) he is a good man. It was not Kevin's good works on snowy days. It required a gracious act by the clubhouse attendant.

The clubhouse attendant—and Bill, of course—took every step necessary to make it possible for Kevin and Bill to reconnect.

But once the clubhouse attendant asked Kevin to wait, Kevin had to decide how he would respond. He could have refused and walked away.

In a similar way, God has taken every step necessary to make it possible for us to reconnect (or, more accurately, reconcile) with him. He has taken every step necessary to make it possible for us to find forgiveness, and for our broken relationship to be healed. He has taken every step necessary to ensure that we can be adopted as his children. He has taken every step necessary to make it possible for us to one day spend eternity with him.

But each of us has to decide how we will respond.

Several weeks into my first semester in college, my friends and I got tickets to see the 1980s band, The Go-Go's, who were coming to campus. Little did I know, as I got ready to head out for the concert, that I would come to look back on that night as the single most important night of my life.

A few weeks earlier, within the first few days of school, in a conversation in our suite late one night, my suitemates asked me what I thought it meant to be a Christian.

I think I said something about believing in God and being a good person. Whatever I said, I am sure now it was not quite right. I asked how they would explain it. One of them used the four-point outline I mentioned earlier in the book to share what they believed.

Here is my paraphrased version of the four points they shared (points I've expanded on in Chapters 12-15 of this book):

1. God's love for the world is astounding, and he created us to know him personally.

2. However, because each of us is sinful, we are separated from him, the holy and righteous God of the universe. The relationship we were created to have with God was broken by our sin, and therefore, we cannot know him personally or experience his love.

3. Jesus Christ is God's *only* provision for our sin. Only his death on the cross makes it possible for us to be forgiven and to experience a right relationship with God.

4. We must individually receive Jesus Christ as Savior and Lord, by faith, in order to receive forgiveness, enter into a right relationship with God, and receive God's gift of eternal life.

As I shared earlier, these four points resonated with something inside me when I first heard them. But my brain still needed convincing. I did believe that some kind of God must exist and did not struggle to believe in his love. Point one made sense. I also had no problem with point two.

If there was a God who is holy, I understood that I was surely not holy. Although I knew that some people might describe me as a good kid, I knew my heart. And looking around at the world, the idea that man's sin (and rebellion against God) had pretty much wrecked everything made sense to me. It still does today.

But I wasn't positive I could trust that points three and four were true. I had questions. That's when I began to read.

The week before The Go-Go's concert, Todd and Keith went away for the weekend. They let a friend, a tennis player from William & Mary who was visiting for the weekend, crash in their room while they were gone. On that Sunday, before he left, I was alone in our suite when he got back from wherever he had been. As we hung out, the subject of Christianity came up. He was a Christian. I still remember the conversation.

I told him I had been thinking a lot about becoming a Christian myself. He asked what was holding me back. This is a great question, by the way, for any person to ask themselves as they ponder the Christian faith.

At that point, I didn't really have a good answer.

He told me that Christianity wasn't only about getting to heaven but also about a relationship with God on Earth—a relationship that was life-changing. He told me that his faith had made a difference in every area of his life and that turning away from his old lifestyle by becoming a Christian and choosing to follow Jesus fully had been profoundly freeing.

He said that his faith gave him a sense of peace and helped shape who he understood himself to be. It also shaped his sense of purpose, from his studies to his future. It shaped how he approached his tennis matches, how he thought about women and dating, and how he tried to treat people.

But the bigger question, he said, is, "Is Christianity true?"

He was right. That was the question that mattered. When he asked, my mind immediately reacted: "Yes. It is." That conversation was a big step in helping solidify much of what I had been thinking and reading about over the previous couple of weeks.

I had not yet decided to follow Christ, but his insight was helpful. That conversation might have been the day everything came together for me.

After reading more and continuing to think about it, I walked into my suitemates' room sometime after 2 a.m. that next Friday night, with my ears still ringing from the concert.

I sat down in a chair by their window and said something like, "I believe. I want to become a Christian. So, now what?"

WHAT DOES IT MEAN TO RESPOND... TO GOD?

Earlier in the book, I mentioned the first part of Romans 6:23, which says, "The wages of sin is death." The second part of that same verse says, "but the free gift of God is eternal life in Christ Jesus, our Lord."

If my friend Morgan wanted to buy a Christmas gift for her sister (and my friend) Reilly, she would decide what she wanted to buy. She would order it online or go to a store to pick it up, and probably wrap it. Perhaps she would then mail it, put it under the family Christmas tree, or hand it directly to Reilly.

At that point, Morgan would have done everything possible to make that gift available to her sister. But Reilly would then have to decide whether to accept, or receive, the gift. Of course, she could also ignore or reject it.

The fourth point I shared earlier said, "We must individually receive Jesus as Savior and Lord." To receive Jesus is to respond to God's offer of this free gift.

John 1:12 says that "as many as received him, to them he gave the right to become children of God, to those who believe in his name."

We receive Jesus by faith. Paul wrote this to the church at Ephesus (in Ephesians 2:8-9): "By grace you have been saved through faith; and this is not of yourselves, it is the gift of God; not a result of works so that no one may boast."

Years ago, I ran across this simple explanation of what it means to receive Christ:

> Receiving Christ involves turning to God from self (repentance) and trusting Christ to come into our lives to forgive us of our sins and to make us [who] He wants us to be. Just to agree intellectually that Jesus Christ is the Son of God and that He died on the cross for our sins is not enough. Nor is it enough to have an emotional experience.
>
> We receive Jesus Christ by faith, as an act of our will."[1]

It is important for a person who is considering Christianity to understand what it means to repent. To repent is to turn—or change direction—away from our sin and self-sufficiency and toward Christ, the heavenly king who has called us to follow him.

When early church leaders in the book of Acts explained how to become a Christ-follower, they often included the word repent. Jesus' own words, as recorded in the book of Mark (1:15), called on people to "repent and believe in the [good news]." Jesus had not yet died for our sins, but he knew then that he had come to take away the sins of the world. Jesus also talked about there being joy in heaven when one sinner repents.[2]

Once we understand the depth of our sin—and the amazing news that Christ died the death we deserved—repentance should be our logical response. If, as I shared in Chapter 4, my friends truly believed that the gym where they were playing basketball was on fire, they'd get out. True belief leads to action. Likewise, we are saved through our faith. But true faith will cause us to act.

If I had to sum up what it means to receive Christ in two words, I'd use these two: repent and believe. But let me be very clear: we must not think that by repenting and deciding to follow Jesus, we somehow *earn* forgiveness. We cannot earn it—it is a gift.

We are saved by grace, through faith. God took every step necessary.

SO, NOW WHAT?
That Friday night in my suitemates' room after the concert, when I asked, "So, now what?" I was really asking what it meant to respond to God.

Todd and Keith reminded me of the four points we had discussed weeks before. They asked me if I truly believed that I was sinful and that I needed God's forgiveness. I had no problem believing either. I said yes.

They asked me if I believed that Jesus died on the cross for the forgiveness of my sins and rose again from the dead.

I knew this demanded faith. My reading had convinced me that such faith was both reasonable and rational. Again, I said yes.

They asked if I was ready to decide to follow Jesus—to become a Christian. For the third time, I said yes.

At that point, they suggested a prayer. They emphasized that the prayer would not save me, but rather that God would save me, by his grace, through my faith. The prayer was simply a way I could express that faith to God. The following is similar to the prayer I prayed that night:

> *Jesus, I confess that I am sinful, and I'm sorry. I believe that you died on the cross for my sins and that you rose from the dead. I place my faith and trust in you for forgiveness and receive you as my Savior and Lord. I repent of my sin and choose now to follow you. Thank you for forgiving me. Please take control of my life and make me the kind of person you want me to be. Amen.*

In that prayer, I received Jesus as both Savior and Lord. To receive Jesus as Savior was to place my trust in his work on the cross (and not in my own ability to be good) for the forgiveness he promised. To receive him as Lord was to decide to turn from sin and align myself with his kingdom by choosing to follow him, the heavenly king.

It was at that moment, I believe, that I became a Christian and that my eternity was changed. Obviously, my becoming a Christian was not about saying a few magic words. Rather, it was about my deciding, as an act of my will, to repent and place my trust in Christ for my salvation.

The next day, I didn't immediately feel much different. Some people do. But over the next few months, I began to sense that God was really changing me, from the inside out. When I learned that baptism was an essential next step—to publicly identify myself with Christ and his church and to make an outward statement about my inner faith—I got baptized.

Since receiving Christ, God has done more in my life than I have space to detail here. He has been faithful, even though I've often been less than faithful to him. He still has work to do in my life, but thankfully, he is not finished with me yet.

WE ARE ALL ON A JOURNEY

Even as I've shared my own story, it is important to point out that everybody's story is different. Some wrestle with questions about God and eventually become convinced, as I did. Then their hearts get in line.

Others, like my wife, Karey, hear the gospel and simply embrace it as true. They respond in faith when they learn that they can find forgiveness for their sin. When Karey first understood the gospel at a camp for high school students in Colorado, she believed, and then later began to learn some of the types of things I've written about in this book. Her transformation was (and continues to be) beautiful.

My friend Brooke became a Christian when she trusted Christ during a humanitarian/construction trip to Kentucky. She pulled me aside as our large group returned from a great evening at a lake where I had just baptized our friends Claire and Emma. She said she had been thinking about becoming a Christian for a while and was ready.

This was her "Now what?" moment.

So, later, at a beaten-up picnic table beside an unremarkable pool in the courtyard of a not-quite-super motel, she responded to God by trusting Christ. And heaven rejoiced. Her eternity was changed forever as she decided to follow Jesus, the one who had formed her in her mother's womb and who loved her so much that he died for her.

I will never forget watching her roommate Kayla's joyful reaction when Brooke told Kayla about her decision. And I will never forget, a short time later, a weekend at our family's river house with my wife, our son Ethan, and about 20 students from Group. That Saturday evening, I had the privilege of baptizing Brooke as the other students hung out in the river and celebrated with her.

It may be my single favorite memory of the many great memories I have of our family and friends at the river house.

My friends Nick and Tyler would describe coming to faith in different ways. Nick would tell you that he simply realized that he believed and decided to follow Christ with his life. He doesn't really remember a specific day that he made that decision—he just did.

Tyler, on the other hand, remembers becoming a Christian on a specific night at my house, but really didn't tell anyone for a while, even as he started to grow in his faith. But I had the honor of baptizing both Tyler and Nick on the same day in a river near Front Royal, Virginia.

It was another day I will never forget.

My friend Amanda became a Christian in our kitchen one night after telling Karey she wanted to know more about what it meant to accept the gift of salvation that Christ offered.

My friend Mike's family was transformed after his mom saw questions about the Bible on the game show *Jeopardy!* She realized she didn't know much about the Bible, so she went out and bought one the next day. The Bible she bought had a page inside the front cover that contained the four points I shared earlier.

She received Christ, trusting him for her salvation. She explained all of this to her husband, and he too came to faith in Christ. Over time, the changes God made in their lives were so dramatic and obvious to their kids that they also became Christians.

My friend Dave was at the top of a ridiculously tall tower, ready to make a base jump (a parachute jump from the top of a tall object or structure rather than from an airplane) when he asked his friend why he had so much peace in his life. Standing atop that tower, his friend said, "Because I know where I'm going when I die." He smiled and jumped. That led to further discussions and, eventually, to Dave becoming a follower of Christ.

My friend Harold was known as Big Hal while he did time in the United States Federal Penitentiary in Atlanta. He intimidated everybody. Everybody, that is, except for a woman named Mary. Mary, whom Harold would later call his "90-pound angel," would visit him and other prisoners and tell them that they needed to turn to Jesus and away from their sin.

Mary wasn't afraid to tell Harold the truth. Eventually, he began to listen. After receiving Christ, his life was so powerfully changed that he decided to personally tell every prisoner about Jesus three times. He thought if he only told them once, they might not get it. The impact God made through Harold—in other prisoners' lives and in the prison as a whole—was so dramatic that on December 21, 1973, U.S. President Richard Nixon commuted Harold's sentence.

Harold was free—physically and spiritually—many years before he was supposed to have been released.

When Harold got out of prison, he married Mary, and they launched the prison ministry of Campus Crusade for Christ (now known as Cru).

I quoted Joe Gibbs earlier about the emptiness he felt even in the midst of a Hall of Fame career as a football coach. He found a solution to that emptiness, and it was a solution that did not come through wins, money, fame, football, or NASCAR. It came through his relationship with God.

Gibbs said this about his journey to faith:

> *You know why I had that emptiness? I started discovering in 1982 that God had made me and he had put that void there, and it didn't matter how much money I tried to put in there or how many football games I tried to win, I still had that empty feeling inside of me... God made us with that empty feeling because he made us for a personal relationship with him.*[3]

I could share even more dramatic stories, of missionaries arriving in some remote village only to have the people who live there ask, "Have you come to tell us about the God we've always longed to know?"

Or of God drawing Muslims around the world to become Christians by speaking to them through dreams.

Or I could share one other story: that my freshman roommate, Mike, came to faith in Christ the same week that I did.

Why do I share these stories? Because they remind us of God's power, providence, and grace. And of his love for people. They remind us that Jesus is the good shepherd who would leave his 99 sheep to find the one who was lost. They remind us that he draws people into a relationship with him in a wide (and sometimes wild) variety of ways.

WHAT REALLY MATTERS

As interesting and encouraging as these stories may be, however, they are not what should matter most to a reader. For every reader, there are two questions that matter far more than any other person's story.

First is the question we've been wrestling with since page one of this book: *Are the central claims of Christianity true?*

This question matters more than how you may emotionally feel about Christianity, how highly (or not highly) you think of Christians you've met, and how highly (or not highly) you think of some of Christianity's more difficult teachings.

The second question is related: *If the central claims of Christianity are true, how will you respond?*

As I begin to wind down this book, I want to consider this question from two different perspectives.

In Chapter 17, we will look at this "how will you respond" question for readers who are Christians. In the remainder of this chapter, however, I'd like to share a story and a thought about this question for my non-Christian readers.

On May 27, 1830, the Circuit Court for the Eastern District of Pennsylvania sentenced a man named George Wilson to die for robbing a mail carrier and endangering the carrier's life. Less than three weeks later, the president of the United States, Andrew Jackson, granted Wilson a pardon for the crime for which he had been sentenced to die. Wilson faced other charges, but none would cost him his life.

Stunningly, Wilson refused the pardon.

At this point, the same government that had just finished trying to prove Wilson's guilt now faced a strange dilemma. Can a man on death row who has been granted a pardon—by the president of the United States—reject that pardon? The question went all the way to the U.S. Supreme Court.

Chief Justice John Marshall, writing for the majority, wrote, "A pardon is an act of grace... which exempts the individual, on whom it is bestowed, from the punishment the law inflicts for a crime he has committed."

But, Marshall then wrote, a pardon must be delivered, and "delivery is not complete without acceptance. It may then be rejected by the person to whom it is tendered; and if it [is] rejected, we have discovered no power in a court to force it on him."[4]

The Supreme Court's conclusion was that if the president's offer of a pardon is rejected, there is no pardon.

When Romans 6:23 tells us that "the free gift of God is eternal life in Christ Jesus," we learn that God has offered us a gift. It is a gift motivated by his love and graciously made possible by Christ's sacrificial death on the cross.

The gift that God offers to all who would turn to him is far better—and was far more costly—than a mere presidential pardon. God has taken every step necessary to make it possible for you to be forgiven for your sin. He has offered you not only forgiveness but also peace, freedom from shame and guilt, freedom from bondage, a restored relationship with him, and eternal life.

But much like the offer of a pardon, God's offer of eternal life is only an offer. It is an offer that must be accepted by the guilty.

When I have had the opportunity to talk to non-Christians who were ready to believe and at a "Now what?" moment, I've asked them if they were ready to accept God's offer of eternal life and to follow Jesus Christ with their lives.

If they've said yes, I've shared the same sort of four-point outline with them that Todd and Keith had first shared with me. This leads me to one final thought in this chapter.

It is possible that at least one person who is reading this book may be at his or her own "Now what?" moment. If that is true of you, perhaps you attended church growing up but walked away. Perhaps you've been attending church but have never taken that decisive step of repenting and placing your trust in Jesus by faith. Or perhaps you have never gone to church or have never seriously considered the claims of Christianity. Perhaps you've been considering them for years.

Whatever the case, if you find yourself at your own "Now what?" moment, I would say to you that your next steps are not difficult to understand. Accept the gift of salvation that God has offered. Confess your sin to God. Trust in Jesus' death on the cross for your forgiveness. Decide to turn away from your sin and to follow Christ. Repent. Believe.

You can use your own words to express this decision to God. Or you can pray a prayer like the one I prayed. But remember, the prayer is not what will save you. A person is saved by grace, through faith in the forgiveness only available as the result of Christ's sacrificial death on our behalf.

If you do receive Christ and become a Christian, your next steps are very important. First, tell another Christian that you have received Christ. Don't be shy; Christians will rejoice with you. I'd love it if you'd let me know—it would be super encouraging to me, and I'd love to pray for you.

Second, find a good, Bible-believing local church and get baptized. You were made by God to flourish as part of a faith community. You were not made to live out your faith on your own. The church is called the "body of Christ," and every believer needs the support that comes from that body. I'll talk more about this in Chapter 17.

Getting baptized should be your very first step of obedience as a Christian. Baptism is a physical act that reflects the spiritual reality that has happened in your life. When we are immersed in the water, it's like a kind of death, spiritually speaking. We die to ourselves and to our reliance on our own goodness or efforts to get us to heaven. When we rise up again, out of the water, we rise to new life.

If you are a college student, it would also be helpful for you to find a faith community on your campus. Good campus ministries that exist at colleges in the United States include Chi Alpha, Christian Union, Cru, Fellowship of Christian Athletes (FCA), InterVarsity, the Navigators, Reformed University Fellowship (RUF), and others. If several of these ministries are active on your campus, one of them will likely be a better fit for you than the others. Try several, but get involved.

To those readers not ready to receive Christ, I'd say that life is short. Eternity is long. If your curiosity is engaged, do not stop here. Read some of the books I've listed in the Appendix. Go back to the Introduction of this book and re-read Pascal's wager. Keep seeking spiritual answers.

In the conclusion, I'll share a few additional thoughts for you to consider.

Faith

He Sought an Answer

In chapter 12, I told the story of a meal I ate with my son Ryan when he was five years old. He had a question about whether the Stormtroopers in the movie *Star Wars* could kill God. His conclusion troubled him.

Here's what I loved about that conversation: He had a doubt (or at least a serious question), so he asked me about it. He didn't let it sit in his brain, unexplored.

He sought an answer.

During his freshman year of college, he and I had one of our many conversations about God, this time at an IHOP over breakfast. This was a very different sort of conversation. He was home for Christmas break, and he shared that he had been dealing with a lot of doubt. In fact, he said, he wasn't even sure he still believed in God.

The conversation concerned me, but not because I was fearful that he would find the best Christian thinkers' arguments to be poor. Rather, I was concerned that, in the busyness of college life, he might not take the time to thoughtfully explore those arguments. I was concerned that he might uncritically accept the skeptics' arguments against the Christian faith and walk away from God without serious and careful thought.

Thankfully, I also managed to recognize that he would have to figure this one out on his own. He was going through the process of deciding whether to continue in the faith he had grown up believing. So even as I sat there during the conversation, I bit my tongue and avoided launching into arguments for God. For all the times in my life that I've put my foot in my mouth and said too much or said the wrong thing (and sadly, there have been a few), in this case I had the wisdom to be patient.

Still, I did ask Ryan to promise me that during this wrestling period, however long it lasted, he would not simply accept his doubts as facts. I wanted him to see that it was possible that his reason for doubt might actually be wrong.

Doubt is not the opposite of faith. Unbelief is the opposite of faith. I mentioned earlier in the book that doubt is not nearly as significant a problem as unexamined doubt.

Over time, many have made the helpful observation that doubts are really just alternate beliefs, and thus we should not accept our doubts (or these new, alternate beliefs) without careful thought.

If I begin to doubt that Earth is round, for example, it is because I am tempted to put my faith in a different idea. That Earth might be flat. Or tubular. Or some other shape.

If we do not examine our doubts, we risk becoming comfortable with them and allowing them to become somewhat set in place. When that happens, they can be hard to shake. It fascinates me that when people explore issues of faith, they tend to ask good questions, like, "Should I believe this?" Or, "Are there good reasons to believe?" But they tend to just blindly accept their doubts—or alternate beliefs—without exploring them with the same degree of care.

One of the things I tried to do in the chapters in this book on evidence for God's existence was to show that people who believe that there is no God also have to believe at least some of what they believe by faith.

To believe that there is no God requires a person to believe: that something (the universe, in this case) could begin to exist without a cause—or that it is eternally old, despite scientific evidence to the contrary; that the fine-tuning we see in the universe happened by chance (despite insanely unlikely odds that it could have); that our sophisticated and highly-ordered world and everything in it (including DNA) came to exist without an intelligent mind behind it; that the objective moral values that many people believe exist do not actually exist; that Jesus Christ was either a liar or a lunatic; and that his apostles pulled off what was certainly the greatest hoax in the history of mankind.

Whatever you believe, faith is important in this discussion because we cannot prove that God exists with 100% certainty. And, of course, we also cannot prove that he does not exist.

In Ryan's case, his doubts were a movement toward the belief that if God exists at all, he is something other than what Ryan had grown up believing. With so much on his plate during college, I was nervous that he would not be intentional about examining these different ideas (or reasons for doubt) that he was tempted to embrace. During this time, though, it seems clear that God's grace was at work in his life.

So was God's Grace.

Grace was Ryan's girlfriend at the time, and she patiently encouraged Ryan during this season of doubt. She sent him articles to read and podcasts to listen to—J. Warner Wallace's podcast was one that was helpful to him—and continued to challenge his thinking in a variety of ways. He was able to hear her in ways he might not have been able to hear me or Karey.

As she encouraged him, he eventually began to examine his doubts with care. He didn't simply accept them. Over time, Ryan concluded that his reasons for doubt were not as strong as his reasons for faith in Christ. He decided that he did believe that Jesus must have been who he had claimed to be, and Ryan has sought to follow God ever since.

Grace (now Ryan's wife and our newest daughter) is now encouraging others to consider and pursue Christ in her role in ministry at George Mason University. To Karey and me, her work with Mason students feels like a very cool, full-circle sort of thing.

And we are thankful for Grace for far more reasons than just the impact she had on Ryan's life in college. But we will never forget her role (and patience) during that time. She never gave up on him.

Neither did God.

DOUBT IS NEITHER FINAL NOR FATAL

In Ryan's case, his season of doubt (because he investigated his doubts well) ended up strengthening his faith. This is a great example of how doubt doesn't have to be fatal to faith.

Doubt is not even necessarily unhealthy, as long as the believer works through it well. In his book, *Reason for God,* Tim Keller wrote this about doubt:

> *A faith without some doubts is like a human body without any antibodies in it. People who blithely go through life too busy or indifferent to ask hard questions about why they believe as they do will find themselves defenseless against either the experience of tragedy or the probing questions of a smart skeptic. A person's faith can collapse almost overnight if she has failed over the years to listen patiently to her own doubts, which should only be discarded after long reflection.*[1]

We should not be surprised when we run into doubt, and we should never fall into the trap of thinking that it reveals some sort of character flaw. We know that even people who take their faith seriously will experience doubt at times. I have.

It encourages me, strangely, that Jesus' own disciples sometimes dealt with doubt. We remember one of them as "Doubting" Thomas. If these men could occasionally doubt despite all they had seen while in Jesus' presence, why should we think we are any less susceptible to it?

It encourages me to read about Jesus' interaction with a man in Mark 9. The man approaches Jesus with a request and, at one point, says to Jesus, "I believe. Help me in my unbelief." What a great prayer. One pastor described this as "a confession of faith and a cry for help."[2] He calls this "a good and appropriate prayer," noting that "even on our best days, we are people of imperfect faith."[3]

Jesus' response is interesting. He challenges the onlookers to believe and then grants the man's request. The man's faith was not perfect, but he did exhibit faith.

We learn an important lesson here: faith matters to God.

FAITH MATTERS

I wrote earlier that Ryan's season of doubt ended up strengthening his faith. I did not write that coming through his season of doubt led him to a place where he could prove, with absolute and unwavering certainty, that Christianity is true.

Now that I've spent most of this book arguing that Christianity is rational and more likely to be true than not to be true, I have to say once more that its objective truth claims cannot be proven with 100% certainty.

Faith matters.

This does not mean, however, that a believer can't have a very high level of confidence that Christianity is true.

Hebrews 11:1 defines faith as "the assurance of things hoped for, the conviction of things not seen." Here we learn that the Christian can have not only assurance but conviction about the truth of those things he or she believes.

When believers see God answer very specific prayers in ways that seem wildly improbable or even impossible to accept as coincidences, their faith grows. I could tell you numerous stories of ways Karey and I have seen God work, often in ways that defy explanation. When we've seen those things happen, our assurance and conviction that God is real (and that he is at work) have grown.

Believers around the world have seen God perform miracles, either on their behalf or in the lives of others.[4] These things have certainly strengthened their faith. As my friend David once said about a medically confirmed miracle that took place in someone's life, "It is amazing when God shows you that he knows your address."

But these lines of evidence may not be convincing for the skeptic.

I understand that. The skeptic might be tempted to call this confirmation bias. I call it confirmation.

Another piece of what I might call a believer's internal evidence is found in Romans 8:16. There, we learn that "the Holy Spirit testifies to our spirit that we are God's children."

This, of course, cannot be proven to anyone else. But for these reasons and others, many believers are fully persuaded that Christianity is true. Many would use the word "convinced" or even stronger language.

But the fact that Christianity can't be proven with 100% certainty seems to be by design. God obviously could have made it clear to each of us that he exists. And he will one day, when Jesus returns to Earth, as he has promised he will do. But he has not yet chosen to do so. Why? We don't know. The Bible doesn't always reveal God's motives or timing, but it does give us insight into the sorts of things that he values. And we know that God values faith. In fact, Hebrews 11:6 tells us that "without faith, it is impossible to please God, since the one who draws near to him must believe that he exists and that he rewards those who seek him."

It is easy to see how much Jesus valued faith. One of the few things he ever rebuked his disciples for was when they displayed a lack of faith. He once criticized Nazareth—his hometown—for the lack of faith he found in the people there.

On the other hand, there is a great story, found in Luke 7 and Matthew 8, of a Roman centurion who comes to Jesus with a request. His faith in Jesus was so strong that both Luke and Matthew record that Jesus was "amazed by" (some translations actually say Jesus "marveled at") his faith.

FAITH, DOUBT, AND COMMUNITY
This chapter is about the importance of faith. But, as I mentioned earlier, we can't ignore the reality of doubt.

If you are in the midst of your own season of doubt, it is important to respond well to that doubt. I've seen too many people experience doubt, not deal with it well, and then really struggle spiritually.

This sometimes happens in the lives of students in their first year of college.

The process often follows a similar pattern, a pattern we've seen happen numerous times in students' lives over the last thirty years.

A student who seems committed to wanting to grow in his faith will sit down with me before leaving for college. He will talk about his plan to get involved with a Christian community at the school he is about to attend. But upon his arrival on campus, everything changes. He either decides against, or simply never gets around to, following his plan.

Sometimes, this happens because he decides that partying or sleeping with his girlfriend is more important than seeking to follow God. Sometimes, such a student is drawn in by the sheer number (and volume) of voices on campus that reject Christianity and embrace a worldview that celebrates the lifestyles of those who live without restraint.

But often, such a student will arrive on campus and simply want to fit in with the people he meets—as all of us do when walking into some new environment. So, the student connects with people in his dorm, a club, a fraternity, or whatever group he happens to feel comfortable with, and jumps in. These things are not necessarily bad in and of themselves, but they can demand the student's time.

And even though he has more available time than he has ever had in his life, he suddenly feels super busy. Before he knows what hit him, he's a month or two into school, committed to a wide variety of activities, and has settled into a pattern. He has not been intentional about finding a community that will help develop the spiritual dimension of his life.

Whatever the reasons, when a Christian student (or adult) does not seek out relationships with other Christians and ends up with mostly non-Christian friends, it is less than ideal from a faith perspective.

When a season of doubt occurs in such a student's life, and the student is surrounded by friends who have a very different worldview, the student will not have the kind of support system to help him examine and work through his doubt in meaningful ways.

If you add to that the tendency we all have to become like the people with whom we spend the most time, we can see why the Bible urges believers to "not stop meeting together."[5]

Karey and I have a friend we love very much who went through this exact process when she moved to a new area.

A couple of weeks after getting settled in, she let us know that she had "found her tribe" and was happy. But the things she told us gave us the impression that this new tribe would not be one that would encourage or strengthen her faith.

The enormous question, of course, was whether she would also seek out a vibrant Christian community. She did not.

We heard from her less frequently over the next year or two. Then we stopped hearing from her at all. Eventually, she let us know that she had been dealing with serious doubt and had struggled particularly with the (important) question as to why God allows bad things to happen.[6]

Because she was not plugged into a thoughtful Christian community that could help her wrestle with her questions in a meaningful way—and she never asked us—her doubts were left untended. And her faith withered.

This is not to suggest that her lack of Christian community was the only reason that her faith withered, but it almost certainly played a role. Karey and I were saddened but not surprised.

And none of this leads us to love her or anyone else in a similar situation any less, of course. The book of Jude calls believers to show mercy to those whose faith is wavering (v. 22). This isn't hard for me, in part because Ryan went through it, in part because others I love have gone through it, and in part because I've dealt with doubt myself. Most honest Christians will likely admit that they have dealt with doubt at some point.

Thankfully, this pattern of students walking away from their faith while in college is not one that is universal. Karey and I have known many students whose faith has grown and thrived during college—even those who have had to spend some time wrestling with some difficult questions about their faith.

Consider Meredith's story. Meredith, who was a part of Group while in high school, attended a great university in the southeast that employs a New Testament professor who doesn't really believe the New Testament.

In fact, he is known for trying to persuade students to reject historic, biblical Christianity. The professor attacked some of the things Meredith had long believed, and it challenged her.

But because Christians on campus were familiar with this professor's arguments, Meredith was able to have conversations and find resources to help her process his critiques in helpful ways. She confronted her doubt, and her faith grew.

Whatever your experience in college or in life, and whether you feel the need for it or not, community matters. It strengthens our faith and helps us thoughtfully process our doubt.

God did not create us to live out our faith on our own. Hebrews 10:23-25 reminds us that we were made to live in community with other believers:

> 23 *Let us hold fast the confession of our hope without wavering, for he who promised is faithful. 24 And let us consider how to stir up one another to love and good works, 25 not neglecting to meet together, as is the habit of some, but encouraging one another, and all the more as you see the Day drawing near.*

There are at least three important takeaways in this short passage.

First, Christians—both students and adults—are challenged to exhibit a faith that doesn't waver. Jesus challenged his disciples to exhibit faith. The writer of Hebrews does the same. Proverbs 3:5-6 remind us to "trust in the Lord with all of your heart and lean not on your own understanding."

Second, we see that we need other Christians who will build us up and encourage us to pursue love and good works. Relationships with other Christians help us fight the human tendency toward self-centeredness, selfishness, and a lack of compassion.

Finally, we see in this Hebrews passage that Christians are to not stop meeting together.

The message here is clear: Christians need each other. Christians today have embraced a worldview that is, (in different ways), out of step with many in our culture. Going it alone is difficult.

Years ago, I heard an illustration that has always stuck with me.

If you start a fire using a pile of charcoal and one of the charcoal bricks tumbles away from the fire, it will cool much more quickly than if it had stayed close to the pile.

When one adds to that the reality of spiritual warfare and the fact that the enemy of God, Satan, would love to isolate believers, our need for each other becomes even more important.

God's plan for community starts with the church. Jesus established the church as the earthly institution that would be a light to the world, declare the good news, and make a public statement about the people who make up the family of God.

If the church is the body of Christ, then all of us who are part of that body are called to participate in the life of the church. If you are a Christian, you need the people in the church. Just as importantly, *they need you.* God has given different members of the body different gifts. Part of the reason he has given you the gifts that he has is so that you can use those gifts to serve or help others in the body of Christ.

A Christian should never believe the lie that going to church is only about what he or she might get out of it. Satan would love to have you believe this. Being part of a local church is about participating in God's visible body on Earth. It is about helping the body be all it can be in this world. And it is about each of us contributing our unique gifts to the life and mission of that body as we grow together.

PEOPLE WHO HELP US GROW IN OUR FAITH

If Christians want to grow in their faith, there are three non-negotiables: learning how to spiritually feed themselves from the Bible, time in prayer (or learning how to pray), and involvement with other believers.

I have already mentioned how important the church is in this process. But to get more specific, there are three types of people who will really help us thrive in our faith.

Each will play a different but important role. You might think of these roles as those of a Paul, a Barnabas, and a Timothy.[7]

A Mentor Like Paul

Timothy had Paul, a mentor, in his life. Timothy could go to Paul with questions. He learned from Paul and looked to his experience in life and ministry for guidance.

My father has been the most influential man in my life, and for that, I am grateful beyond words. When I was in college, Todd, Keith, and later an older student named Mark invested significant time, intentionally, in helping me learn how to live out my faith. Since college, a mentor named Spencer has played an extraordinarily important role in my life for more than 30 years. He has had a profound impact on my walk with the Lord, my ministry, and my life in general.

We all need mentors who will help us grow into Christlikeness. The Bible calls this discipleship.

Friends Like Barnabas

Barnabas was a peer of Paul's. A friend. In the book of Acts, we see Paul and Barnabas as two men of faith who experienced wild adventures on their journeys together. We might think of them as partners in crime—even if their crime was ignoring Rome's attempts to get them to shut up about their faith.

Relationships with Christian friends are incredibly important. We need a Barnabas, or several of them, in our lives. We need to develop go-to friendships with people who take their faith seriously, pray for us, walk alongside us, lift us up when we fall, and encourage and challenge us as we seek to pursue Christ together.

Without friends like this, it is easy for our faith to become stagnant.

Younger Believers Like Timothy

Finally, Paul had younger men like Timothy in his life. He took Timothy under his wing to help him grow.

Paul challenged him to invest in others (who would invest in others) in the same way Paul had invested in him. In his second letter to Timothy, Paul wrote, "The things you have heard from me in the presence of many witnesses, these things entrust to faithful men, who will be able to teach others also" (2 Tim. 2:2).

That baton has been passed to us today. It was passed to me by Todd and Keith. And by Mark. And Spencer. I have sought to pass it on to others.

If you are new to Christianity, relationships with people who might become like a Timothy to you will come in time. Begin asking God to bring people like this into your life, even now. It is never too early to learn how to talk to others about your faith.

Consider all I've written in this book about Todd and Keith and the ways God used them in my life. Now consider that they were only 19 years old when they led me to faith. You are never too young, or too young in your faith, for God to use you to make a difference in the lives of others.

It may sound strange to say that we grow in our faith by helping others, but this seems to be the way God has made us. It is a dynamic I've seen to be true not only in my life but in the lives of many others. We'll explore this idea further in the Conclusion.

This chapter has focused on the reality of doubt. And on the importance of faith. We know we cannot please God without faith that God exists and is a rewarder of those who seek him (Hebrews 11:6).

But God calls us to a faith that is more than just a set of beliefs. He calls us to a vibrant faith that shakes up everything. The Bible makes it clear that we are to *live* by faith. But what does it mean to live by faith?

We will consider this question in our final chapter.

The Great Reversal

MORE THAN 200,000 BASEBALL GAMES have been played in Major League Baseball history. Hundreds of thousands of minor league games have been played across America. Add to that all of the pro, semi-pro, college, summer league, high school, travel, Babe Ruth, Little League, and other games played around the world by people of all ages, and I'd guess that the total number of baseball games that have ever been played must easily be in the tens of millions.

Whatever the number, I suspect that a game my son Ethan was part of on June 17, 2013, ended in a way that few other games have ever ended.

Ethan and a friend, Jake, were named to a 10- and 11-year-old all-star team that was to take part in a local postseason tournament. Their team was talented, though most of the best pitchers played on the 12-and-under team that would try to earn a spot in the Little League World Series.

So, although teams in this younger tournament could all hit, there was not a ton of pitching depth. As you might guess, the tournament featured some high-scoring games.

This particular game was played in Northern Virginia at a field called LLV. Ethan and Jake's team was losing by 11 or 12 runs as they came to bat in what would turn out to be the final inning of the game. Then they began a furious comeback.

The fact that they were able to come all the way back to take the lead in one inning after being that far behind was great. But that was not what made this game memorable. It was what happened after they scored the go-ahead run that I will never forget.

Our team's coaches knew, even during the comeback, that they were facing a challenge on two fronts.

Obviously, the boys had to score enough runs to catch up. But beyond that, they had to do so quickly. The game was running late, and the field had a hard deadline of 11 p.m., at which point the field's lights would be turned off. If the lights went off during an inning, the game score would revert, by rule, to the score at the end of the previous inning.

The timing was going to be tight.

As the team began to score runs, we all knew that the lights could go out at any moment and that they'd lose. But the boys kept scoring runs and eventually managed to take the lead.

It was at that moment that everything got wacky.

To win the game, the single most important goal for each team suddenly became the exact opposite of everything a team is supposed to try to do in baseball.

Beginning at that moment, our team—which was batting—needed to make outs as fast as possible to end the inning and ensure that all of the runs they just scored would count. The team in the field, on the other hand, needed to extend the inning and still be in the field when the lights went out. They wanted to avoid getting any of our batters out and needed our players to get on base and even score runs. The more runs *our* team scored, the more likely *their* team was to win.

This is not how baseball usually works.

The player who was set to bat next for Ethan and Jake's team was instructed to strike out by swinging at the first three pitches. He was told to swing no matter what, to swing at every pitched ball, and to swing in such a way that he could not possibly hit the ball. I cannot remember if the other team changed pitchers, which obviously slows everything down, but they did not hurry.

Eventually, their pitcher began throwing ridiculous pitches, trying to walk our batter. Our batter made three equally ridiculous and entertaining swings. The most bizarre strikeout you'll ever see ended the inning. The lights went off moments later, and the game became official. It was a comeback for the ages.

An offense trying not to score. A defense trying to let the other team score. Even if you've never watched, played, or cared much about baseball, you can probably imagine how bizarre this situation was. For Ethan and Jake's team to win, everything we know about baseball had to be utterly turned upside down.

You could call the final moments of that game a great reversal.

This idea of a great reversal—of everything being turned upside down—is a good description of Christianity.

CHRISTIANITY'S GREAT REVERSAL

In this chapter, we will explore the same question we asked in Chapter 15, but here from the perspective of a Christian: If Christianity is true, what will I do about it?

There are two ways that thinking about this "great reversal" can be helpful for us. First, as we consider Christianity, we find incredible encouragement in Jesus' great reversal on our behalf. He turned everything upside down for us.

The most brilliant depiction I've ever seen of this great reversal was a video written by Jason Dyba for a Good Friday gathering at his church in 2015. I have included the link in the Endnotes.[1]

The video is made up of words that scroll from the bottom of the screen upward until they scroll off of the top of the screen.

Good Friday
how can one describe such a day?
the wrongdoing of all humanity
putting to an end
an innocent man
the son of God
this is the story of Jesus
death, by way of a cross
all in one moment, bringing death to
the bright light of our future
He never stopped loving us
and yet, this is the incredible part of it:
our sin stopped his heart
our sin drove the nails
firmly in the hands of God
all along, these were the plans
we told ourselves that we were in control
and this was deemed sufficient for all of us
the brutal beating
the inhuman flogging
the naked humiliation
Heaven watched and saw it all:
our rebellion, our guilt, our shame
erasing the very notion of
reconciling us with God
our sin and our debt
overcoming
Jesus
here is our King
obliterated
the enemy laughing: his plans
unstoppable—there's no longer the sound of
freedom rising, now God's people are
utterly broken—behold
the chains of mortality
yes, this is what is true
we had heard the stories of old:
the lost are found
the blind can see
the weak are made strong

but now we are witnesses to this reality:
God is dead
we had almost believed
there is a way of redemption
there is a life of fulfillment
there is a peace beyond understanding
now we know better
for us
we can say that God is
encapsulated in this one realization:
the single greatest sacrifice in human history
is finished...
how clearly we can see it[2]

As you finished reading that text, of Jesus being obliterated and of Satan laughing, you might have thought, "Sure, that's interesting, Patrick. But would you really call it brilliant?"

Yes, I would—because of what happens next in the video.

It says, "So what's so good about Good Friday? Just one thing: that the blood of Jesus can reverse the curse of sin and raise the dead to life."

At this moment, the video literally does its own great reversal.

The words begin to scroll in the opposite direction. As the exact same lines of text reverse and start to move back down the screen, the creative brilliance of the video begins to become clear.

Go back to the text above and re-read it. But this time start at the bottom, with "how clearly we can see it." Read the lines from the bottom to the top, ending with "Good Friday."

The exact same lines, when read in the opposite order, focus no longer on Satan's victory and Jesus' death but rather on Jesus' victory on our behalf. Reversed, they tell the story of Jesus' great reversal. The power of this piece is simply extraordinary; its creativity is breathtaking. Seriously, if you didn't go back and re-read it from bottom to top, please do so now. Or make a point to watch the video. It is one of the most creative things I've ever seen.

✛ ✛ ✛

Nearly five hundred years ago, a theologian and pastor named John Calvin wrote, in his own creative way, about Jesus' great reversal. If you are unfamiliar with 1500s-era English, this will read a bit oddly, but it is worth the effort.

> *[Jesus] was sold, to buy us back; captive, to deliver us; condemned, to absolve us; he was made a curse for our blessing, sin offering for our righteousness; marred that we may be made fair; he died for our life; so that by him fury is made gentle, wrath appeased, darkness turned into light, fear reassured, despisal despised, debt canceled, labor lightened, sadness made merry, misfortune made fortunate, difficulty easy, disorder ordered, division united, ignominy ennobled, rebellion subjected, intimidation intimidated, ambush uncovered, assaults assailed, force forced back, combat combated, war warred against, vengeance avenged, torment tormented, damnation damned, the abyss sunk into the abyss, hell transfixed, death dead, mortality made immortal. In short, mercy has swallowed up all misery, and goodness all misfortune.*[3]

Calvin noted a range of things that Christ accomplished for Christians, each its own sort of reversal. This should lead us to worship. Calvin then transitioned to the impact that this great reversal should have in the life of a Christian:

> *We are comforted in tribulation, joyful in sorrow, glorying under vituperation [verbal abuse], abounding in poverty, warmed in our nakedness, patient amongst evils, living in death. This is what we should in short seek in the whole of Scripture: truly to know Jesus Christ, and the infinite riches that are comprised in him and are offered to us by him from God the Father.*[4]

I love Calvin's perspective here. We should seek "truly to know Jesus Christ, and the infinite riches that are comprised in him and are offered to us by him from God the Father."

This is what the Christian life is about: getting to know—and walking with—the God who loves us so much that he came to Earth as a man, was tortured, and ultimately killed in our place.

One historic document on the Christian faith says that "the chief [purpose] of man is to glorify God and enjoy him forever."[5]

But how do we go about pursuing such a thing?

Even as I write this paragraph, I wonder how many Christians sense that they know what it means to "enjoy" God. Recently, a high school student sent me an email that said, "For a while, I have had trouble connecting to Christ. It's like I'm not really sure where to begin, and it is a little overwhelming." When I responded, I told her that she was not alone in that feeling. This is a question that many Christians ask.

The short answer, for anyone asking the same question that the student asked, would have three parts. First, I would ask the person if he or she has ever truly made a personal decision to become a Christian, as we discussed in Chapter 15.

It may surprise some to read that I would not ask if the person was religious, went to church, or was raised by Christian parents. These questions do not get to the heart of what matters. What matters is whether the person had responded to God's offer of salvation by trusting Christ for the forgiveness of his or her sin.

If so, the second thing I'd point out is that, like any relationship, our relationship with God is unlikely to grow unless we invest time in that relationship. There are no shortcuts.

James 4:8 tells us that if we draw near to God, he will draw near to us. It is a promise. Two of the best (but not only) ways to draw near to God are through prayer and reading his word.

It should never fail to amaze us that the God who spoke our entire universe into existence invites us to spend time with him. It is astonishing that God wants to know us! But God's enemy, Satan, would rather have us do just about anything other than pray. He would even rather we do good things. This is why it is not surprising that it can often feel hard to find time to pray.

As we spend time with God and begin to really understand the width, length, height, and depth of his love for us, our faith will grow. It will be strengthened, and our walk with God will become increasingly mature. Our relationship with Christ will grow.

Each of these things, plus being in community with other believers, is mission-critical. But if we truly want to experience life the way God intended it, we have to be willing to take a much bigger step than merely starting to pray or read the Bible, as great as those things are.

We have to be willing to die.

I obviously do not mean that we need to literally die, in the physical sense, but rather that we have to decide for whom we will live. Will we live for ourselves, our own desires, and our own interests? Or will we seek instead to "die" to ourselves and fully pursue God's ways, desires, and interests? This is more easily said than done.

Matthew records two different times that Jesus taught this idea: "For whoever wants to save his life will lose it, but whoever loses his life because of me will find it." (Matthew 10:39 and Matthew 16:25)

This is the great reversal to which God calls his followers, and it is a hard teaching. We are to lay down our lives to gain life and find true joy. But what does that even look like?

Let's consider one answer, from the book of Romans.

WATER SKIING THROUGH THE FIRST FEW CHAPTERS OF ROMANS
Romans is one of my favorite books in the Bible. It explains Christianity in a way that has always made sense to me. Some have observed that Paul's style, in what was originally a letter to the church in Rome, reminds them of a lawyer making a case.

Throughout the book, Paul makes a point, predicts how readers might respond to that point, and then addresses the responses he guesses he might get. The first 70% of the book (Chapters 1-11) teaches theological truth. The last 30% of the book (Chapters 12-16) focuses more on practical application, or how we should live in light of that truth.

In Chapters 1, 2, and the first part of Chapter 3, Paul addresses the same thing I wrote about in Chapter 13 of this book: our sin.

He reminds us that our sin is a massive problem for religious people, non-religious people, Jewish people, and non-Jewish people. It is even a problem for those who consider themselves to be good. In fact, the middle of Chapter 3 reminds us that "there is no one righteous" and "there is no one who seeks God. All have turned away." (Romans 3:10-12)

Then, in the second half of Chapter 3, he introduces what might be called the thought bomb that is at the very heart of Christianity: that "God has revealed a righteousness that comes through faith to all who believe." He explains that Christians are, amazingly, declared righteous in God's eyes "by his grace through the redemption that is in Christ Jesus." (Romans 3:21 and 3:24)

The idea that we (as sinful and broken people) could be declared righteous by God through faith—and not by religious ceremony, good works, or our own merit—is astounding. This is what I wrote about in Chapters 14 and 15.

In different ways, Paul then unpacks and explains this righteousness that comes through faith in Romans Chapters 4-8. The end of Romans 8 is highlighted by Paul's sheer wonder at how incredible God's goodness is toward us:

> If God is for us, who is against us? He did not even spare his own Son but gave him up for us all. How will he not also with him grant us everything? (Romans 8:31-32)

And then:

> ... in all these things we are more than conquerors through him who loved us. For I am persuaded that neither death nor life, nor angels nor rulers, nor things present nor things to come, nor powers, nor height nor depth, nor any other created thing will be able to separate us from the love of God that is in Christ Jesus our Lord. (Romans 8:37-39)

If you were to read the book of Romans straight through, as it was originally written (a letter to the church), you'd feel the power of Paul's emotion here. You would understand how moved he was by the gospel and by God's grace.

We, too, should be similarly moved.

SCUBA DIVING INTO ROMANS 12:1-2

When Paul gets to Romans 12, he turns the corner from teaching theology to teaching, in very real and practical ways, how that truth should change how we live.

He begins with two powerful verses:

> *Therefore, brothers and sisters, in view of the mercies of God, I urge you to present your bodies as a living sacrifice, holy and pleasing to God; this is your true worship. Do not be conformed to this age, but be transformed by the renewing of your mind, so that you may discern what is the good, pleasing, and perfect will of God. (Romans 12:1-2)*

Our Source of Motivation

Here we begin to learn what it means to die to ourselves.

Paul first addresses our motivation by starting with "in view of the mercies of God." For 11 chapters in Romans, Paul has written about the mercies of God—the amazing, unfathomable, overwhelming grace of God to believers. He has reminded us of the lengths to which God has gone to rescue us from our sin.

This matters because we will be most motivated to live God's way not by some sense of guilt or fear that God is looking to smack us when we mess up, but rather when we are motivated by our thankfulness for God's mercies toward us.

A Living... Sacrifice?

So, in light of God's mercies, Paul instructs us to do three things. He starts by calling us to present our body as a "living sacrifice." Again, we are not called to do this to earn God's favor nor to earn our way to heaven. We are to do this as a response to all that God has done for us.

This idea of being a living sacrifice would certainly have been a jarring thought to people familiar with the sacrificial system in the Old Testament. In the Old Testament, of course, the animal to be sacrificed actually had to die.

As a *living* sacrifice, however, we are to put God's desires, cares, and values above our own. We are to offer him our lives and give our bodies to his service in any way that he sees fit.

Paul writes that presenting our bodies as living sacrifices is our "true worship." He means here that this is our most reasonable, or logical, response to God's mercies. If God has done all of this for us, Paul writes, it makes sense for us to be living sacrifices.

As in Penn Jillette's quote earlier in the book, imagine that my friend Bridgette was about to get hit by a truck she never saw coming. But just before impact, imagine that our friend Riley jumped in to save Bridgette's life. Bridgette would feel incredible gratitude toward Riley and would do anything she could for her out of thankfulness. This would be Bridgette's logical response.

But even if it is logical, it is not easily done.

Instead, we are tempted to want to only give parts of our lives to him. We are tempted to see Jesus' role in our lives as if he is some sort of supernatural hitchhiker who might make our journey easier or more enjoyable. Perhaps we'd pull over to pick him up and nod to the back seat, saying, "Hop in" as we move clothes, basketball shoes, and the Chick-fil-A bag from lunch out of the way to make room.

But we'd learn that Jesus wants to drive. We might shrug and say, "Okay, Jesus. You can sit in the front. But I'm driving." Still, Jesus wants to drive. So, we sigh and say, "All right, all right. You can sit in the front, and you can even have the aux. But I'm driving." Still, Jesus wants to drive.

I know people who seem to view Jesus not as a king for whom they would lay down their lives but rather as a sort of add-on to make their lives happier or better. They might view Christianity as helpful, but not as something that will make a difference in the decisions they make on a weekend night. Or with their finances, career, or future. They might love the promise of God's forgiveness and might even think of Jesus as their savior, but the idea of letting Jesus drive goes a bit too far.

As a minister named Alexander Moody Stuart once observed, "Many are willing that Christ should be something, but few will consent that Christ should be everything."[6] These people enjoy the idea that they will benefit from Christianity—at least until Jesus calls them to live differently.

This is a problem.

Although it is true that Jesus is the savior who came to save us from our sins, he also came to be our Lord. Our king. Jesus did not come to be some sort of add-on to our lives.

Jesus said, "If anyone wants to follow after me, let him deny himself, take up his cross, and follow me."[7] When Jesus called his disciples, he said, "Follow me." And they dropped whatever they were doing and followed. He calls us to do the same.

Make no mistake: Jesus' call to follow him is a call to obey.

And that is the final thought I would have for the student who sent me the email about not feeling connected to Christ. Nothing will short-circuit a Christian's closeness—or connection—with Christ more quickly than when he or she is not obeying God in some area of his or her life.

The night before Jesus was crucified, as he was spending time with his disciples, he shared three different variations of this thought. First, he said, "If you love me, you will keep my commands (John 14:15)." Six verses later (in v. 21), John records that Jesus said, "The one who has my commands and keeps them is the one who loves me." Later, Jesus said, again, "You are my friends if you do what I command you." (John 15:14)

Christ calls his followers to obey. And along with that call, he promises rest, peace, joy, and abundant life to all who follow. But this is a calling that has caused many to turn away in sadness.

To help us further understand how to live out this idea of being a living sacrifice, Paul gives us two more instructions in Romans 12:2. The first is to "not be conformed to this age."

Do Not Be Conformed to this Age
Christ-followers are called by God to stand out. He calls us to *look* different than the rest of the world because he calls us to truly *be* different. To not conform to this age is to be willing to say no to the crowd. To not drink

our culture's (or any political party's) Kool-Aid. To be different from the world in our thoughts, motives, and actions.

The call to avoid conforming to the world means we must, in a variety of ways, be willing to be rebels. We must not fear rebelling against the prevailing or popular views held by those in our society today. Jesus never played to the crowd. Nor should we.

This requires hard decisions. It demands hard decisions on Friday and Saturday nights. It demands hard decisions in our relationships and in our finances. It demands hard decisions when the easy way out of a situation seems profitable or beneficial, but we know that it is wrong. It demands hard decisions when those around us are openly rebelling against God and encouraging us to do the same.

When we choose not to conform to the world, we understand that we may face possible rejection or even persecution. I've known kids from Group who have made wise decisions to change how they were living, even though those decisions caused a few of their friends to ridicule or even drop them as friends.

As Tim Keller wrote:

> This upside-down pattern so contradicts the thinking and practice of the world that it creates an "alternate kingdom," an alternate reality, a counterculture among those who have been transformed by it. In this peaceable kingdom there is a reversal of the values of the world with regard to power, recognition, status, and wealth.
>
> In this new counterculture, Christians look at money as something to give away. They look at power as something to use strictly for service. Racial and class superiority, accrual of money and power at the expense of others, yearning for popularity and recognition, these normal marks of human life, are the opposite of the mindset of those who have understood and experienced the Cross. Christ creates a whole new order of life.
>
> Those who are shaped by the great reversal of the Cross no longer need self-justification through money, status, career, or pride of race and class. So the Cross creates a counterculture in which sex, money, and

power cease to control us and are used in life-giving and community-building rather than destructive ways.[8]

Be Transformed by the Renewing of Your Mind

Paul's second instruction in Romans 12:2 is to be transformed. How? By the renewing of our minds. Our minds are renewed when we spend time in prayer, time reading God's word, and time with other believers.

We need to have our minds renewed often as we navigate life in this fallen world. When my friend Bella talks about spending time with God or reading the Bible, she talks about how it "sets her heart's posture for the day." That is a beautiful picture of how God's word can transform us.

Zach, a friend who was involved in Group during high school, told me one day that he had been reading First Corinthians, a book in the New Testament. He said he had read Chapter 13 (often called the famous "love chapter"). Later that day, after working a twelve-hour shift, one of his co-workers didn't finish a task the way he should have and left early.

The burden to do it fell upon Zach, whose shift suddenly became longer. But he said he remembered what he had read that morning about love and was surprised to find that he did not have a bad attitude about having to stay even later to cover for his co-worker.

His heart and attitude had been transformed by the renewing of his mind.

We also need to have our minds renewed because we so often forget the great things that God has done for us. In the Old Testament, we can read on one page about something God did to deliver his people from danger or drama, only to turn the page and discover Israel's tendency to immediately forget what God had just done. We then see Israel complain, whine, forget, and sometimes blatantly turn their backs on the same God who had just rescued them in some way.

When I was new to the Bible, I would read this type of story and think, "How could they have been like that?"

And then I realized that—far too often—I am exactly like that. I might see God provide or work in some way, but then, when a new trial or challenge arrives, forget how he provided or showed up the last time.

To say that a life is being transformed is not to suggest that it is without struggle. Few thoughtful people would say that their lives are perfect or struggle-free. And it is definitely not to say that such a life is without sin. Rather, it is to say that a person is increasingly seeking to yield to God's leading, confessing their sin to God, and repenting.

As Christians, we will not be fully set free from all sin and struggles until we are in heaven. So, while we are still here, we will not obey God perfectly. But as our minds are renewed, we are reminded of all that is true. We are reminded that we have been forgiven by God's grace. We are reminded how amazing that grace really is. And we are reminded that our culture's dominant worldview is bankrupt and does not lead to true flourishing.

As our minds are renewed, we begin to see God changing our hearts, thoughts, and desires. We see him change our perspective on things going on around us. We discover that our compassion is growing, and we find an increased capacity to love our friends (and even enemies) well. We become more others-centered and begin to hold healthier views on our money, career, possessions, relationships, and life itself.

And transformed people do tend to look different than much of the rest of the world, in some very real and meaningful ways.

Transformed people tend to be hopeful. Why? Because they wake up and ask, "What do you have for me today, Lord?" And then they live with their eyes wide open, trusting God to show up or to work in different situations.

Transformed people see prayer as an opportunity, not a chore. They have seen God answer prayer, and they trust his goodness when the answer is no. So, they make time to pray.

Transformed people are deeply thankful. Why? Because they know they did not do anything to earn God's kindness and mercy.

Transformed people are generous. Why? Because they are totally aware that everything they have that is good was made possible by God. They understand that God gives us things, in part, so that we can meet the needs of others. So, they give, trusting that in God's economy, you can't outgive God. This is not just about money. Transformed people are generous with their things, their time, their talent, and their treasure.

Whatever their circumstances, transformed people tend to be content. Why? Because they trust God, even during really hard times.

Transformed people tend to be gracious and not judgmental. They are deeply aware of how much they have been forgiven by God and understand how desperately they needed God's forgiveness. So, they do not look down on anyone who is struggling or battling with sin. Instead, they react with understanding and compassion.

Finally, transformed people have a deep-seated sense of purpose. They recognize that the greatest investment they could ever make in life is in knowing God and helping others discover the grace and forgiveness that can come only through Christ. So they pursue that purpose.

In my life, I see myself growing in these areas, even if progress seems slow sometimes. During the 39 years since I became a Christian, there have been seasons when I have yielded as fully to God's leading as I know how. But there have also been seasons when I have not—seasons when I have stubbornly taken back the steering wheel.

This is evidence of what many call the spiritual battle, a battle that is a daily one: *Who am I going to let drive today?* As Frank Turek once asked, "Are we going to follow Jesus, or are we just going to follow our desires?"[9]

I can say without hesitation that the best and most fulfilling times of my life have been those when I was most yielded to God, letting him drive, and trusting that he can run my life better than I can.

To die to ourselves so that we can experience a life of joy, purpose, and fulfillment? *That* is a great reversal.

It is also a great adventure.

Saddle Up Your Horses

I SPENT THE SUMMER AFTER MY SOPHOMORE YEAR of college at a camp in western North Carolina called Windy Gap.

One of the other college students who worked there was named Amy. She was a horse wrangler, so her job was to care for the horses and take campers on horseback rides. She was also cute.

On a day off, she found me at breakfast and asked if I wanted to go on a horseback ride with her. I was planning to play basketball, but (again) Amy was cute. If she wanted to spend what I imagined might be a romantic day riding horses with me, who was I to say no?

When it was time to go, I headed off for the horse barn. When I got there, I quickly realized that my vision for how this ride might go was very different than Amy's. She had invited a ton of other people to go on the ride with us.

I immediately wondered if it was too late to escape so I could play basketball. But I got on the horse, and we headed out to explore trails in the beautiful Blue Ridge Mountains. As we rode, I had to admit that it was fun. It was a cool way to spend a morning.

Near the end of the ride, Amy stopped us before we went out into a clearing. She told us to turn our horses to the left in the clearing because if the horse turned right, it would see the barn and immediately want to run for it.

We came out into the clearing and turned left. Amy rode around in front of us and explained that in just a moment, we were going to turn and run for the barn. She explained that we should try to keep our weight on our feet in the stirrups, squeeze in with our knees, and hold on to the reins with one hand and the horn of the saddle with the other. She said to try to lean forward and to stay in an athletic posture.

That all sounded good. I assumed we would trot. Or prance. Or some other word that meant "horse jog for beginners."

I couldn't have been more wrong.

We turned around, and, before I knew what was happening, I found myself in the middle of the Kentucky Derby. We were in an all-out run, at what seemed to be about 400 miles per hour.

I had a horse running right beside me and could hear the rest of the horses' hooves pounding behind me. It was thrilling. It was also terrifying. Horses are enormous.

But my fear was short-lived. It was quickly replaced by my competitiveness as I realized that not only was I *in* the Kentucky Derby, I was *winning* the Kentucky Derby. Even if nobody else thought we were racing at that point, I definitely did. If I was going to die, at least I would go out in some sort of imagined blaze of glory.

It was at that moment that I saw the most incredible sight I had ever seen. It was a fence. And it was coming at us at about 400 miles per hour. It wasn't just that we were moving at 400 miles per hour. The fence itself was also moving that fast, directly at us. You may be thinking, "No, Patrick. The fence was not moving. Only the horses and riders were moving." To this, I can only say that you were not there. I was.

I quickly calculated that I was about to have a collision at approximately 16 billion miles per hour. My math may have been a little off; I'm not a math guy. And I had other things to worry about at the moment, like my impending death.

It seemed to me that the horse had three options (note that, at this point, I thought the horse had taken over all control of the situation).

First, it could decide to jump the fence. If it did that, I thought, at least my parents would still have my younger brother to enjoy.

A second option was that the horse would skid to a stop like you'd see in a cartoon, with its front legs extended out in front of it. It might stop, I thought, but it would catapult me halfway to Tennessee.

The final option, as I mentioned above, was that the horse didn't see the fence, and we were about to crash into it. I had no clue what would happen next, but I knew it was going to be exciting.

✛ ✛ ✛

Obviously, I did not die that day. As it turns out, there was an open gate that was at an angle that made it hard to see until we were fairly close to it. Of course, we weren't going to run into the fence; the horses had done this before. They knew the drill.

We came over a subtle hill that hid the path in front of us, made a couple of small turns, and ran smoothly through the gate and to the barn. Thankfully, all fatalities were avoided on the ride that day. And thus, this story's build-up was far more exciting than its conclusion.

But even if I had fallen off the horse during the sprint, I could have died. And that's one of the odd things about death: many of us will wake up on our last day on Earth without having any clue that we will die that day.

As I was writing this part of the book, I read about yet another senseless and horrific school shooting. In this case, I read an article about a kid named Tate, a high school junior. I saw his photo and a tweet about his visit to a college that was interested in having him come play football there after graduation.

According to reports, while everyone else was running away from the danger, Tate ran toward it. He selflessly ran toward the shooter to see whether he could stop him. Tragically, he was shot. He died while on the way to the hospital. But his efforts were heroic. In the days after he died, nearly 300,000 people agreed and signed a petition to rename the school's football stadium after him.

As I read, I couldn't get past the thought that Tate had woken up on that cool fall day with no idea that it would be his last on this planet.

I do not know when my last day on Earth will be. Neither do you. I'm sorry if this seems morbid, but we must understand that life is short. None of us is guaranteed a tomorrow.

We know that life is short, at least in theory. But, because we all tend to think, "I've got time," too few of us allow the brevity of life to drive us toward living intentionally with whatever time we do have left.

DON'T SETTLE

Sadly—and far too often—most of us (myself included, at times) settle for less in life than God's best for us. Blaise Pascal pointed to what could be called a God-shaped vacuum in each of our hearts, a vacuum that only God can fill. And we try to fill that vacuum with all sorts of other things.

C.S. Lewis addressed this in a sermon called *The Weight of Glory*:

> *It would seem that Our Lord finds our desires not too strong, but too weak. We are half-hearted creatures, fooling about with drink and sex and ambition when infinite joy is offered us, like an ignorant child who wants to go on making mud pies in a slum because he cannot imagine what is meant by the offer of a holiday at the sea. We are far too easily pleased.*[1]

Many of us too readily believe that the things of this world will satisfy us. We touched on this in Chapter 1. Each of us pursues these things, not realizing that people who have obtained those very things are also searching. We really are just like Lewis' imagined ignorant child who is content to play in the mud.

We settle. And yet, God offers us something so much better.

Jesus said (as recorded in John 10:10) that he came to Earth that we "might have life, and have it abundantly." Other versions of the Bible translate the last part of the verse as "so that they could live life to the fullest" and "to give them a rich and satisfying life."

MY HOPE FOR THE NON-CHRISTIAN

My sincere hope for you, if you are not a Christian, is that a hunger to continue the exploration you've begun will have been awakened in you as you have read this book, and that you'll continue to seek answers.

My hope is that you will re-examine your reasons for doubt and ask yourself the question that I was once asked: What's holding you back from turning to Christ?

My hope is that one day soon you will discover that he who knows you the best also loves you the most. And that you will recognize your need for forgiveness, put aside the pride that makes it hard for us to admit we need a savior, and be drawn to the God who willingly laid down his life so that you could live.

God has invited you to turn to him and to accept the forgiveness he offers by trusting Christ's work on the cross and deciding to follow Jesus. He has invited you to experience a restored relationship with him. But as strange as this might sound, this is a limited-time offer. It is only available during your lifetime.

My most profound hope is that one day soon you will receive Christ, get baptized, and discover joy and peace as you begin to truly yield to his leading in your life. If Christianity is true, the decision to repent and believe will be the best decision you will ever make. It will change both your eternal destiny and your present experience in life.

So, what is your next step? What is holding you back?

To have read this book, I hope, has been a good thing. To act on something as a result of having read it would be far better. Every reader may have a slightly different next step. Pause for a moment and consider yours.

If you are not a Christian, a next step might be to talk to someone about questions you still have about Christianity. It might be to read one or more of the books in the Appendix in search of answers to questions you still have. It might be to decide to turn to Christ by repenting and believing.

It might be to say yes to that friend who invites you to go to church or—if you are a student—to decide to check out a Christian group on campus.

A great next step might also be to pray something like this: "God, if you are real, would you reveal yourself to me? Would you show me in some way I can understand?"

And then keep your eyes open for an answer.

MY HOPE FOR THE CHRISTIAN

My hope for the Christian reader is the same that I'd want you to hope for me: that you will draw near to God, trusting his promise that if you draw near to him, he will draw near to you.

That you would seek to glorify God and enjoy him forever. That God's mercies (the gospel) would drive you to yield to his leading in every area of your life. And that you'd do this not out of duty or obligation but out of gratitude.

In Colossians 3, we are called to set our minds on things above, not on things here on Earth. Jesus told us to take courage because he has overcome the world. Put differently, God calls us to live for the upper story. The lead pastor of my church, Brett, often talks about God's upper story and our lower story. The lower story is our experience on Earth. The upper story is all that God is doing to accomplish his purposes.

When Jesus was crucified, for example, things looked so bad in the lower story that the disciples took off. Viewed through the lens of the upper story, however, God allowed—and Jesus willingly went to—the cross. They knew that if Jesus didn't die, we would have no hope of forgiveness.

The question for all Christians, of course, is whether we will live our lives focused on the upper story or the lower story.

Living for the upper story requires trust but eliminates so many of the things that can cause us to be overwhelmed by stress, worry, and fear in the lower story.

When we choose to live an upper-story life—a life not conformed to this world—and as we yield our lives to God, he promises a quality of life that is unavailable anywhere else. This does not mean a life invested in walking with God will always be exciting in an adrenaline-fueled way. In fact, when we read the Bible, we learn what many of us know from experience: that the Christian life will sometimes involve suffering and pain.

Jesus suffered while on Earth. So did his first followers. It should not surprise us, then, when we suffer at times—we are not in heaven yet. And Jesus warned us that in this world we will all face troubles of different kinds (John 16:33). But he promises us peace in the midst of the trials. He promises to meet us in our suffering and walk through it with us.

My hope for you is that you will invest in your relationship with God and be transformed as your mind is renewed. He is the supernatural, all-powerful, all-knowing, all-wise, and all-loving creator and king. Never stop being amazed that this king invites you to spend time with him. According to John 1, if you are a believer in Christ, you are his child. He loves you. Bask in that reality.

But you are more than just his child. You are also, according to Second Corinthians 5:20, his ambassador. You are called to represent him and his interests here on Earth. If you are a Christian, when you wake up and are given a new day to live, you have the opportunity not only to watch God work but to participate with him in that work. You have the opportunity to embrace your role as his ambassador and to seek to deploy the gifts, skills, and interests God has given you for his glory.

Part of your role as an ambassador is to love people well and to help introduce them to the God who so loved the world that he gave his only son. Jesus told us, in Matthew 28, to "go into all the world and make disciples of all men." This is God's plan for reaching the world. It is not about big initiatives or strategies, nor is it about pastors and missionaries doing all the work. He wants to use us—everyday people—to accomplish his upper-story purposes.

One might view this as a responsibility God has given us, and that's not wrong. But I view it differently. I'd call it an opportunity. An opportunity for us to be involved in something incredibly significant every day. To be involved in something far larger than ourselves.

When I was still in college, I heard Josh McDowell speak at a conference outside of Charlottesville, Virginia. He challenged us to invest our lives in something that would outlive us. I've never forgotten that challenge. And I am absolutely convinced that nothing (for a Christian) is as fulfilling as being involved in helping others come to faith or grow in their faith.

Years ago, a Steven Curtis Chapman song called *The Great Adventure* was popular among many Christians. It wasn't my favorite style of music, but the words reflect a desire that most of us share—a desire for adventure and a life that is well-lived.

Here are some of the lyrics:

> *Come on get ready*
>   *for the ride of your life.*
> *Gonna leave long-faced religion*
>   *in a cloud of dust behind.*
> *And discover all the new horizons*
>   *just waiting to be explored.*
> *This is what we were created for.*
>
> *Saddle up your horses*
>   *we've got a trail to blaze*
> *Through the wild blue yonder*
>   *of God's amazing grace*
> *Let's follow our leader*
>   *into the glorious unknown*
> *This is life like no other, whoa*
> *This is the great adventure*
>
> *We'll travel long, over mountains so high.*
> *We'll go through valleys below.*
> *Still through it all we'll find that*
>   *this is the greatest journey*
>   *that the human heart will ever see.*
> *The love of God will take us*
>   *far beyond our wildest dreams.*[2]

Chapman writes here of a life that "we were created for." He writes of a life that is the exact opposite of one settling for mud pies.

I do believe that God has called us to a great adventure. But if we want to experience that adventure, we have to invest in it. If we aren't promised a tomorrow and we know we will have to give an account to God for how we lived, it is time to get serious about living the way God would have us live.

As Andy Dufresne said to Red in the famous line from the film, *The Shawshank Redemption*, "I guess it comes down to a simple choice, really. Get busy living or get busy dying."

For all of us who are Christians, we must never forget that life is a vapor. We are wise to remember what Paul wrote in Ephesians 5:15-16: "Pay careful attention, then, to how you walk—not as unwise people but as wise—making the most of the time."

If we only have one life to invest, we should live intentionally in a way that will bring us the greatest possible return on the investment of our life. None of us wants to get to the end of our lives and discover that we wish we had invested it in different things.

That's one reason I was moved so powerfully by the Johnny Cash video of the song "Hurt" that I mentioned in the first chapter. The video was partially filmed in Johnny's old museum. In the video, we see that his museum was closed and in disrepair. To film the video there, of a song in which Johnny sings about his "empire of dirt," was perfect.

Johnny achieved tremendous fame, financial success, and artistic acclaim during his lifetime. These are the types of things people spend their lives chasing. But we see, in the video, Johnny's recognition that those things do not bring lasting satisfaction.

Thankfully, Johnny was a Christian. That's why I loved the clips near the end of the video of Christ on the cross, dying for Johnny's sins. And ours. They hint at Johnny's Christian faith and at the reason he could face his eventual death with hope.

WHAT'S NEXT?
On the first page of the Introduction to this book, I wrote that some things matter very much, and a few things matter immensely. I will conclude with the same idea.

How we live, how we influence others, and how we invest our lives and resources really matter. They matter... immensely.

Whatever your stage of life, what is your next step?

A few pages ago, I listed possible next steps for a non-Christian. If you are a Christian whose spiritual life is not where you'd want it to be, a next step might be to ask God to reveal areas in your life where you are settling for mud pies, living for the lower story, and/or not yielding to God—and to repent. To turn away from that sin and back to God.

Your next step might be to find a small group Bible study or to go back to church, however long you have been away. If you are a believer but have never been baptized, that is a very clear and obvious next step.

If you want to walk with God and become more of the person he wants you to be, do a personal and spiritual self-inventory. Be honest about where you are, and talk to God about it. And then, as Paul challenged us—by the mercies of God—offer your life to him as a living sacrifice.

If you are walking closely with the Lord but have never gotten involved in the adventure of discipling others, perhaps it is time to start. Talk to your pastor, a mature Christian that you know, or a mentor to explore what that might look like in your life.

Whatever it looks like, I hope that you will take a next step. And when you determine what your next step is, that you will talk to another believer about it. As I've mentioned, we were not built to run this race on our own.

As for me, I have no idea when the Lord will call me home. But in whatever time I have left in this life, I hope to continue to pursue the adventure God still has before me and Karey. I want to live for the upper story and never stop battling against the temptation to settle for mud pies.

I want to continue to pass on the baton of faith by investing in others in the same way others have invested in me.

Obviously, I won't (and don't) get it right all the time, but I am encouraged and challenged by Paul's tremendous perspective, found in his letter to the church at Philippi (3:12-14, J.B. Phillips version).

It captures how I want to live:

> *I do not consider myself to have "arrived," spiritually, nor do I consider myself already perfect. But I keep going on, grasping ever more firmly that purpose for which Christ grasped me. My brothers, I do not consider myself to have fully grasped it even now. But I do concentrate on this: I leave the past behind and with hands outstretched to whatever lies ahead I go straight for the goal—my reward the honor of being called by God in Christ.*

Wherever you are spiritually, and however old you may be, please join me, Karey, and Christian brothers and sisters across the globe in the pursuit of this great adventure in your life. It is a pursuit you will never regret.

Saddle up your horses.

Thank You...

To Jesus, for grace I did not deserve.

To my wife, Karey, for encouraging (and even pushing) me to finish this book. Also, for the extraordinary love, wisdom, and encouragement you provide every day. Thank you for being so much like Jesus in so many ways and for loving me unconditionally. You continually amaze me.

To Mom and Dad, for your love and for your encouragement about this book. Mom, your edits have been great—I've never been more thankful for your professional experience and expertise. If a typo or grammatical problem still exists in these pages, it is because I've changed something since your "final" edits.

To my most committed and thoughtful readers throughout the process: Grace and Ryan. Both of you were incredibly insightful and perceptive— on so many levels—with your feedback.

To Megan, for the ridiculously great art you created for the beginning of each chapter. Seriously—what can't you do?

To Ethan, for simply being you. I love and respect how your mind works, your sense of humor, and so much more about you. You've had more of an impact on this book than you might suspect.

To Kayla, Ryan C., Randy, Pat F., Madison, Megan G., and Tim. Each of you challenged me, encouraged me, and helped make this better. I couldn't be more thankful for the time you invested in this project and for your thoughtful feedback.

To my sister-in-law Kim and my friend Abby, for your input and proofreading. And to my Group test readers and proofreaders who took the time to review and provide feedback on different parts of the book along the way. A special shout out to Tyler, Nick, Brooke, Emma, Tanner, and Robbie.

To my friend Curt, for your encouragement.

To Brett, my friend and pastor, for continually challenging me to live for the upper story.

To Spencer, for your decades-long investment in my life.

To Mark, for your significant investment in me when we were both college students.

To Todd and Keith, for introducing me to Jesus and to this great adventure.

To Colonel Mansur, for permission to use the "No Greater Love" article, for your graciousness when we talked, and for your life of service, both to our nation and to our God.

To my friends Dan, Wendy, Dave, and John, for your willingness to contribute your time and professional expertise to specific chapters.

Finally, to Chick-fil-A, for your chicken sandwiches. As Peter Kreeft once wrote about something else entirely, "You either see this one or you don't."

Endnotes

A few final thoughts that didn't fit into the book—plus sources.

INTRODUCTION

1. "A Gift of a Bible," YouTube video, accessed on April 10, 2020, https://www.youtube.com/watch?v=6md638smQd8

2. Some atheists believe that God does not exist. Others argue that they "lack a belief" that God exists. I've talked to people in both camps. In my view, to "lack a belief" in one thing is to hold a different belief. If you lack a belief in thing A (whatever thing A is) it is almost certainly because you have an alternate set of beliefs (say, in B, or C, or K, for example). But the "lacks a belief that God exists" definition can sometimes feel like a way to avoid having to defend what one does believe.

3. Tim Keller, *Reason for God,* (Riverhead Books, 2008), xvii-xix. I will talk more about unexamined doubt in Chapter 16, but I credit Keller for this line of thinking. Also, for the 'doubting your doubt' idea.

4. See 1 Peter 3:15-16. Sadly, some Christians have not always been careful to engage in discussions of faith with "gentleness and respect." I hope I have done so here.

5. There are exceptions to this, of course. If a person lives in a part of the world where he or she is persecuted, imprisoned, or otherwise harassed for his or her Christian faith, a believer may face significant risk.

6. I have chosen to paraphrase Pascal's Wager here. Blaise Pascal, *Pensées,* (E.P. Dutton & Co., Inc, 1958), Section III, #233. This version is available online as part of the Gutenberg Project (accessed December 11, 2021, https://www.gutenberg.org/files/18269/18269-h/18269-h.htm).

1. Jean Chrétien, *My Stories, My Times,* (Random House Canada, 2018),62-63.
2. Henry David Thoreau, *Walden,* (Peter Pauper Press, 1966), 8.
3. Quoted by Thaddeus Metz, *Meaning in Life,* (Oxford University Press, 2013) 23.
4. The mention of George Floyd is not intended to be some sort of covert or overt political statement. His killer was convicted of second- and third-degree murder, though as I write, I understand that the conviction is under appeal. But I mentioned it because—regardless of the state of the appeal and regardless of whether it can be legally called murder or not—it was an example of something that we saw and *just knew* was wrong.
5. Stefani Germanotta, Mark Ronson, Anthony Rossomando, and Andrew Wyatt, "Shallow," Interscope Records, 2018.
6. I first heard late-night television host Johnny Carson say this line many years ago; the original quote is attributed to John Rockefeller, perhaps the first American billionaire.
7. "Jim Carrey at MIU: Commencement Address at the 2014 Graduation," YouTube video, accessed on August 10, 2020, https://www.youtube.com/watch?v=V80-gPkpH6M
8. "Joe's Story," joegibbsstory.com, accessed September 4, 2020, http://www.joegibbsstory.com/joes-story-page-2/
9. NF, "Interlude," from the album, "The Search," (NF Real Music / Caroline, 2019).
10. "Johnny Cash – Hurt," YouTube video, accessed on July 29, 2020, https://www.youtube.com/watch?v=8AHCfZTRGiI
11. Trent Reznor, "Hurt," from the album, "The Downward Spiral," (A&M Studios, 1995).
12. The two verses quoted here are from Romans 7:15 (ESV) and Romans 7:24.
13. C. S. Lewis, *Mere Christianity,* Mercy House Publishing, 2019, accessed via Apple Books, 136.
14. "Paste Magazine's Top 100 Living Songwriters," trouserpress.com, accessed July 29, 2020, https://trouserpress.com/forum/read.php?1,5470
15. Bill Mallonee, "Blister Soul," from the album, "Blister Soul," (Capricorn Records, 1995).
16. Dale Ahlquist, "Who is this Guy and Why Haven't I Heard of Him?," accessed May 8, 2020, https://www.chesterton.org/who-is-this-guy/
17. G.K. Chesterton, Letter to the Editor, London's *Daily News,* August 16, 1905.
18. Beyond the spiritual nature of the brokenness we face, many also deal with emotional and/or mental health challenges—challenges that may well require the help of a professional counselor. Others deal with very real physical types of problems or challenges.

   Whatever other challenges we may face, the idea that we all have a spiritual problem is still both real and very significant. And it applies to all of us.

CHAPTER 2

1. 1 Corinthians 15:12-19 says, "12 Now if Christ is proclaimed as raised from the dead, how can some of you say, 'There is no resurrection of the dead'? 13 If there is no resurrection of the dead, then not even Christ has been raised; 14 and if Christ has not been raised, then our proclamation is in vain, and so is your faith. 15 Moreover, we are found to be false witnesses about God, because we have testified wrongly about God that he raised up Christ—whom he did not raise up, if in fact the dead are not raised. 16 For if the dead are not raised, not even Christ has been raised. 17 And if Christ has not been raised, your faith is worthless; you are still in your sins. 18 Those, then, who have fallen asleep in Christ have also perished. 19 If we have put our hope in Christ for this life only, we should be pitied more than anyone."

2. Books like *Evidence that Demands a Verdict,* and this book, fit into a genre known as Christian "apologetics." This comes from the Greek word "apologia." In the Classical Greek legal system, when someone was facing charges in a courtroom, they would reply with an apologia, or defense. Thus, Christian apologetics is the discipline of study and thought concerned with reasoned arguments to defend the truth and rationality of Christianity.

CHAPTER 3

1. https://en.wikipedia.org/wiki/The_dress
2. Taylor Swift, via Twitter, February 27, 2015, accessed May 7, 2020.
3. Demi Lovato, via Twitter, February 26, 2015, accessed May 7, 2020.
4. Anna Kendrick, via Twitter, February 26, 2015, accessed May 7, 2020.
5. Justin Bieber, via Twitter, February 26, 2015, accessed May 7, 2020.
6. Kim Kardashian, via Twitter, February 26, 2015, accessed May 7, 2020.
7. Josh Groban, via Twitter, February 26, 2015, accessed May 7, 2020.
8. Ariana Grande, via Twitter, February 27, 2015, accessed May 7, 2020.
9. Rashida Jones, via Twitter, February 27, 2015, accessed May 7, 2020.
10. https://en.wikipedia.org/wiki/The_dress
11. A Buzzfeed poll revealed that 75% of those who took the poll saw the dress as white and gold (https://says.com/my/fun/people-on-the-internet-are-arguing-about-the-colour-of-this-dress, accessed May 7, 2020). But you can also find polls that say a majority saw it as blue and black. The fact that polls can't even agree on this entertains me tremendously.
12. I'm thankful for the freedom of religion—to the degree that we can keep it. What I did not write is that this freedom is being whittled away in America. This is a hot-button topic for me. When Thomas Jefferson wrote (in a letter) of a "wall of separation" between the church and the state, the idea was that the church should be protected from intrusion or the influence of the government—*not* the other way around. This is massively important. He assumed people's faith would shape

their politics and had no problem with that. Today, that has been flipped, as if the government somehow needs protection from the church. This is bogus, and it makes me crazy because many of the values upon which America was founded were derived from the Judeo-Christian worldview.

13. This idea for this came from a pastor named Stephen Bilynskyj.

14. Social media platforms have openly admitted to censoring (in different ways) accounts of people with views that disagree with their ideology. Thoughtful voices who defend Christianity and historic biblical values, for example, have been removed from different platforms for their views. Even Amazon, which (in theory) is in business to make money for its shareholders, has removed books with which it disagrees. This is nothing other than blatant censorship, and it should be troubling, whatever you believe about an idea.

15. Tim Keller, via Twitter, December 29, 2021.

16. If you haven't already done so, please be sure to watch the Netflix film, *The Social Dilemma*. It chronicles how social media platforms have been carefully designed in a way that has resulted in people often getting their information only from like-minded people. The resulting echo chamber causes people to ridicule and demean those who might disagree—even if there might be good reason for dissent.

17. Desmond Tutu once said this, in *Desmond Tutu, a Spiritual Biography of South Africa's Confessor,* by Michael Battle, Westminster John Knox Press, 2021.

18. John 14:6

19. Frank Turek, via Twitter, August 9, 2020.

CHAPTER 4

1. Charlie Warzel, quoting Karen Freund in Buzzfeed News, accessed May 7, 2020, https://www.buzzfeednews.com/article/charliewarzel/226-how-two-runaway-llamas-and-a-dress-gave-us-the-internets

2. Ibid.

3. Lucie Zhang, via Twitter, February 26, 2015.

4. Rebecca Traister, via Twitter, February 26, 2015.

5. This is an inside joke for my family, a nod to a video my kids loved when they were young. If curious, search Google for the "No, llama, no original video."

6. This conversation took place seven years ago. I have a clear memory of the conversation, but in case I somehow misquote the man with whom I was speaking, I will not name him.

7. Sir Harold Kroto, from a video of a presentation he gave. https://www.mediatheque.lindau-nobel.org/videos/31303/creeativitee-sans-frontires-2011/meeting-2011, accessed June 21, 2020.

8. Freeman Dyson, "Does a Fine-Tuned Universe Lead to God?," An interview on the Closer to Truth website: https://www.closertotruth.com/interviews/4582, accessed February 27, 2021.

9. Peter Wehner, "NIH Director: We're on an Exponential Curve," *The Atlantic,* accessed on September 23, 2020, https://www.theatlantic.com/ideas/archive/2020/03/interview-francis-collins-nih/608221/

10. Edwin M. Glaser, *An Experiment in the Development of Critical Thinking*, (Columbia University, 1941), as cited on https://www.criticalthinking.org/pages/defining-critical-thinking/766

CHAPTER 5

1. Counting to 100 billion is based on the fact that 90% of the numbers you'd have to count have at least nine digits. The average amount of time it takes to *say* a nine-digit number is just under 4 seconds. Feel free to debate my methodology; I could be wrong. But if I'm wrong, I suspect I've erred on the conservative side.
2. NASA, "Hubble Reveals Observable Universe Contains 10 Times More Galaxies Than Previously Thought," https://www.nasa.gov/feature/goddard/2016/hubble-reveals-observable-universe-contains-10-times-more-galaxies-than-previously-thought, accessed on July 6, 2020. Also, "A Universe of 2 Trillion Galaxies," on Phys.org, cites the team's work from the *Astrophysical Journal,* https://phys.org/news/2017-01-universe-trillion-galaxies.html, accessed July 9, 2020.
3. The currently accepted size of the universe seems to be 93 billion light years wide. One reference I saw for this is from a book by Itzhak Bars and John Terning, called *Extra Dimension in Space and Time,* (Springer Science + Business Media, 2010), 27.
4. "How Big is the Universe... Compared with a Grain of Sand?" YouTube video, https://www.youtube.com/watch?v=AC7yFDb1zOA, accessed July 7, 2020.
5. Stephen Hawking and Leonard Mlodinow, *The Grand Design,* Kindle edition, (Random House, LLC, 2012), 130.
6. Ibid.
7. Peter Kreeft and Ronald K. Tacelli, *Handbook of Christian Apologetics,* (InterVarsity Press, 1994), 59.
8. Some have pointed to radioactive decay as an example of something that seems to begin to exist without a cause. But in reading a variety of views by scientists who conclude different things on this, it seems to me that this subject is not even close to settled. Some scientists conclude that there is a cause. Some do not. Many say we just don't know if this truly happens without a cause. It is also at least possible that we've simply not yet been able to figure out a cause. Based on what I've read (and admittedly, as a non-scientist), I remain confident that things don't happen without a cause. I see this not only as a question of science but also of logic.
9. Anthony Walsh, *Answering the New Atheists,* (Vernon Press, 2018), 60.
10. Ibid.
11. This argument, about the impossibility of crossing an actual infinite, is fascinating. You can read more about it in a great book by J.P. Moreland, called *Scaling the Secular City.* William Lane Craig has also addressed this article in books, articles, and videos you can find at ReasonableFaith.org. One such video can be accessed at https://www.reasonablefaith.org/videos/short-videos/explaining-hilberts-hotel
12. Adam Curtis, "A Mile or Two Off Yarmouth," an interview on BBC, February 24, 2012, accessed July 8, 2020.
13. Robert Jastrow, *God and the Astronomers,* (Norton, 1978), Chapter 9.

14. Malcolm W. Browne, "Clues to Universe Origin Expected," *New York Times,* March 12, 1978, p.1.

15. Steven Ball, "A Christian Physicist Examines the Big Bang Theory," p.6, accessed July 8, 2021, https://www.letu.edu/academics/arts-and-sciences/files/big-bang.pdf. To repeat something I said earlier in this chapter, some Christians believe in a far younger Earth than many who believe in the Big Bang theory. I lean toward an older Earth, but it is (far) beyond the scope of this book to dive into questions about the Earth's age here and how different biblical passages about the Earth's creation should be undetstood. It is important for Christians to know that there are bright minds— and Christians who are trained scientists—on both sides of this discussion.

16. Alexander Vilenkin, *Many Worlds in One,* (Hill and Wang, 2006), 176.

17. Dr. Craig has spoken and written about this, using this language, often. A brief overview of these ideas is found in his great animated video: "The Kalam Cosmological Argument - Part 1," YouTube, https://www.youtube.com/watch?v=6CulBuMCLg0, accessed July 10, 2021.

18. Ibid.

CHAPTER 6

1. Billy Graham in Cleveland, date unknown, https://www.youtube.com/watch?v=hYSgg3WvYeE, accessed February 27, 2021.

2. This number is based on Mars' average distance from Earth, 142 million miles.

3. Francis Collins, *The Language of God,* (Free Press, 2007).

4. Bill Gates, *The Road Ahead,* (Viking, Penguin Group, 1996, Revised Edition), 228.

5. Stephen Meyer's three books: The first is *Signature in the Cell: DNA and the Evidence for Intelligent Design.* The second is *Darwin's Doubt: The Explosive Origin of Animal Life and the Case for Intelligent Design.* Finally, his most recent book is *The Return of the God Hypothesis: Compelling Scientific Evidence for the Existence of God.*

6. "Stephen Meyer: DNA and Information," YouTube, https://www.youtube.com/watch?v=7c9PaZzsqEg, accessed July 9, 2020.

7. Ibid.

8. Ibid.

9. "Information Enigma: Where Does Information Come From?," YouTube, accessed July 10, 2020, https://www.youtube.com/watch?v=aA-FcnLsF1g

10. Stephen Meyer, *Signature in the Cell: DNA and the Evidence for Intelligent Design,* (Harper Collins eBooks, 2009), 300.

11. If anyone is tempted here to point out that artificial intelligence can now write books or create computer code, they are correct, of course. But someone—an intelligent mind—had to initially create the AI hardware and code.

12. Kreeft and Tacelli, 55-56.

13. Ibid.

14. "Information Enigma: Where Does Information Come From?," YouTube, accessed July 10, 2020, https://www.youtube.com/watch?v=aA-FcnLsF1g

15. Antony Flew & Roy Abraham Varghese, *There Is a God,* (Harper Collins eBooks, 2007), 91.

16. From the "Faith and Reason" television program, by PBS, accessed on July 12, 2020, https://www.pbs.org/faithandreason/transcript/coll-frame.html.

17. Ibid.

18. Ibid.

19. "Press Conference Statement by the Rev. Dr. John C. Polkinghorne," accessed December 16, 2023, https://www.templetonprize.org/laureate-sub/polkinghorne-press-conference-statement/.

CHAPTER 7

1. Robin Collins, "God, Design, and Fine-Tuning," accessed on February 20, 2021, http://home.messiah.edu/~rcollins/Fine-tuning/ft.htm.

2. Ibid.

3. Stephen Hawking, *A Brief History in Time*, (Bantam Books, 1988), 126.

4. Anil Ananthaswamy, "Is the Universe Fine-Tuned for Life?," accessed on February 23, 2021, https://www.pbs.org/wgbh/nova/article/is-the-universe-fine-tuned-for-life/.

5. Ibid.

6. I've seen an almost identical quote from Davies cited in many places, including in his book *Cosmic Jackpot*, (Houghton Mifflin, 2007), 149. But this quote is more up-to-date and I've seen it cited in multiple places, including here: https://ubcgcu.org/2014/08/22/mind-expanding-quotes-on-fine-tuning/.

7. Freeman Dyson, *Disturbing the Universe*, (Pan Books, 1979), 250.

8. Freeman Dyson, "Does a Fine-Tuned Universe Lead to God?," From an interview on the Closer to Truth website: https://www.closertotruth.com/interviews/4582, accessed February 27, 2021.

9. Ibid.

10. Ibid.

11. Fred Hoyle, "The Universe: Past and Present Reflections," "Annual Review of Astronomy and Astrophysics," Volume 20, September 1982, 16.

12. Hawking, *A Brief History in Time*, 125.

13. Philip Goff, "Our Improbable Existence is No Evidence for a Multiverse," from *Scientific American*, https://www.scientificamerican.com/article/our-improbable-existence-is-no-evidence-for-a-multiverse/, accessed on February 27, 2021.

14. This number, cited by Goff, is from Lee Smolin, *The Life of the Cosmos*, (Oxford University Press, 1997), 45.

15. Numbers this large are hard to get our heads around. If you are reading this note, you are obviously curious, so I'll give one more example. In his book, *Creator and the Cosmos* (NavPress, 1993, p. 115), Hugh Ross tries to help readers understand the size of a different enormous number, 10^{37}. He writes that if we were to cover the entire continent of North America with dimes in a pile high enough to reach the moon—and then create *one billion more* identically-sized piles—we'd have approximately 10^{37} dimes. That's a lot of dimes. If you took *that* number of dimes and multiplied it by 10,000,000,000,000,000,000,000,000,000,000,000,000,000,000, 000, you'd end up with 10^{80} dimes.

Aidan's odds, in our illustration, of 1 in 10^{80}, would be like finding one specific dime from this new, absurdly large number of absurdly large piles of dimes.

16. Amir Ancel, "Why Science Does Not Disprove God," https://time.com/77676/why-science-does-not-disprove-god/, accessed July 27, 2021

17. Smolin, *The Life of the Cosmos,* 45.

18. Natalie Wolchover and Peter Byrne, "In a Multiverse, What Are the Odds?" From *Quanta Magazine,* November 3, 2014, https://www.quantamagazine.org/the-multiverses-measure-problem-20141103/, accessed July 28, 2021.

19. Dyson, "Does a Fine-Tuned Universe Lead to God?," https://www.closertotruth.com/interviews/4582, accessed February 27, 2021.

20. Sarah Scoles, "Can Physicists Ever Prove the Multiverse is Real?" From *Smithsonian Magazine,* April 19, 2016. https://www.smithsonianmag.com/science-nature/can-physicists-ever-prove-multiverse-real-180958813/ accessed July 27, 2021.

21. "Why We Gamble Like Monkeys," from bbc.org, https://www.bbc.com/future/article/20150127-why-we-gamble-like-monkeys, accessed on December 19, 2021.

22. Philip Goff, "Our Improbable Existence is No Evidence for a Multiverse," from the *Scientific American* website, https://www.scientificamerican.com/article/our-improbable-existence-is-no-evidence-for-a-multiverse/, accessed on February 27, 2021.

23. William Lane Craig, "Why Can't the Multiverse Be Eternal?" from ReasonableFaith.org on YouTube, https://www.youtube.com/watch?v=l1ScQ9EBFKM, accessed on February 27, 2021. See also William Lane Craig, "Multiverse and the Design Argument," from https://www.reasonablefaith.org/writings/question-answer/multiverse-and-the-design-argument, accessed on December 19, 2021. Here he points to the book, *Many Worlds in One: The Search for Other Universes* (Hill and Wang, 2006). If you are really interested in the multiverse, please also see this article by Dr. Craig: https://www.reasonablefaith.org/writings/popular-writings/existence-nature-of-god/has-the-multiverse-replaced-god.

24. William Lane Craig, "The Big Bang, Multiverses, and the Anthropic Principle," a podcast in two parts: https://www.youtube.com/watch?v=-J5D7R3pyro (Part 1) and also https://www.youtube.com/watch?v=jyQMGBmPkdI (Part 2), accessed December 19, 2021.

CHAPTER 8

1. I realize that a man who had fought for Germany in World War II but now lives in America may be unlikely to admit to an American that he supported the Third Reich's aims during the war. But I had no real reason to doubt him. And even if he was shading the truth about what he personally believed, it is certainly true that Hitler faced widespread opposition from many Germans.

2. C.S. Lewis, *Mere Christianity,* (Mercy House Publishing, 2019), 17. I cite here the ebook version of this book, found at https://books.apple.com/us/book/mere-christianity/id1488426288. This book was first published in 1952 and was adapted from a series of radio broadcasts made by Lewis between 1942 and 1944.

3. Ibid, 43.

4. Slavery is still an enormous problem in our modern world. Anyone who thinks otherwise has his or her head in the sand. I wrote that "in many countries today, slavery is still not illegal." This is true. Although the article I'll cite below does say that "legal ownership of people was indeed abolished in all countries over the last two centuries," it goes on to say that "but in many countries it has not been criminalized... In 94 countries, you cannot be prosecuted and punished in a criminal court for enslaving another human being." This means that more than half of the world's nations (as of 2020) had not yet put laws into place against slavery. Further, more than 40 million people are estimated to be trapped in slavery worldwide today, 25% of whom are children. The stats about the laws around the world were cited in the article, "Slavery is Not a Crime in Almost Half the Countries of the World – New Research," accessed December 13, 2021, https://theconversation.com/slavery-is-not-a-crime-in-almost-half-the-countries-of-the-world-new-research-115596. The number of people trapped in slavery comes from https://www.antislavery.org.
5. Peter Hoffman, *The History of the German Resistance, 1933-1945*, (McGill-Queen's University Press, 1996), xiii.
6. If you like reading science fiction, *The Man in the High Castle* was originally a 1962 novel of the same name, by the renowned American science fiction writer, Philip K. Dick.
7. Sean McDowell has used this formation of the argument in a few places, but here is a short video in which he unpacks it: https://www.youtube.com/watch?v=yTMN7NElISU, accessed August 22, 2021. Watch any of McDowell's YouTube videos—he is a great thinker and communicator.
8. J.L. Mackie, *The Miracle of Theism*, (Clarendon Press, 1982), 115-116.
9. William Lane Craig has created a series of fantastic, animated videos on arguments for the existence of God. The video that explains the moral argument makes the point about a cat killing a mouse: https://www.youtube.com/watch?v=OxiAikEk2vU, accessed August 22, 2021. The larger list of his animated videos on apologetics arguments can be found at: https://www.youtube.com/playlist?list=PL3gdeV4Rk9EfL-NyraEGXXwSjDNeMaRoX.
10. The often-asked question about why God might allow bad things to happen is an important one. Here are a few thoughts, though a more complete treatment of this subject would obviously demand much more than a few pages in this Endnote.

Some may ask this question while wrestling with intense or very real pain. Generally speaking, these people are not looking for a philosophical or theological answer. What most people need in the midst of pain is compassion—someone to cry with them or to simply be there, even if in silence, through the pain.

Philosophical and/or theological answers will not typically ease our pain and may even sound cold or uncaring. Years ago, I made the mistake of giving a theological answer when someone in pain stopped by my house to talk. I didn't help. But I learned. Thankfully, I have never repeated that mistake.

If you are currently experiencing some sort of pain, you may find that the things I will write next feel somewhat empty or unhelpful. But when we are not in the middle of pain or suffering (and not feeling somehow broken or highly emotional), it is important to think about this topic thoughtfully.

Even the idea that we'd think to call something "bad" hints at God's existence. Chapter 8 explores this idea. The skeptic may suggest that if God does exist, he is either not good (because he can stop evil from happening and sometimes does not) or that he is not all-powerful (because he might want to stop evil but sometimes cannot). But there is a third option: that he is good *and* all-powerful, even if he sometimes allows things to happen that we wish he would not have. During any experience of pain and suffering, it is important to remember that there is a bigger picture that we cannot see.

When my son Ethan was a toddler, my wife took him to get blood drawn for tests that a doctor had ordered. The nurse who was assigned to draw blood from his arm was not particularly good at this part of her job. She had to repeatedly insert the needle in order to actually find a vein from which to draw the blood. Ethan was, as you might imagine, screaming.

As Megan, who was about six years old at the time, watched the nurse repeatedly jab her little brother, she also got upset. She cried, "Mommy, make her stop!" Ethan was too young to understand the suffering he was going through. He just knew that it hurt. Megan felt compassion for Ethan and did not understand why Karey would let this continue. Karey was experiencing her own sort of agony.

Even as Karey allowed Ethan to go through what she knew would be temporary pain, she was being a good mom. And she chose to allow it, at least for a little while. Eventually, she requested a new nurse, but when the new nurse arrived, Karey allowed her to restart the process of drawing Ethan's blood. Karey had the power to fully stop Ethan's pain but did not. Why? Because she saw the bigger picture—a picture that neither Ethan nor Megan could even begin to grasp.

As Tim Keller, who recently went home to be with the Lord after a long battle with cancer, said often, just because we cannot imagine a good reason that a loving, all-powerful, and all-knowing God might allow something to happen certainly does not mean that a good reason does not exist. We are finite beings. From our finite perspective, we see something bad and are quick to judge that *God* must be wrong for allowing it. But if God is real, it seems arrogant for us, with all of our limitations, to judge the actions of the eternal, all-knowing, and all-wise creator of the universe.

The Bible does not provide complete answers as to why God might allow any one instance of suffering to happen in our lives. But it does give us insight that is helpful.

First, we live in a world that is fallen and completely broken. I've written about this in Chapters 1 and 13. The fall of man messed up everything: our hearts, desires, actions, and even our motives. Further, it has even corrupted our physical universe. When humanity, as a race, chose to turn away from God, the result was that everything that was a part of his creation broke. As a result, we can expect to go through difficulties and trials of different kinds in this life.

A second part of an answer is that mankind's turn away from God was possible because God does not force us to love or follow him. He did not want us to be robots and will not force anyone to go to heaven. He gives us the freedom to make moral decisions. And, as we all know, moral decisions have consequences.

We've all seen terrible things happen in other people's lives as a result of a bad decision. Most of us have seen bad things happen in our own lives as a result of a bad decision. Sometimes, as in the case of a drunk driver, a rapist, or an active shooter, that person's awful decision can have a horrible impact in the lives of others.

Sometimes, as in the case of a murderous dictator, that person's awful decisions have a horrible impact in the lives of many, many others. This has been called moral evil.

Some bad things, however, like natural disasters or sickness—things we might call natural evil—are not necessarily the result of a bad decision or due to something a person did wrong (in the Bible, see John 9). This type of evil can be harder for many of us to stomach because it feels so random.

It is worth pondering that we have no clue how often God actually *does* stop evil on a given day—or how often he might intervene on a person's behalf. But this doesn't soften the pain we feel when we recognize that God could have stopped a particular thing from happening but did not.

The reality is that every one of us will suffer in this life. This should not surprise us. Jesus himself suffered, brutally and unfairly. So did his first followers. When facing suffering, we must not forget Jesus' reminder in John 16:33 that in this world we will face trials, but that we should take courage because he has overcome the world.

Sadly, to be human in this fallen world is to suffer in different ways at different times. In the midst of suffering, God may not reveal his rationale for allowing it to happen. But the Christian can take great comfort in knowing that God promises to provide resources to help us face suffering with strength, dignity, and hope. He promises that in all things, even bad things, he is at work for good in the lives of those who follow him and are called according to his purpose (Romans 8:28).

The Apostle Paul—who suffered immensely—obviously had it right when he wrote, "I consider that the sufferings of this present time are not worth comparing with the glory that is going to be revealed to us" in Romans 8:18. That thought, by Paul, points us to our most significant reason for hope in the face of evil and suffering: we are not home yet. God will resolve evil once and for all, in eternity. We rejoice that one day, believers will be with God in a place where there will be no more sin, no more pain, no more moral or natural evil, and no more tears.

And compared to eternity, whatever we might go through in this life is very short by comparison. Is that line of thought fully satisfying? Perhaps not. But I'd argue that it is far more satisfying than the atheist's answer: "Stuff happens."

I'll stop here, but I have listed several books on this topic in the Appendix. I'd particularly recommend Clay Jones' book, *Why Does God Allow Evil?* It is helpful, thoughtful, and accessible. For a far shorter treatment, John Lennox's booklet *Where is God in a Coronavirus World?* is only 62 pages long but is very good.

CHAPTER 9

1. Yes, Fred Krueger was actually his name. This case took place long before a horror movie would introduce millions to a different Freddie Krueger.
2. First Corinthians 15:12-19; specifically verse 19.
3. Paul Maier, *The Very First Easter*, (Concordia Publishing House, 2000), 120.
4. Paul Althaus. *Die Wahrheit des kirchlichen Osterglaubens* (Gutersloh: C. Bertelsmann, 1941), 22.
5. Cited by Jerry Pierce in "The Towering Truth of the Resurrection," from *Decision Magazine*, https://decisionmagazine.com/towering-truth-resurrection/, accessed September 15, 2021.
6. Matthew 26:35
7. Conrad Hackett and David McClendon, "Christians Remain the World's Largest Religious Group, but they are Declining in Europe," Pew Center Research, https://www.pewresearch.org/fact-tank/2017/04/05/christians-remain-worlds-largest-religious-group-but-they-are-declining-in-europe/, accessed January 14, 2022.
8. Sean McDowell, in a lecture on his book, *The Fate of the Apostles*, https://www.youtube.com/watch?v=_sy1BwLBIU8, accessed on September 16, 2021.
9. Ibid.
10. Ibid.
11. Ibid.
12. Ibid.
13. Ibid.
14. 1 Corinthians 15:5-8.
15. John Warwick Montgomery, *History and Christianity*, (Bethany House Publishers, 1964), 78. Here, Montgomery may be quoting Frank Morison's book, *Who Moved the Stone?*

CHAPTER 10

1. Scott Allen, "How U.S. Marshals Used Redskins Tickets to Bust Fugitives in 1985 Sting," *The Washington Post*, December 18, 2015, accessed at https://www.washingtonpost.com/news/dc-sports-bog/wp/2015/12/18/how-u-s-marshals-used-redskins-tickets-to-bust-fugitives-in-1985-sting/on August 14, 2021

2. Ibid.

3. Ibid.

4. Simon Greenleaf, *An Examination of the Testimony of the Four Evangelists by the Rules of Evidence Administered in Courts of Justice*, (A. Maxwell & Son, 1847), 73. Note that this page number is from an eBook edition.

5. Tim Keller, via Twitter, April 8, 2021.

6. While Christians in India widely believe that Thomas brought the gospel to their country, we should admit that this does rely on church tradition.

7. Kreeft & Tacelli, 189-194.

8. Bart Ehrman, *Forged*, (HarperOne, 2011), 285.

9. We do not actually know for certain which specific instrument of pain was used to scourge Jesus. That said, any non-Roman who was to be crucified by the Romans was typically flogged, most often using a flagrum, as I have described here. It is helpful to note that Jesus was scourged before it was clear that he would be crucified. Pilate said in Luke 23, "I will have him flogged and release him." Pilate did not find Jesus to be deserving of death and thus tried to release him instead of crucifying him (see John 19). In John 19:5, after the scourging, Pilate said, "Behold, the man!" Here, he seemed to say to the crowd, "This surely isn't a king." Many have speculated that by scourging Jesus brutally, Pilate thought he could dissuade the crowd from demanding Jesus' death. He was wrong.

10. Terry McDermott, "The Physical Effects of the Scourging and Crucifixion of Jesus," *Catholic Insight*, March 13, 2020.

11. Ibid.

12. Ibid.

13. William Edwards, Wesley Gabel, Floyd Hosmer, "On the Physical Death of Jesus Christ," *Journal of the American Medical Association*, 255: 1455-63.

14. Cited by Pierce, "The Towering Truth of the Resurrection."

15. For a variety of sources and resources on prophecies Jesus fulfilled, see Chapter 9 of the recently updated *Evidence that Demands a Verdict*, by Josh McDowell and Sean McDowell, (Harper Collins, 2017), 209-231.

16. I'll recommend two books: J. Warner Wallace's *Person of Interest*, and Alvin Schmidt's *How Christianity Changed the World*. Both are listed in the Appendix.

17. See Baruch Shalev's *100 Years of Nobel Prizes*, (Los Angeles, 2005), 57-61.

18. The internet seems to attribute this to a columnist named Don Marquis.

19. James Allan Francis, *The Real Jesus and Other Sermons*, (The Judson Press, 1926), p.121.

CHAPTER 11

1. Many people have made this same point, but it is covered briefly but clearly by J. Warner Wallace here: https://coldcasechristianity.com/writings/how-many-angels-were present at jesus tomb/, accessed May 27, 2021.

2. Mark Strauss, "Bible Contradictions Explained: 4 Reasons the Gospels "Disagree," ZondervanAcademic.com, https://zondervanacademic.com/blog/bible-contradictions-explained, access May 28, 2021.

3. J. Warner Wallace, "Why I Rarely Share My Personal Testimony and Why You Shouldn't Be Quick to Share Yours," https://www.youtube.com/watch?v=dFdYXzz2-P0, accessed on May 27, 2021.

4. Ibid.

5. Ibid.

6. Ibid.

7. J. Warner Wallace, "Why the Differences in the Gospel Accounts Make them More Reliable," https://www.youtube.com/watch?v=jp-cn6rVFO8, accessed May 27, 2021.

8. Ibid.

9. J. Warner Wallace, "Ten Principles When Considering Alleged Bible Contradictions," https://coldcasechristianity.com/writings/ten-principles-when-considering-alleged-bible-contradictions/, accessed May 27, 2021.

10. Frank Turek and Norman Geisler, *I Do Not Have Enough Faith to Be an Atheist,* (Crossway, 2004), Chapter 11.

11. Ibid.

12. William Ramsay, *The Bearing of Recent Discovery on the Trustworthiness of the New Testament,* (Hodder and Stoughton, 1915), 222.

13. Ibid.

14. I first saw Hemer's work cited in Turek and Geisler's *I Do Not Have Enough Faith to Be an Atheist,* (Crossway, 2004).

15. Nelson Glueck, *Rivers in the Desert: A History of the Negev,* (Farrar, Srauss, and Cudahy, 1959), 31.

16. "A Tunguska Sized Airburst Destroyed Tall el-Hammam, a Middle Bronze Age City in the Jordan Valley Near the Dead Sea," Scientific Reports, September 20, 2021, https://www.nature.com/articles/s41598-021-97778-3, accessed October 1, 2021.

17. If you are curious about the historical reliability of the Old Testament, this essay (and footnotes) by Dr. Richard E. Averbeck: "The Reliability of the Old Testament" is a good place to start. Accessed at https://www.thegospelcoalition.org/essay/the-reliability-of-the-old-testament/ on September 2, 2022.

18. Stanley E. Porter and Andrew W. Pitts, *Fundamentals of New Testament Textual Criticism,* (Eerdmans, 2015), 50.

19. McDowell and McDowell, 56.

20. Ibid.

21. Ibid.

22. Sean McDowell and Peter Gurry, "Avoiding Big Mistakes in Defending the Bible: Interview with Dr. Peter Gurry," https://www.youtube.com/watch?v=EPXY2PF7eB0, accessed on May 27, 2021.

23. Greenleaf, 41. (Again, this is from Apple books, so the page numbering may be different for viewers reading the eBook on different platforms.)

24. Owen Barfield, "Chronological Snobbery," from https://www.owenbarfield.org/chronological-snobbery/, accessed May 27, 2021.

25. My friend was paraphrasing a famous Paul Harvey quote here.

26. This illustration is my modern re-telling of one of Blaise Pascal's thoughts in his book, *Pensées.* (#217)

27. Romans 1:16

CHAPTER 12

1. John Mansur, "No Greater Love," *The Missileer*, February 13, 1987. Here is a great story—about this great story. "No Greater Love" first appeared in *The Missileer*, a U.S. Air Force newsletter. *Reader's Digest* later reprinted it, and theirs was the version I found at the barber shop. While writing this book, *Reader's Digest* could not give me permission to use the story because permission was not theirs to grant; they had received permission from the Air Force newsletter. But the newsletter no longer exists. Thankfully, I was able to track down Colonel Mansur himself, and he graciously extended permission for me to use it here. It turns out that Col. Mansur is a decorated combat veteran who received a Silver Star and served our nation with distinction during a long Air Force career. I was also encouraged to learn of his deep faith in Christ. We had a wonderful conversation in which he shared some remarkable ways that God has used this article. Thank you again, Col. Mansur.
2. John 15:13
3. John 10:11
4. Clayton Brumby, *The Parable of the Strings*
5. Luke 22:44 records that, "being in anguish, he prayed more fervently, and his sweat became like drops of blood falling to the ground." Today we know of a medical condition we now call hematohidrosis that is caused by overwhelming stress and can result in a person sweating blood.

CHAPTER 13

1. Andy Greenberg, "The Confessions of Marcus Hutchins, the Hacker Who Saved the Internet," *Wired*, June 2020.
2. Ibid. All of the details I share about the Marcus Hutchins story in the next two pages are taken from this same *Wired* magazine article.
3. Ibid.
4. Wayne Grudem, *Systematic Theology*, (Zondervan, 1994), 490.
5. Jeremiah 17:9 ESV. Some translations say that the heart is "incurable," while others say it is "desperately sick."
6. Randy Newman, *Bringing the Gospel Home*, (Crossway, 2011), 64-65.
7. Ibid.
8. Grudem, 497.
9. Ephesians 2:1
10. Romans 6:23
11. Ephesians 2:3
12. A.W. Tozer, *The Knowledge of the Holy*, (Harper & Row, 1961), 106.
13. Matt Chandler, *The Explicit Gospel*, (Crossway, 2012), 44.

CHAPTER 14

1. This story was passed along to me directly from a now-second lieutenant in the U.S. Army that I've known since the day she was born.
2. Eminem Ft. Rihanna, "The Monster," (Sony/ATV Music Publishing, Universal Music Publishing Group, MBG Rights Management, Reach Music Publishing), Track 12 on "The Marshall Mathers LP2," 2013.
3. Michka Assayas, *Bono, in Conversation with Michka Assayas*, (Riverhead Books, 2005), 204-205
4. Ibid.
5. Lewis, *Mere Christianity*, 202 (in eBook format, this page number will be different on different devices).
6. Grudem, 574-575.

CHAPTER 15

1. Bill Bright, *Knowing God Personally*, (BMF and Cru, 1965-2022).
2. See Luke 15.
3. "Joe's Story," joegibbsstory.com, accessed September 4, 2020, http://www.joegibbsstory.com/joes-story-page-2/
4. United States v. George Wilson, https://www.law.cornell.edu/supremecourt/text/32/150, accessed on December 8, 2021.

CHAPTER 16

1. Keller, xvii.
2. Matthew Breeden, "I Believe, Help My Unbelief," a sermon delivered on January 10, 2021, at Southern Hills Baptist Church in Round Rock, TX.
3. Ibid.
4. If you find yourself doubting that God is still in the miracle business, I'd recommend that you challenge your own thinking by reading either Eric Metaxas' book, *Miracles*, or Craig Keener's massive two-volume work by the same name. I have not yet read Lee Strobel's 2018 book, *The Case for Miracles*, but I have heard from someone I trust that it is very good.
5. Hebrews 10:25-27
6. I have briefly addressed the question of why God allows bad things to happen earlier in the Endnotes, Chapter 8, Note 10.
7. I heard this concept years ago in a talk somewhere, and it has always stuck with me. My friend Jay mentioned that it may have originated with Howard Hendricks.

CHAPTER 17

1. "What's So Good About Good Friday?" YouTube, https://www.youtube.com/watch?v=FzxXvEtf9D0, accessed January 12, 2022.
2. Ibid.
3. John Calvin, from the preface he wrote for Pierre Robert Olivétan's French translation of the New Testament (1534). English translation from Joseph Haroutunian, ed., *Calvin: Commentaries, The Library of Christian Classics.*
4. Ibid.
5. "The Westminster Shorter Catechism," by the Westminister Assembly, 1647.
6. Alexander Moody Stuart, as quoted by Frank Turek in a tweet on December 9, 2021. I could not find the original source for this quote from Dr. Moody Stuart, a pastor from the 1800s.
7. Matthew 16:24
8. Keller, 204.
9. Frank Turek, via Twitter, May 5, 2021.

CONCLUSION

1. C.S. Lewis, "The Weight of Glory," in a sermon preached in the Church of St. Mary the Virgin, June 8, 1942. This sermon was later included in a collection called *The Weight of Glory and Other Addresses,* (Simon and Schuster).
2. Steven Curtis Chapman, "The Great Adventure," track 2 on the album "The Great Adventure," Sparrow Records, 1992.

For Further Review

I have not included every book by the authors in the list below, and I certainly couldn't list every person who has done great work in the area of apologetics. So, this list is not even close to exhaustive. My hope is to introduce you to some of these authors and that you'll explore their other books as well.

By including these books or quoting their work, I am not suggesting that I totally agree with every belief of every author, of course. The authors don't fully agree with each other on some topics. One writer I've listed below, Peter Kreeft, is a Roman Catholic. I am not. But he is a tremendous thinker and writer, and I could not recommend the books I've listed of his any more highly. To my knowledge, David Berlinski, who wrote a book I've recommended below, is not a Christian.

The fact that these authors might have different takes on certain topics should neither surprise nor bother us. When we read authors with a wide range of views, we are challenged to think.

I should note here that I have chosen not to list books by writers who attack Christianity or would be likely to oppose the arguments I've made here. To anyone wanting to dig into those sorts of books, I'd suggest becoming deeply familiar with Christianity's best arguments first. And then engage with thoughtful writers and thinkers who disagree.

I've heard, though I've not been able to verify, that countries, including the United States, train agents to spot counterfeit currency primarily by having them study genuine currency so thoroughly that it becomes easy to spot a fake.

Similarly, while I believe it is very important for believers to understand what the opponents of Christianity write, say, and believe, a person who is grounded in the Bible and in Christianity's best arguments first will have a solid foundation that will help immensely when diving into the critics' arguments.

Ultimately, the more we learn about Christianity—and about opposing arguments—the more we will be ready to "give a reason for the hope that is within us" (1 Peter 3:15).

67 BOOKS (IN ALPHABETICAL ORDER BY AUTHOR'S LAST NAME):

Michael Behe
- ☐ *Darwin's Black Box*
- ☐ *A Mousetrap for Darwin*
- ☐ *Darwin Devolves*

David Berlinski
- ☐ *The Devil's Delusion: Atheism and Its Scientific Pretensions*
  Note: Berlinski, a mathematician, calls himself a "secular Jew."

Craig L. Blomberg
- ☐ *The Historical Reliability of the Gospels*

G.K. Chesterton
- ☐ *Orthodoxy*
- ☐ *The Everlasting Man*

William Lane Craig
- ☐ *Reasonable Faith*
- ☐ *The Son Rises: The Historical Evidence for the Resurrection of Jesus*
  Visit ReasonableFaith.org web site for hundreds of Dr. Craig's talks, articles, videos, and responses to critiques from skeptics. His animated video series offers fantastic high-level overviews of various arguments for God's existence.

William Lane Craig and J.P. Moreland
- ☐ *Philosophical Foundations for a Christian Worldview*

William Dembski, Casey Luskin, and Joseph M. Holden
- ☐ *The Comprehensive Guide to Science and Faith: Exploring the Ultimate Questions About Life and the Cosmos*

Greg Ganssle
- ☐ *A Reasonable God: Engaging the New Face of Atheism*

Simon Greenleaf
- ☐ *An Examination of the Testimony of the Four Evangelists By the Rules of Evidence Administered in Courts of Justice*

Gary Habermas
- ☐ *Evidence for the Historical Jesus: Is the Jesus of History the Christ of Faith?*

Gary Habermas and Michael R. Licona
- ☐ *The Case for the Resurrection of Jesus*

Julie P. Hannah
- ☐ *A Skeptic's Investigation into Jesus*

Joseph M. Holden, *General Editor*
- ☐ *The Comprehensive Guide to Apologetics*
  This book features 75 different articles on a wide range of topics from a wide range of great writers and thinkers. In fact, some of the people whose books I recommend in this list have written articles for this book. For example, Dr. Clay Jones is a thoughtful person to read on the problem of evil. Holden's book contains an excellent four-page article on the topic by Dr. Jones. Jones unpacks that argument in much greater depth in his own book, which is the next book on the list, below.

Clay Jones
- ☐ *Why Does God Allow Evil?*

Craig Keener
- ☐ *Miracles: The Credibility of New Testament Accounts, 2 Volumes*

Tim Keller
- ☐ *Reason for God: Belief in an Age of Skepticism*
- ☐ *Making Sense of God: Finding God in the Modern World*
- ☐ *Walking with God Through Pain and Suffering*

Gregory Koukl
- ☐ *The Story of Reality: How the World Began, How It Ends, and Everything Important that Happens in Between*

Peter Kreeft

- *Between Heaven & Hell*
  This book is an imagined conversation—after their deaths—between C.S. Lewis, Aldous Huxley, and John F. Kennedy, all of whom died on the same day. Lewis (as imagined by Kreeft) defends Christianity using apologetics in this fascinating "conversation."
- *Socrates Meets Jesus*

Peter Kreeft and Ronald K. Tacelli

- *Handbook of Christian Apologetics*
  I'd recommend this book very highly, to have as a resource. For clarity, this book is a different book than the *Handbook of Catholic Apologetics*, written by the same authors. I have not read that book and thus cannot comment on it.

John Lennox

- *Cosmic Chemistry: Do God and Science Mix?*
- *God and Stephen Hawking: Whose design is it, anyway? (2nd Ed.)*
- *Where is God in a Coronavirus World?*

C.S. Lewis

- *Mere Christianity*
- *The Problem of Pain*
- *The Abolition of Man*

Josh McDowell and Sean McDowell

- *Evidence That Demands a Verdict: Life-Changing Truth for a Skeptical World*
- *77 FAQs About God and the Bible*
- *Evidence for Jesus*

Sean McDowell

- *The Fate of the Apostles*
- *Evidence for the Resurrection*

I've only listed five of McDowell's books but he has written and co-written many more. I'd also point you toward the great content on his YouTube channel. See also: SeanMcDowell.org.

Rebecca McLaughlin

- *Confronting Christianity: 12 Hard Questions for the World's Largest Religion*

Eric Metaxas

- *Is Atheism Dead?*
- *Miracles What They Are, How They Happen, and How They Can Change Your Life*

Stephen Meyer

☐ *Signature in the Cell: DNA and the Evidence for Intelligent Design*
☐ *Darwin's Doubt: The Explosive Origin of Animal Life and the Case for Intelligent Design*
☐ *Return of the God Hypothesis: Three Scientific Discoveries That Reveal the Mind Behind the Universe*

Mark Mittelberg

☐ *The Questions Christians Hope No One Will Ask (with Answers)*

J.P. Moreland

☐ *Scaling the Secular City*
This is certainly one of the most intellectually rigorous of the books I'll list. I once heard Dr. Moreland say in a class that he wrote this book so that the "typical graduate student would only understand 70% of it upon the first reading." I may remember the percentage wrong, but the number was lower than I would have expected.
☐ *Love Your God with All Your Mind*
☐ *The God Question: An Invitation to a Life of Meaning*

Randy Newman

☐ *Mere Evangelism*
This book explores principles used by C.S. Lewis to help Christians think well about talking about issues of faith with those who are not Christians.

Blaise Pascal

☐ *Pensées*

Alvin Plantinga

☐ *God, Freedom, and Evil*
☐ *Warranted Christian Belief*
☐ *Where the Conflict Really Lies: Science, Religion and Naturalism*

Nabeel Qureshi

☐ *Seeking Allah, Finding Jesus: A Devout Muslim Encounters Christianity*

Tom Rudelius

☐ *Chasing Proof, Finding Faith: A Young Scientist's Search for Truth in a World of Uncertainty*

Alvin Schmidt

☐ *How Christianity Changed the World*

Lee Strobel
- *The Case for Christ*
- *The Case for Faith*
- *The Case for a Creator*
- *The Case for Miracles*
- *The Case for Easter*
- *The Case for Christmas*
- *The Case for Heaven*

Frank Turek and Norman Geisler
- *I Don't Have Enough Faith to Be an Atheist*

J. Warner Wallace
- *Cold-Case Christianity: A Homicide Detective Investigates the Claims of the Gospels*
- *God's Crime Scene: A Cold-Case Detective Examines the Evidence for a Divinely Created Universe*
- *Person of Interest: Why Jesus Still Matters in a World that Rejects the Bible*

I've only listed three of J. Warner Wallace's books here, but he has written a number of excellent books. As I mentioned previously, Wallace has posted tremendous apologetics-related content online, at ColdCaseChristianity.com, and updates it often. From podcasts to videos to blog posts, he does a fantastic job. Wallace's content was very helpful to my son Ryan as he worked through his season of doubt. If you have enjoyed this book and are new to books like this, my guess is that you will really enjoy Wallace's books.

N.T. Wright
- *The Resurrection of the Son of God*